£2

Highway Cello

Kenneth Wilson is a poet, a cellist and a dreamer. He is also an ex-vicar, failed property developer and reformed vegetarian who once ran an India travel company. He lives in a treehouse in rural Cumbria.

www.kennethwilsoncello.com

HIGHWAY CELLO

Kenneth Wilson

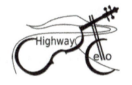

City Village Books
www.cityvillage.co.uk

"Highway Cello is a rare and strangely joyful read. I guarantee it will stay with you long after you reach the last page; a journey on which you really feel you've accompanied the author and his cello, meeting interesting characters and learning new facts about all manner of weird and wonderful things along the way. Highly recommended."
Louise Voss, author of *His Other Woman, The Venus Trap*, etc.

"A musical cycling journey that hits all the right notes. An adventure with a cello, told with humour and filled with unexpected encounters along the road."
Lesley Caple, Canada.

"A joy to read, with beautiful imagery and language… Marvellous."
Barbara Nienaber, Australia.

"To travel with Kenneth Wilson on his extraordinary bike ride from Cumbria to Rome is to participate in a wealth of fascinating experiences: visual, musical, literary and more. He does what all great travel writers do – enable you to see wonderful landscapes, explore ancient places, meet fascinating people, and excite you with unexpected and curious incidents. And all that with a cello on the back of his bike! Take up his invitation and come along for the ride."
Christine Roberts, UK.

"An intelligent tome of discovery, adventure, music, history, epiphanies, and nostalgia as observed and shared by a uniquely talented and adventurous cellist."
Bob Morrow, USA.

Published by City Village Books, 2023

A CIP record for this book is available from the British Library.

ISBN 978-1-7393182-0-8

Cover design and typesetting by Jasmine Aurora

Cover photo by Enrico Coviello Photography

Printed by Biddles

DISCLAIMER: This book contains elements of storytelling, speculation, reflection and fantasy, as well as non-fiction. Where the author is describing real people, some names have been changed to protect the privacy of others. As is sometimes the case when events and people are described in hindsight it is possible, in that famous political phrase, that "recollections may differ". If you believe you feature in these pages and have been misrepresented in any way, please accept the author's apologies and his assurance that he intended to offend no-one. Please advise the publisher, who will ensure that no notified errors persist through any future edition.

In memoriam

Joan Wilson
who always
answered the
phone when a son
called
and who thought
faraway places
overrated.

THE CELLO DARE

Play it here, play it there,
I'd play my cello anywhere.
On the top of Snowdon? Easy.
In the rain and snow, then? Peasy,
Simples.

On a double decker bus
there isn't room enough to bow,
and the driver makes a fuss,
no music when the bus has no
conductor.

Here's a dare then: get you home
then pack that cello on a bike;
pedal South – go down to Rome
be careful where you aim its spike.
Go on!

Play it every day en route
in squares and streets, in parks, on roofs;
posh restaurants where the food's *en croute,*
low dives where no-one gives a F - hoot.
If you dare!

Play some concerts overnight
in homes, halls, churches, left and right;
And if this madness doesn't fail
then back at home write down the tale
of Libre on a bike –

The *Highway Cello.*

CHAPTERS

CHAPTER 1

Over the Alps

SATURDAY 25 JUNE

I'm nine thousand and sixty-eight feet above sea level, on the highest proper road over the Alps, twelve hundred miles from home, on a nearly fifty-year-old Dawes Galaxy bicycle. Also on the bike, precariously, dangerously heavy and wobbly, is my beautiful black, curvy, shiny companion, Libre.

Libre is a cello.

Yesterday was the first day since we left home that Libre didn't come out of her case. She didn't like Val d'Isere any more than I did.

But it was a good decision to stop there, in a town that's really only a town in the winter, and the rest of the time – like yesterday – a bit ghostly. The weather was bad – thundery, blustery and wet. The Col de l'Iseran has been on the Tour de France's punishing route several times, and on a quarter of those occasions the day has had to be curtailed because of snow. In July.

So on a wet and windy afternoon in late June, before the winter has convincingly ended at this altitude, and after a tiring climb up to the ski resort, it would have been unwise to risk it.

Today the weather is altogether better. There's wall-to-wall sunshine and, in Val d'Isere, hardly a breath of wind. It's warm enough to breakfast outside in the sunshine.

Most of the town's hotels are winter-only establishments. All the houses and apartments I could see were shuttered, and not because of the heat that had slowed me for the past few days, lower down. Finding a place to stay in Val d'Isere, where most of the accommodation was empty, was frustratingly difficult.

But the Hotel Bellier was pleasant, and there were a few other guests rattling around. I was impatient for an early breakfast so I could get back on the road, and pedal the few thousand feet up to the top of the *col*. People go to hotels like the Bellier, in places like Val d'Isere, though, for holidays. So you can't get a hotel breakfast until about mid-morning, especially if it's a Saturday.

You need a big breakfast, I was always telling myself, when you're cycling like this, so curb the impatience, and stock up properly. Even if that means a disgracefully late start. Smile nicely for the hotel, so they can take a picture of this comically eccentric arrangement of cello on bicycle. But don't wave as you pedal away, or you'll fall off. Let the climb begin.

Tomorrow, Sunday, is going to be one of those special days when the Col de l'Iseran road is closed to motor vehicles for half a day so that cyclists can really enjoy it in peace. But I can't wait that long. Certainly not in Val d'Isere; soulless and dispiriting place. It's the same D902 as terrorised me yesterday. But today it's empty enough. No lorries on Saturday. Later there would be armies of motorbikes; but not yet.

When you're on an old steel-framed bicycle, with all the luggage you need for six weeks away, plus a non-pedalling companion like Libre, you need a strategy for climbing big hills. The Hartside strategy – I'll tell you about that later if we get that far – isn't going to work today. Instead I've mentally divided the four-thousand-foot climb into five equal stages. Try and do eight hundred feet between rests. I know that doesn't sound much, but I'm a bit weary, OK? In the last two days I've climbed a total of more than ten thousand feet. Since I left home, a month ago, more than twice the height of Everest.

The main thing, I'm telling myself, is there's no hurry. Stop as long as you like. This turns out to be good advice; there's so much to see, and it's breathtakingly beautiful.

Actually, it's the climb and the altitude that are doing most of the breath-taking. I did prepare for it being a good deal cooler at nine thousand feet, but I don't think I reckoned on the shortage of oxygen. Really? Does it make a noticeable difference?

Well, whatever it is, I'm seriously short of breath by the time I reach the top, nearly nine thousand one hundred feet (did I say that already?) above sea level.

For the first hour I climb in almost perfect solitude. The mountains are beginning to open up. I stop on a stone bridge, just above an overnight park-up for campervans, where I could look down on a now harmless town and up to meadows, scree, peaks, snow, ski-lifts and magnificence.

The air was sharp, with that kind of clarity that makes you think distant summits are just a mile or two away. The stream under the Pont St. Charles gushed. There were flowers, tiny as befitted their alpine altitude, but with ambitiously bright colours. Two cyclists pedal hard past me, clearly on a severe deadline.

When the road, with its evenly punishing gradient, turned around on itself, and the view suddenly changed, I had to stop again. There were more flowers, and huge vistas of green and grey and cream and white. And it would have been rude, I thought, not to properly acknowledge the walkers who had also come up from Val d'Isere, the steep way, and who wanted to know what was in that case on the back of the bike.

It's about then that the motorbikes began to pass me. For the rest of the day they were constant, mostly quiet and respectful, as they should be in the mountains, but occasionally loud, fast, terrifying or suicidal. Uncountable numbers of them. Why do they always hunt in packs? And a couple of touring cyclists from Sheffield, with very little luggage, on nice light carbon fibre bikes, who couldn't believe what they were seeing.

"See you at the top," they said, in tones of cheerful dismissal. They clearly didn't think I'd get that far.

Then the first little wall of snow at the edge of the road. Then bigger patches, a bit brown with accumulated wind-blow, but still bright with glare.

And every kilometre a small painted concrete block of encouragement by the side of the road telling us how far we still had to go, what altitude we'd reached and what average gradient we faced for the next kilometre, all under a schematic picture of a cyclist whose ascent looked impossibly quick and easy.

And then suddenly the *col* itself, a little disappointingly flat-topped, with the iconic sign, two surprised cyclists from Sheffield, lots of bare rock and snow and tiny bright flowers, and a shuttered building that proclaimed itself a restaurant (though presumably only in the summer, which it wasn't yet). A biting wind and an urgent and sweaty need to put on every possible piece of extra clothing. The high point of the journey, twelve hundred miles from home and (I might have already said) nine thousand and sixty-eight feet above sea level. Take that, you doubters.

At the top, lots of the motorbikes are parked up and cyclists are appearing regularly from the other direction, each arrival loudly cheered, before everyone jostles for a spot to have their photo by the Col de l'Iseran sign.

There's also a *Vespa Society of France* convention, and they're coming in droves up the other side.

Several of the bikers ask if there's going to be a concert. Of course there is. I perch on one of the stones, and struggle with cold fingers. In the thin air Libre sounds weak and reedy. She's also gone very sharp.

But the audience is large, and appreciative, and everyone wants to video this idiotic madness. A good number sing along loudly to *My Bonnie Lies Over the Ocean*, without minding when I conduct them into my tempo not theirs.

Getting to the top of the Col de l'Iseran is an achievement for anyone who does it under their own steam. And the cello just adds to it all.

But you can't stay long, because it's too cold. Take some pictures, and set off again, brakes complaining.

Coming down from the *col* to the village of Bonneval ("the highest inhabited Alpine village" by some claims, though I've no idea if it is) the scenery is unquestionably the most dramatic and beautiful I've ever seen. It's wilder, wider, steeper and whiter than the way I came up. But I don't imagine every day is like today. As the story of the Tour de France testifies.

Stop at Bonneval, which you first see as a little toy town of sparkling interlocking buildings, quite a long way below you, to admire the rock-lapped construction of their roofs. Park the bike and wander a little through the narrow streets, where I suspect the houses huddle closely because of the winter.

There's a small church among the old stone and timber houses, and some new houses, built to imitate the old ones. Old rickety wooden balconies, new solid balconies, stacks of firewood everywhere. Tourists, and places for the tourists to sit, and to eat. And a war memorial, a group of bikers who've lined their helmets up at the foot of the war memorial on a bench, and pots of flowers.

Go a little further down the hill, because it still isn't warm enough here, and settle by the shallow river for a bread and cheese lunch, and a little doze in the nearly-warm sunshine.

There are some bikers doing the same, not far off, and one of them comes over. She gives me twenty Euros. "I know you weren't asking for anything, up at the top, but you made a lot of people very happy today," she says.

I eat my Bonneval cheese, then sleep the sleep of the blessed.

CHAPTER 2

The A69

The journey began a few weeks ago. In one sense, anyway. A journey's a story, and the beginning of a story is almost as arbitrary as an ending. One day is always followed by another. There's no stopping. You just pick a point to begin and another to end – but only so you can print a front and back cover, and say what kind of story it is.

Pick a moment. When you close the front door, with a click that sounds the same as it does every day, but with the tell-tale giveaway that you look upwards – why upwards? – as though for inspiration. When you don't quite know how to deal with the nagging thought that something vital is being left behind – something like a passport, or a pair of socks, or everything that counts as sanity.

It's a disorientating moment – a moment of madness, of abandon, of idiotic freedom – scary but slightly optimistic. There's a "normal" life, which we structure in hundreds of little ways – so we know what we're doing, and we can do it without (too much) thinking. We're not inventing ourselves every day.

At the same time I chafe against that normality. I find it boring and constraining. From time to time I call it *soul-destroying*. It seems like a prison, in which I might even be serving a life sentence, from which I crave escape. I want freedom.

But not too much. Because freedom means thinking; the

17

examination of every moment, the making of choices, the taking of responsibility. Which is exhausting if done too much of the time.

So we negotiate, and compromise, looking for the right balance of freedom and structure, routine and invention...

I could give you a precise time for that moment of beginning that I claimed and then immediately disclaimed. It's no more really a beginning than many other moments I might have chosen. So I'm going to pick a different one, and start somewhere else...

Driving along the A69, eastwards from my home in northern Cumbria, to Newcastle and Gateshead, on a Saturday morning in September. The A69 is a great road. Much of it is straight and Roman. The temptation to go faster than the law and single carriageways sensibly permit was strong. Recently, "average speed checks" have been introduced.

The country's wild in places, and nowhere thickly inhabited. The Romans who traversed this route, guarding the limits of their empire, and allegedly wearing socks under their reinforced Mediterranean sandals, must really have felt on the edge of an abyss. It's a real boundary road, following quite closely the line of Hadrian's Wall. Civilisation a long way to the South and Pictish chaos and savagery too close for comfort. (I'm talking about then, not now. Of course.)

The cello's in the boot of the car, and I'm feeling a bit of a fraud.

I've never been a professional cellist. But I'm going to play with a professional orchestra, the Royal Northern Sinfonia, at the Sage in Gateshead.

The Sage is a beautiful and spectacular building. It's a bulbously-curved steel and glass structure sitting right by the Tyne, next to the Baltic Art Gallery and the Millennium Bridge. It looks proudly across the water at Newcastle, challenging that city to a battle of the arts. Which it would win.

Twenty years ago I took a day off work and went to see it when it was under construction and all there was of it was an unfeasibly curvy, sexy, steel frame. Steel frames for buildings used to be straight and right-angled, built by numbers, functional and without much pretension – except perhaps a rather masculine one. And then some engineers got together with some computers, and started dreaming dreams in steel, and drawing the things that filmmakers had been putting on other planets for decades.

The Sage is one of those sketched dreams. Conjure up something that might have been made out of fruit peel, and then get a computer to make it out of steel instead. And a thousand times bigger. Total magic.

You can't of course get into a professional orchestra under false pretences. There's no question of fudging a CV, for example. Entry is by audition. Normally.

But the Royal Northern Sinfonia is a small orchestra, with some big ideas. They had an idea for a massed performance of Verdi's *Requiem*, which is a big work however you look at it, with the professional players shepherding an equal number of amateurs, and a chorus about the size of a football crowd. I was to be one of the drafted-in amateurs.

I live with that feeling of being a bit of a fraud. Sometimes it's just a well-developed sense of not wanting to represent too much. Sometimes I think it's almost full-blown impostor syndrome. But then again, I wouldn't want to claim it's something it might not be.

So I was wondering and worrying, if I should really have put myself forward for this, when that familiar train of thought was suddenly side-swiped by something quite different:

There are two kinds of musician. Well, obviously, there are lots of kinds, but this is a facile generalisation to make a point, ok? There are those who read the music on the page, and don't really play if they haven't got the copy in front of them. And there are those – who may or may not actually read written music – who learn it and play it without the part in front of them. I'm very definitely, and incurably, the first kind.

But recently I've started doing some solo performance of music and poetry, and I find I want an audience connection that isn't mediated by a music stand, and the notes written in front of me.

I just couldn't do it. Hours and hours of learning the notes, and weaning myself off the copy, so that I could play it fine in front of the mirror, with what result? Stage fright, and sudden mental blankness in front of an audience – even if the audience was a single person. I would be playing a tune perfectly and then suddenly not know what the next note was.

And there's a limit, I thought, to how often you have to tell them this was a tune "based on" *Danny Boy*, or *Yesterday*, or a Bach *Sarabande*, while you fish around in a kind of helpless improvisation, looking for the tune again.

So I took to busking.

The idea was that perhaps I could train myself out of it. I thought if I practised on an audience that wasn't really a real audience, a Schrödinger's cat kind of audience, that was at the same time there and not there, it might help. Not of course that buskers don't have real audiences, or that if you're walking along the street you're not really listening. But the audience is mostly transitory. And it hasn't paid up front, so it doesn't feel quite so entitled. An audience without teeth, or something like that.

It hasn't quite worked out, yet. The stage fright isn't tamed or diminished. But I found that I really enjoyed the busking. I like watching the passing parade, and all the different reactions. I love the way children stop and stare – and sometimes dance, totally disrupting the family progress. I love the way they put coins in the open cello case, not quite sure how to do it, and the challenge of thanking them without losing the music.

It's wonderful how the outside tables at the café across the way all stop and applaud together.

I smile at the people who pointedly ignore me – they should take acting lessons, they're so transparent. And I'm still bemused by those who actually don't notice me – I'm not a shy retiring violet when I'm on the street – and sometimes almost walk into me.

And the people who tell me how lovely it is and is that a cello and they used to play the cello and do I give lessons and can I play Elgar's cello concerto for them or the *Jaws* theme tune or something I've never heard of or they haven't got any cash but could they buy me a coffee? And the boys on their bikes doing wheelies in front of me, pretending to show off because they're not sure it's cool to be listening to a cello or whatever it is. I love it.

But I live in a remote place, and Penrith is half an hour away, and any other towns are too far, and soon Penrith – if it isn't already – will be busked out with cello. I need to go further afield.

Further afield is a big place. So, in idle moments, I've been thinking about how to get there – further afield, that is. Maybe I should travel around Europe with my cello – and play in squares, and outside cafés, in the sunshine? Go by train. Maybe I should make my way East, go to India, maybe not come back. There's sunshine there, too.

Cumbria is – there's no doubt about it – the best place to live a settled life. But if there was just a bit more sunshine… Just a bit more sunshine.

These thoughts don't survive much examination. First of all, the cello doesn't like the sunshine. Talk about incompatible partnerships. It doesn't like the rain, either. It's really only happy in a moderately warm room, with all the atmospheric conditions identical to yesterday's, and every day it can remember. Changes in temperature, or humidity, give her the sulks and put her out of tune. If she gets wet, she gets pneumonia. Five minutes of sunshine and she'll split apart.

Apart from that, she's heavy. And she's big. Tall, and broad in the beam. She has to travel in a hard case, and she doesn't fit easily through doorways. She couldn't walk across town, to make a connection from one station to another. She couldn't easily even get from one square to the next if she found the crowd unfriendly.

Most cellos, by the way – and you'll just have to trust me on this for now – are male. They have names like Sebastian (after Johann Sebastian Bach who wrote the *Six Suites for Unaccompanied Cello*, which is still the best cello music *ever*, even three hundred years after it was written, since you ask).

Why my cello turned out to be a lady, I don't know. But she has to be treated like one.

So I couldn't realistically drag her around Europe, in the sunshine. And certainly not to India. (Trans-Siberian railway to Beijing, the new Chinese railway to Lhasa, three or four days' drive to Kathmandu, and over the border near Kushinagar, final resting place of the Buddha, since you ask. It would take about a month.)

No, it just couldn't be done. Unless…

What about leaving the sun-sensitive proper lady cello at home, and taking an instrument not made of wood at all? An electric cello. Cheap, and sometimes nasty. With the right amp a powerful beast that would make anyone sit up and take notice. Slightly sensitive to the rain, I admit, but fine in the sunshine.

Yes, but then you've got to take an amp around as well. You'd need more hands than average, and a strong back. It just wouldn't work.

And then suddenly, that Saturday morning, driving to Gateshead on the A69, making sure the needle didn't too often pass sixty; the solution. Everything fell into place. All those problems resolved. Dissolved. A few more, of course, precipitated themselves out of that solution in due course. But in essence, the single factor that would make it all feasible presented itself. It was obvious:

Go on a bicycle.

I laughed. As did everyone I told, and I suspect everyone *they* told. But you're not laughing, because – if you've read this far – *you know it works*.

So this is the moment, in the story I'm telling, that I'm calling the beginning. The moment when an unformed, nebulous, pie-in-the-sky, daydreaming, idle sort of idea, suddenly becomes a plan. It might still be nebulous, pie-in-the-sky, and all the rest of it, but the Idea has become a Plan. That's it; that's all it takes.

When it's gestating, it's an Idea. When it's taken birth, it's a Plan.

Twenty minutes later, when I had to abandon all further attention to it, just to follow Google Maps' not-quite-timely-enough instructions on how to get through Newcastle and onto Gateshead Quayside, the Plan had Legs. I mean Wheels.

How quickly little plans can grow up. Already I miss those early days. Still dazed from the birth, and here we are with a screaming, mobile, toddler.

CHAPTER 3

Blown off the bike

FRIDAY 27 MAY

And now, a bit more than half a year after that beginning day, here I am at the beginning of the *real* day, that most people would recognise as a real beginning. Three or four sleepy people have come out in their pyjamas, the morning after the birthday party of the night before, to wave me off, and then, I suspect, to go back to bed thankful it's me and not them.

The bike is loaded. Two smallish panniers on the front, with the very minimum of clothes, below a lopsided bag with some pristine poetry books and fifty CDs. The cello, in its pink chequered case plastered with reflective yellow strips, on the rack stretching out behind and making the bike twice as long as it would otherwise be. Squashed between the cello and the saddle, a smaller bag, sideways on the rack, with some tools, waterproofs, high-energy food, and a few other quick-access essentials. Under the cello another pannier with cello accessories – an expanding stool, a lightweight music stand – and a padlock thingy long enough to chain the bike to a tree.

It's all too heavy, unwieldy and unbalanced to ride up the gravel drive. So it's an ignominious start, and a damp squib of a send-off. There's a limit to how much waving and good-lucking you want to do when you're in your pyjamas, the morning after the night before, and wanting to get back to bed.

I push up the drive, trying to look jaunty, trying to make it look less heavy than it is. I turn round briefly at the top, to see the farewellers drifting away, still half-waving, back to bed.

It's a lonely moment. One of those when the self-doubt is so overwhelming you just don't know what to do with it. When speaking sternly to yourself isn't enough. How stupid, I said, probably aloud, to feel this way after so much planning, so much preparation, so much effort to get to this moment of beginning, which seemed for so long so far in the future as to be fiction.

Well, it isn't fiction now.

Due to some mismanagement, a late cancellation, the birthday being on an inconvenient day, and a number of unanswered emails, today is going to be a difficult day. It would be difficult *without* the tidal wave of self-doubt, the chronic lack of practice on the fully-loaded and lorry-length bicycle, and the compulsive checking of everything I might have forgotten.

I planned to ride the eighteen hundred miles to Rome in manageable, fifty-mile, chunks. A bit more on flat days. A lot less on mountainous alpine days. Today, for all the reasons above, I have to ride seventy miles. I have to go up and over the Yorkshire Dales, which are big hills, and which will add six thousand feet of climbing to the day's effort. And then I have to perform a two-set concert in the Town Hall at Masham.

Seriously, that's not a sensible first day. And, seriously, I'm not sure I can do it.

I push off, wobbling, grateful that the send-off has gone off back to bed. I should have done more practice riding a fully loaded bike. But that felt silly. I would meet people I knew. "Where are you going?" they would ask, and I'd have to tell them I wasn't actually going anywhere, yet, I was just practising. But, believe me, if you're used to riding a bare bicycle, you really need some practice with the cello on the back, and some panniers on the front. It isn't the same thing at all. Imagine driving your Cinquecento with a caravan on the back, and a brown bear sitting on the steering wheel.

At least I know where Kirkby Stephen is. It's twenty-eight miles away, on not too hilly, and very quiet, roads. The White Hare Café will be open, and Maz will be pleased to see me, and it will be coffee time.

I know where it is because I went there, three weeks ago, on my only proper practice ride with the cello. I set the borrowed GPS thingy, pointed the bike in the direction it said, and set off. I could see the GPS thingy and I were going to have to work out who's boss. And it's going to have to be me.

Are you joking? I had to ask it, more than once. Roads that were little more than tracks, wide enough for two sheep to pass, but not a bike and a Range Rover. Potholes that made the cello squeak and moan in protest. Twice I had to stop, and open the case, and give us both a tranquillizer.

And then the firing range. Warcop, it's called. Seems a fair name. *No entry. Do not enter. Do not stop. Do not get out of your vehicle. Beware live firing. No entry – unexploded ordnance.* Etc., etc. But the red flags weren't actually flying, and I didn't hear any actual explosions. There's mile after mile of it, though, and I didn't like it. At least there was no traffic.

Kirkby Stephen (which no-one knows how to spell, even if they live there) is, as the advertisements claim, a beautiful place. I was welcomed by pealing church bells. (That was actually for a grand wedding, not for me, but never mind.) I rode up and down the main street a couple of times, trying to muster the courage to stop and get the cello out.

After a couple of passes I picked a spot at random and parked up. I went into the pub, waited my turn, and then pointed at the bike through the window. Could I play my cello on the pavement outside your pub?

Of course, of course, that would be nice, make yourself at home!

I played for an hour, wishing it was just a little bit warmer. Lots of passing cars lowered their windows. One elderly couple passed me three times, looking slightly doubtful. A young Kirkby Stephenite, who described himself as a photographer, was very pleased when I asked him to take some photos. The proprietor of the café next door came out in a quiet moment and was very keen to have some photos with his café in the background.

The sun came out as I drank tea, inside, and then went in again as soon as I got back on the bike. But I got home, and all day it hadn't rained, and I'd met some very interesting people in Kirkby Stephen, and I gave Warcop a very wide berth on the return, despite the borrowed GPS flashing red lights at me in displeasure, and I thought maybe – just maybe – I can do this, after all.

So today Maz and his café would be a good first staging post, I thought. Through Ousby, which, according to the road sign, is "a doubly thankful village". Are we supposed to know what that means? Overtaking an old man on a bike, turning his pedals very slowly, who called after me, "I saw you on the telly!" Yes, a couple of days ago the local news had done a short feature, in its "this will make you laugh" sign-off slot.

It's still a couple of weeks until Appleby Horse Fair but already, as I approach Appleby, on the way to Kirkby Stephen, the defences are up. You can see why gypsies and travellers feel persecuted. Everywhere there are newly erected palisades. Anywhere a couple of caravans could park up there are fierce notices forbidding it, except in some places for a week or so, on strictly specified dates. About ten thousand travellers will come, and among the big cars and big white caravans there will be hundreds of horses and horse-drawn wagons.

Appleby Horse Fair claims a charter from James II. It's part of the history, and the mythology, of European gypsies. The young men, and quite small boys, canter and gallop bareback up and down the main drag, the "Flashing", and drive their horses into the river. The young women parade in small packs, in high heels and short skirts. Marriages, as well as horse trades, are contracted. Very flashy cars, perfectly polished, specially hired for the occasion, crawl through the crowded streets, shirtless men hanging their elbows out of open windows.

But it causes a lot of controversy. Instead of making hay, many local businesses shutter their shops. Petty criminals converge on the town, knowing the gypsies will be blamed. There are accusations of animal cruelty – a dehydrated horse makes headlines; but a dog dying in a visitor's unventilated car doesn't. And the litter. *Don't get me started on the litter*, a spluttering local warned me loudly. Have you seen the aftermath of a music festival, I wanted to ask him; and does the local authority put out enough bins? But it doesn't help. You're either for it, or against it. I shall be sorry to miss it this year.

The café was full. The bike was propped up outside the window. Maz welcomed me like an old friend, and announced generally that this man and his cello were on their way to Rome.

The table with the only free seat invited me to join her. She knew all the official cycle routes across Europe. Presumably, she said, I was going on the Eurovelo 5 most of the way? There were advantages to the Eurovelo 15, of course, and the EV19 was pretty, but it abandoned you in the middle of nowhere. Which was I doing?

I couldn't admit that I didn't know what she was talking about. I mumbled something about it being a road bike, and I couldn't really go off-road with a cello, and I was following the *Via Francigena*, the old pilgrim route, and some of the Roman road lines, at least in a general sense. Ah, she said, the EV5; yes, that's what I would do.

She wished me luck, and paid my bill without telling me.

Out of Kirkby Stephen and the road is suddenly steep. The sign says it's 20%. I can hardly pedal up that. But getting off to push would be a worse option. It settles down to 14%, but it's still a very long way from the Eden Valley up to the glory of the Yorkshire Dales.

I was blown off the bike. Literally. Over the top of the Yorkshire Dales the wind was – I'm guessing – 60mph. Later, a bit lower down and feeling slightly safer, I met several people who said places had closed everywhere because they weren't safe.

Down to the Tan Hill pub – the "highest in England" – with that dark, dour, besieged look common to all high-altitude inns. But no time to stop. I need to get down to Reeth, fifty miles from home, before I can sensibly stop for lunch. It would be a pretty place if the big village green wasn't a huge car park. I sat on a bench. It wasn't quite warm enough.

A bevy of Scottish cyclists want to know all about it. A white van stopped to make a delivery to the hotel. Its driver said he saw me wobbling about on the top, and nearly stopped to offer me a lift. "I thought that was a boat on the back," he said. "You didn't look happy." I wish he had stopped. Then I was glad he hadn't – it would have been a temptation, and probably a defeat. It's a bit soon for that.

An old lady approached me, waving a paper. "Have you come to play the festival tomorrow?" she asked.

When I said I didn't know about the festival she went to get a programme to present me with. The Swaledale Festival featured the eight cellos of the Hallé Orchestra, and one of the younger Kanneh-Masons, in its extensive programme. Maybe out of my league, then; but nice of you to ask.

It's still twenty miles to Masham, and although it's mostly downhill, I still shouldn't dawdle. Masham, with a more or less silent "h". I've been saying it wrong all the time.

A few miles before Masham the imposing ruin of Jervaulx Abbey requires a big kink in the road. There's a £5 honesty box, and almost no-one there. I wonder how many Cistercians there would have been here in its heyday – it's huge. Like most of the other ninety or so Cistercian abbeys in the UK, it was founded in the middle of the twelfth century. It lasted just shy of four hundred years, before Henry VIII dissolved it, and hanged its abbot for good measure. I couldn't really cycle past without paying a visit, I thought.

It's atmospheric and beautiful. I went back to the bike, parked at the gate, and fetched Libre. I wondered if someone would come and stop me, but I played for half an hour among the ruins, and felt renewed, much less tired. This, after all, I reminded myself, is what *Highway Cello* is about. Libre isn't just baggage; she's an essential part of the enterprise. She should sing. This would be the first impromptu performance en route, where something significant made an intersection that required our musical response.

A Cistercian expert came by, with a big camera. Yes, he said, but it's not a patch on Rievaulx, is it? Have you come from there, or are you going there next? He was one of those experts who behave as though you share their agenda, and much of their knowledge, who expect proper Wikipedia contributions to the conversation.

They don't really, of course. If by chance you do know as much as them, they're likely to go off quite quickly in a bit of a sulk. But he was safe with me. I'd heard of Rievaulx, but I wasn't sure I could spell it, and I didn't know it was barely thirty miles away. Not today, I said; deadlines.

Then, of course, I was late getting to Masham. I was exhausted, and dehydrated. I'd brought two bottles of water from home, and still had one and a half left. That was stupid, I remember telling myself, before I fell over, in a state of dizzy amnesia, on the bed of the shepherd's hut the good burghers of Masham had kindly provided for my accommodation that night.

I couldn't do anything else. I only just managed to get up in time to go to the grandly named Town Hall to play. I'd had no tea. I was still dizzy. I couldn't remember the name of the town I was in. I couldn't remember anyone's name. I forgot my own poems as I was performing them.

But the audience was lovely, and very sympathetic to the hunger and everything else. We had to have a slightly longer interval than planned while a very kind gentleman went to his car and brought me a local pork pie about the size of a football. While I ate it, with sounds of appreciation that probably shouldn't be made in public, I re-jigged the second set so I could perform the poetry with the words in front of me.

It could have been worse. But there are some days the ending of which is cause for great relief. This was one of those days. Tomorrow will be gentle.

CHAPTER 4

Not a real cello

If the bicycle was the moment of birth, when the gestating idea became a nappy-filling plan, and therefore by my unilateral decision the beginning of this story, there was still a fair amount of growing up to do.

Neither of my cellos, on any measure, was up to making such a journey. A proper cello, by which I mean an expensive, delicate, wooden *prima donna*, does not go out in the sun. It doesn't go out in the rain. It certainly doesn't get strapped to the back of a bicycle, to get bounced around all day on the road, and then respond well to any expectation that it might stop and make some music.

An electric cello, on the other hand, would do most of that – with some caveat over the rain thing – but it has difficulties of its own. Most electric cellos look pretty good, once you get used to them being rather skeletal. They don't need all the reverberating body of a conventional cello, so they tend to dispense with that. All they need is a simple up and down structure on which you can tension the strings, and a couple of sticking out bits so you can hold it between your knees and play it. They look elegant and airy.

And you can have them any colour you like, because the wood (if they're even made of wood) doesn't have to breathe and resonate, so it can be painted. They draw attention to themselves and like to be noticed. Which, of course, is an advantage if you're busking.

But they're just as heavy as a real cello; often heavier. And you need a suitcase-sized amp, and a lead, and some batteries, and ideally a roadie to carry it all.

On the back of a bike? It's a big ask.

There's a third kind of cello though, which on that Saturday morning on the A69 I knew nothing about. I'd seen pictures of it, that's all. It looks quite like a real cello – by which you know I mean a wooden one with four curves and four corners, made out of five different kinds of wood, to a pattern perfected in the early eighteenth century and hardly changed since.

This third kind of cello isn't made of wood at all. It has the curves, but no corners. Why, come to think of it, does a real cello have so many corners? Not for any musical reason. Only that without the corners it wouldn't be strong enough to hold together under the tension of the strings. It's a compromise between strength and function.

So, if you built a cello out of a material that weight for weight is stronger than steel, you'd ditch the corners, wouldn't you?

Then your cello, being all curves, would be – what's the word I'm looking for? – quite sexy.

This is a cello inspired by a racing catamaran. And made out of the same material – carbon fibre.

From a standing start I learned a lot about carbon fibre cellos that weekend. And by Wednesday I was playing one.

The story of the carbon fibre cello isn't a long one. A cellist called Luis Leguia, who'd played in the famous Boston Symphony Orchestra for nearly forty years by then, was inventing it in his basement at about the same time as I was taking the day off work to go and see the steel frame of the Sage Gateshead under construction. Both of us enjoying the curves.

He'd played a real cello in a really real orchestra for forty years, and then decided he wanted to make something better?

Yes, really, that's the story.

As well as a cellist, he was a sailor. Seeing the smooth and shining hull of a racing boat in the water one day, and hearing it hum, he realised a cello made out of the same stuff would be a lot less damageable than a real one. It would look good, too. And it might even sound like a cello.

Luis Leguia was, by the way, an extraordinary cellist. If you want to be really good at the cello you have to start learning it absolutely no later than your first day at school. And by the time you're halfway through school you need to be practising it several hours a day.

But Luis Leguia didn't pick up a cello until he was fifteen. Far too late for any normal person to make a success of it. But he worked very hard, and by the time he was seventeen, the great – the greatest – Pablo Casals had taken him on as a scholarship student.

Some cellists become legendary. Mstislav Rostropovich, for instance, Russian dissident and later hero, who's had about a hundred concertos written for him and dedicated to him, who shares a birthday with me, and was friends with Shostakovich, Leonard Bernstein, and Benjamin Britten. What a giant.

And Pablo Casals. Pablo – Pau in his native Catalan – was born in 1876, and by the time he was four, allegedly played the violin, the flute and the piano. His first cello, a few years later, was amateurishly made for him by his father out of a hardened gourd and a broom handle. Allegedly – this is all hagiography now.

Casals is famous, and revered among cellists, for two great things, one of which changed the world. He rediscovered the Bach *Suites for Cello*, in a second-hand bookshop in Barcelona (and the rest is history). And in all his concerts in exile from Spain during the Civil War, every single one of them, he goaded General Franco by playing a simple Catalan melody, the *Song of the Birds*, which he said was a song of love and freedom. Every cellist, all over the world, now plays the Bach *Suites* and the *Song of the Birds*.

Luis Leguia, now retired from the Boston Symphony Orchestra, and unable to play the cello because of damage to his hands, sometimes laments, he says, that he will be remembered for his carbon fibre cello, and not for being a cellist. Well, he was a great cellist, definitely. Not a world-changing one like Casals, admittedly – those don't emerge more than once or twice in a century. His carbon fibre cello though is definitely world-changing.

When he started making his prototypes in his Boston basement, Luis Leguia's wife was not a believer. She was, she admits, slightly scornful of the self-indulgence and waste of time, as she saw it.

But when the first prototype was finished, and Luis Leguia expressed his disappointment that it didn't sound like a great cello – a cello, yes; but not a great one – Mrs. Stephanie Leguia was an instant convert.

"It sounds like a cello!" she said.

And you can imagine the surprise, the amazement, the greatest kind of reconciling apology a husband can ever hope to hear.

Only a few prototypes later and Luis Leguia was satisfied. The carbon fibre cello was born. A manufacturing company was set up; Mrs. Stephanie Leguia took her proper place in charge, and that was that.

It was a bit slow to catch on, though. In the first couple of years only a handful were sold. Even when Yo-Yo Ma, another cello legend, bought number 4, it was still slow. Yo-Yo Ma; who played for the inauguration of President Barack Obama, who played all six of the Bach *Cello Suites* at one marathon Prom concert at the Royal Albert Hall in London, who normally plays a 1733 Montagnana cello said to be insured for $3m.

Yes, Yo-Yo Ma, who founded the Silk Road Ensemble in 1998, to connect music from China to America, and all points in between.

But cellists are a conservative lot. The answer to the traditional question, *how many cellists does it take to change a light bulb?* is, *Change?! What do you mean, change?*

So twenty years later the total world population of Luis and

Clark cellos, as they are called, is still only about 1350. They're all numbered. And mine is number 580.

Well, I didn't buy it new. I had a bit of a budget in mind, as I drove back along the A69 later that day, for the cello I was going to buy for this expedition. It would be what the industry slyly calls a *student model*. Maybe not quite as cheap as the plywood ones that come out of Chinese factories, bought perhaps to be abused in mass lessons in schools where music is only taught, like prayers, on sufferance, and to be thrown away when it's fallen apart after a couple of years.

Maybe not quite that cheap, but definitely not expensive. It wasn't a difficult decision, I thought. I needed not to worry about it being out in the sun, even being rained on occasionally, and bouncing around on the back of the bike. When I got home again it could show the scars of war with some pride. And if it suffered a fatal wound on the battlefield, well, it would be lamented of course, but not for too long.

Then I remembered the picture I'd seen of Yo-Yo Ma playing this beautiful shiny black cello without corners, and Stjepan Hauser, the handsome one from the famous 2Cellos, and I thought maybe there's no harm in asking a few questions. Just having a look.

Honestly, I was just having a look. I learnt about the Luis and Clark carbon fibre cello, and listened to it a bit. But you can't tell online, because you don't know what electronic jiggery-pokery has been done to the recording; adding reverb and chorus and whatnot. All the recordings sound as though they've had some reverb added, but the sound is clear, and strong. In the lower registers they sound like real, and very expensive, cellos. In the upper registers they sound a bit more electronic, with a sound that's less complex than that of a real cello. But still magnificent.

Shipped new from the workshop in Massachusetts they cost about five times the (admittedly rather vague) budget that's in my head. So out of the question.

Until I found a second-hand one for sale about three hundred miles away.

What's a budget, anyway? You can't take it with you, can you? And what else am I going to spend it on?

You can tell where this is going, can't you?

He wanted me to drive three hundred miles to collect it. But I told him if it's as strong as they say, you can just put it in the post. And if it doesn't arrive in one piece, I don't want it anyway.

It arrived in one piece, and a day earlier than scheduled. I nearly kissed the postie from excitement. But he was wearing a floral sun hat (in the rain), and he was quite large, and I thought maybe it wouldn't be wise. It isn't always easy to show your appreciation wisely.

If I had driven those three hundred miles to see it and test it out, I would have discovered its injury, presumably a childhood trauma. The fingerboard was a little detached from the neck. And then I might not have bought it. A traumatised cello is hard to home – a bit of a risk.

I rang Mrs. Stephanie Leguia, to ask her how to fix it. She sent me a link to an automotive epoxy resin which, she said, was the stuff they used.

An automotive resin? On a cello?

So how then do I detach the fingerboard where it's still attached, in order to re-attach the whole thing?

You have to use a hammer and chisel, she said.

A hammer and chisel? On a cello?

Well, that's how strong it is, she said.

God's teeth, I thought. Or something like that.

CHAPTER 5

Going Viking

SUNDAY 29 MAY

As soon as it opened, I had scrambled eggs in the campsite café at Masham, where the little shepherd's hut lived. I haven't properly recovered from yesterday's ride and the disorientating, dizzy, brain emptiness that followed. It wouldn't be an exaggeration to say I was frightened by it. Have I ever had amnesia before? I can't remember.

Sorry.

But if it's brought on by exhaustion and dehydration then I'm definitely going to be more careful. It's still a long way to Rome.

Fortunately, I don't have far to go today. I'm going to stay with some good friends in Harrogate, and on the way I'm going to stop in Ripon.

In an earlier version of the plan there was going to be a concert in Ripon. The cathedral had kindly included me in their lunchtime concerts series. But that had to be changed when someone remembered there was a Jubilee, and they should probably put on a massed choir instead. At least, that was the reason that reached me.

Ripon is on the way to Harrogate, and I've not got much riding to do. Besides, playing to an empty abbey that was dissolved and de-roofed nearly five hundred years ago is one thing, but playing to a living breathing crowd of Saturday shoppers is another thing altogether. And I think I'd like to see the cathedral anyway.

Ripon isn't a big place and finding the town centre isn't difficult. Today isn't market day, but there are still a handful of stalls to one side of the square, which is dominated by an enormous obelisk. It's far too tall to see who might be standing on the top of it, who it might be a memorial to. In fact I don't think it's dedicated to anyone; I think it's just an obelisk, for obelisk's sake.

The plinth around the base looks like a good place to sit and play. Lots of other people are already sitting there, exhausted from shopping, or not doing very much, and I think I might join them. A fitting place, I think, for the first public busking of the *Highway Cello* project.

Surely there could be no better place to play a cello, sitting in the sunshine, serenading the market?

But it didn't go well. Perhaps the good burghers of Ripon have more (or maybe – I don't know – less) exalted tastes. I was comprehensively ignored. I persevered for forty minutes and earned £1 – from a gentleman who appeared to be selling paint rollers (though perhaps he'd just bought them, and didn't really know how to carry them).

He had a story to tell – he was writing a book about arithmetic, explaining why it didn't work. I couldn't quite follow the argument, but no doubt it will be persuasive when it's published.

I should have analysed the busking failure. Instead of just feeling sorry for myself, and thinking the Riponites were Philistines, I should have asked what I was doing wrong. I don't know. Why was it important? I wasn't relying on the income, so why did it matter? Ah well, perhaps next time would be better.

I packed up and pedalled the short way to the cathedral. The bike looks good, propped in splendid isolation against the imposing West Front. It's hard to believe this was just an ordinary parish church until 1836. It looks as though the entire town could sit in the nave facing the red tiered seats, put out, no doubt, for the massed Jubilee choir. Lovely windows, and little painted saints and martyrs in comfortable cosy niches.

But this is no place to busk; there's no-one here. I should have stopped longer in Ripon and found something for lunch, but the accumulation of disappointment was a bit much. So instead I pressed on, to Harrogate, looking for better luck. Have I not learnt from yesterday? If you're hungry, eat. Don't forget to drink.

And then another argument with the GPS thingy. I haven't yet got the measure of it. Paper maps are so last decade. These days you're supposed to plan a route on an app on the phone, and transfer it to the GPS, for the GPS to give you reliable and uninterrupted instructions as you progress. It works well when it works. But the app I'm using has a particular liking for farm tracks. Especially if they're steep and strewn with boulders.

I met the farmer. I couldn't ride up this, and I was very crossly and very slowly pushing the bike up the boulder-strewn hill. The track showed all the signs of doubling as a raging torrent in wet weather. Churlishly I didn't get out of his way, as he came down in his 4x4, which I could have done.

He asked if I needed help. Yes, he said, it was a bridleway, and a public right of way, but he owned it, and if he didn't maintain it eventually people would stop using it, wouldn't they?

The GPS thingy also didn't tell me – which a paper map would have done – that I'd passed within a mile or two of Fountains Abbey. If I'd known I would certainly have added it to my list of important, dissolved and ruined, Cistercian sites visited en route, wouldn't I?

And so, after only thirty miles, but more than a day's worth of emotional turmoil, I found the house in Harrogate. I drank three cups of tea straight off, ate Daniel's beautiful Spanish lunch at tea time, segued neatly into dinner and, just before bedding down on the living room floor, played them a few tunes.

Nearly-three-year-old Samu had never seen a cello before. The delight on his face, and his wild clapping when he heard it, transformed the day.

I didn't really want to get up. I've only ridden two days, one long and one deliberately short to allow some recovery from the long one. But they were both, in their way, difficult. Here I am, with friends I've known almost since they were the age of their own offspring now, and I don't want to venture out again into the unknown.

The point of this journey, of course, is to go out into the unknown. To see what's there; to see what happens; to meet the unexpected. But the unknown and the unexpected scare me, especially in prospect. I imagine all kinds of things, all of them mistakes, disasters, accidents, embarrassments or dangers. I don't relax out in the unknown.

Samu, of course, is up before anyone else. He makes it clear the day has begun. We should be on our feet and doing things; not lying down, boringly.

I've planned another short day today – two days to recover from the badly-planned excesses of the first day. So I'm not in a hurry. I linger. Then I linger a bit longer. Then I start to pack the bike again. It's amazing how long that can take if I do it thoroughly.

It can't be put off forever, though. I'm beginning to get the measure of the GPS thingy. I've learnt how to give it instructions, and then how to interrogate the thick blue line of its suggested route. There's a button that has to be pressed to lift the blue line temporarily, so that I can see what's underneath it. The blue line makes you think there must be a decent road. Take it away, and you can see where the GPS has chosen little roads, and where those little roads disappear into tracks and minefields and goods yards and glaciers. And adjust the route accordingly.

There's one such bit of the route just outside Knaresborough. A small diversion eliminates it – victory over the GPS, and an achievement to be celebrated.

Wiggle around the little roads of Harrogate, north of the town centre. Sometimes a cul-de-sac has an escape for pedestrians and cyclists. Sometimes it doesn't. Take the diversion on the edge of Knaresborough and find yourself, suddenly, on the main bridge looking down on a bigger river than you expected – the eccentrically-named Nidd – and a long line of red and green rowing boats.

Somewhere around here, presumably up one of these hills, must be the remains of Knaresborough Castle, where the murderers of Thomas Beckett holed up after the dirty deed. But there's no time to look for it. I'm on a deadline.

I was in correspondence with York Minster. Could I, I asked, play a *pop-up* concert in some suitable place – outside if the weather's ok – as part of my journey? Yes, they said, after they had established that a) I could play the cello and b) the journey could almost be called a pilgrimage. They suggested a spot outside St. William's College, facing the Green, and with the great East Window looking down on me. Perfect, I said. 12.30 on Sunday then.

I was planning to go to the Sunday service beforehand, it not being very far from Harrogate. But as you know I had a late start. And by the time I'd gone too far along the river (it's called the Nidd, you know) in Knaresborough, and backtracked, and pushed up a cobbled hill far too steep to ride, and tried to cross the railway line by a pedestrian underpass with steps, and given up, and found another way, it was after 12.30 before I got to the Minster.

A small audience was waiting. They'd circumambulated the Minster looking for me and were, I think, on the point of giving up. They greeted the bike like a long-lost friend, then settled at a picnic table on the Green with obviously high expectations. Maria had heard my playing before, and now brought her friends to hear it too. Afterwards she wrote to me, inviting me to make a tour to Greece, where all her family were, scattered about, all of whom would be honoured to host me, she said. Wasn't that nice?

But it was cold, and I wasn't in the sun, and too much of the crowd was just passing by. So after Maria and her friends left, I ate the remains of the pizza Daniel made last night, and set off into town to look for a different kind of place to play. I was thinking that a more confined space, where the passers-by pass by a bit closer, might be better – by which I mean, might solicit more contributions.

So now here I am, playing my cello in an occasionally sunny spot in York. When the sun comes out it's warm and lovely. The rest of the time it's neither. There's no room for cars here, but the streets are full of people wandering. A lot of ice cream is being eaten.

Within the crowd, and usually more purposeful in their passage than the obvious tourists, are quite a lot of people rather unconventionally dressed. I'm guessing it's some kind of medieval pageant somewhere.

No, I was told, when I stopped a couple of them, we're Vikings. Do you need any pillaging doing?

I think I can do my own pillaging when required, thank you for asking, I said, but today I'm just playing the cello.

I played quite a lot on the streets of York, here and in a couple of other places, mostly outside ice-cream and chip shops. A small girl with very new front teeth stopped, and grinned, and had her picture taken with me. I asked her if she would like to dance to the music, which she did very beautifully. A proud parent filmed. That was nice.

Then Caitlin stopped, having recognised some Bach. She was a pianist, and experimental musician, she said; but it was so hard to make a living from music in a pandemic. We gave each other a bit of encouragement, and I admired her strikingly pink hair.

York is a really nice place. I had a cup of coffee in a nice tea shop where a plate of cakes and tea for two could be had for not much more than the price of a small family's weekly shop. And afterwards, feeling that I'd achieved something today, I went off in search of my *Warmshowers* host, Tim.

CHAPTER 6

Cellos are complicated

The relationship between player and cello is intense. It can also be complicated. I'd had my shiny black curvy and cornerless Luis and Clark cello for three days, and the complications were screaming.

In the whole of my life, until now, I've had seven real cellos (plus the electric one, but that's different, and it's not complicated).

Before the cellos there was a violin. That was very unfortunate. My father played the violin well enough to be in some demand as an amateur quartet player. He believed the most important part of his children's education was the learning of the violin.

I have an older brother who's infinitely more musical than I've ever been, or ever will be. He sat down at a piano at a very early age and played it. He picked up the violin, and never looked back. He's also a mathematical genius. He's going to win a Nobel Prize one day, but that's not this story.

So, thirteen months younger than him, and practically tone deaf, I was never going to compete with him in the musical stakes. And I was an obnoxiously competitive child. Especially where the older brother was concerned. I think it should be recorded that for all his musical and mathematical abilities I could do at least the following things much better than him: climb trees, ride a bike, shout (and make grown-ups shout), break things, make a mess, and lie.

The little violin was a horrid thing. Elder Brother had grown out of it, so it wasn't even really my violin. It made a nasty noise. It was boring, pointless, and a torture for everyone involved.

Father did his best, but he belonged to the *no tea until he's done his practice* school. And encouragement wasn't in his vocabulary. If he'd known any child psychology (which my mother had done a course in, but he wouldn't be told) he would have known this was never going to work.

Then one day the horrid little violin was found in its case, mysteriously and irreparably broken. Irreparably. At least Father knew he'd been beaten. He retired from the ring. I was a cruel child – which even now is a painful recollection, and an embarrassing admission.

A few years later I saw someone playing a cello, and decided on the spot that I wanted one of those. It had lots of advantages over the violin, mostly to do with size, which is quite important to small boys, especially if they have an older brother.

I didn't know it then, though of course I discovered it as soon as the half-size cello called Sebastian came into my possession, that it had a spike. A very manly piece of kit, that – oh happy day! – I found could be weaponised against the younger brothers who by then were beginning to need more aggressive treatment.

I still wasn't musical. I still didn't like practising. But for some reason the *no tea until he's done his practice* regime now worked, up to a point, and I grudgingly and impatiently persevered.

Two paedophile teachers later – one who served a long prison sentence, and one who many years later killed himself when a police investigation was at an advanced stage – I got a bigger cello. I think Sebastian is still in a cupboard somewhere. But this bigger cello has disappeared. At some point in the last twenty years I lent it to someone – I can't remember who – and it never came back.

Then an almost proper cello. It came from a factory in East Germany, though the certificate was insistent it had been constructed and finished by a named maker. So it was a slight step up from a factory

45

cello, but probably not very much. I think by then I'd reached an age at which the naming of cellos seemed infantile.

Ah, the gendering and naming of cellos. Not all cellists get it. And it's practically Masonic, in the sense it isn't something you really talk to non-cellists about. Well you wouldn't, would you? But soon there are going to be two more cellos, whose naming and gendering need some explanation – if only to justify myself in the light of the complications I mentioned.

But we need to return to Mr. Luis Leguia's motivation for making the carbon fibre cello, in the light of Mrs. Stephanie Leguia's initially less-than-fulsome support. He didn't want specifically to make a cheaper instrument, or a more robust one, though of course he knew he would do that. That was incidental.

What he wanted was to make a *better* cello. That is to say, a cello that sounds like a cello, only more so. He was going to make a cheap cello that sounded like a really, really expensive one. Well, cheap in the scheme of things, when a good old instrument costs millions, and even a back desk player in a professional orchestra has an instrument instead of a pension fund. In a world where the mortgage goes on the instrument, not the house.

I only know one other person who has done something similar from a similar motivation.

My father was not a young man about town. He didn't spend money on himself, and he didn't see any need to spend it on anyone else. As a result, in those far off days, and before they became real film star items, he found himself with a year's accumulated Civil Servant's salary in his bank account, and he could afford to buy an eighteenth-century violin by a named maker. He spent the year's salary on a violin by Johannes Gagliano, *circa* 1790.

Leaving aside the fact that he really wasn't a good enough player to have such a thing, he bought it. It came with a certificate of authenticity from the most famous dealers of the day, who went out of business years ago so they can't now be sued.

He insured it for the value they certified. He played it. And his playing was consequently admired. One of the paedophile teachers, who *was* a proper violinist (and not a cellist at all) coveted it to the point where he nearly committed a crime that might have got him jailed. And then he might not have had to commit suicide later. Who knows how things could have turned out differently.

It wasn't until Elder Brother inherited it that it was discovered to be a fake.

Actually, not really a fake. The dealers had just misattributed it. It's a perfectly good violin; it's just that it's now worth 10% of what it had been worth before. All those wasted insurance premiums.

The point is, though, that Father decided after he'd bought it, it really was quite expensive and maybe he should have put a deposit on a house instead. And more importantly, surely he could make one just as good?

He tried. He tried hard. I have memories of bonfire nights in the garden when we smashed up rejected instruments and put them on the fire. Even then I felt this was a wanton destruction we shouldn't be undertaking.

Father was adamant. An instrument that wasn't good enough wasn't to go out in the world with his name on it. It was pointless telling him to take the label off, and sell it anyway, and use the money to buy me a bike.

I don't know about violins. I don't play the violin, remember. But Elder Brother tells me eventually our father made quite good ones. He never sold one though. He said it would make his income tax too complicated. He lived in mortal fear of making a tiny mistake on his income tax form and being marched off to jail. He just lent them to people, and never asked for them back. No-one knows where they all are now. Even how many of them there are. Like some famous people and their rather too many children.

He also made three cellos. And where Mr. Luis Leguia succeeded so spectacularly, my late lamented father failed.

The first cello met the bonfire fate. Very deservedly. He'd made the front plate far too thin. It's complicated, but basically if the front's too thick it makes a dead sound, and if it's too thin the cello's "wolfy". This one was so thin it warped under the weight of the strings tensioned over the bridge.

The second cello was a bit better. I played it for a couple of years, despite its unorthodox mauve colour – a fault in the staining – and all its other deficiencies. Until the third cello. By then I wasn't quite such a cruel child, and I knew that gratuitous honesty wasn't called for. I said nice things about it and tried hard to make a nice sound on it. It was, of course, *mine*, so there was some incentive.

The third cello was a bit better again, and a much better colour. I played it for years, until I had to admit to myself that actually the East German factory-begun-and-hand-finished cello was still better. By then I'd left home and thought perhaps I might swap back to it without it really being noticed. But I still played it guiltily.

The third cello wasn't a bad instrument. It's a bit heavy, but it's sound and even-tempered. It's now my daughter's, and she tells me it, too, is a Sebastian.

No, no, said Elder Brother; that's not how it happened at all.

As well as inheriting the violin, Elder Brother had received Father's archives (surely only people who know they're important keep *archives*?) So he could consult Father's 1940s tax returns – yes, really; kept forever in case the Inland Revenue should ever raise a question – and say with confidence that Father had only spent one-sixth of his salary on the violin. Cremonese antiques were not so important then.

It was fifteen years later, and with a young family, that Father decided he should upgrade, and found he couldn't afford to. A combination of child costs and fiddle inflation. That's when he decided he could make a better one.

When it comes to family history, it always depends who's

telling it. I think mine's a better story, but Elder Brother's more likely to be right.

Aren't they always?

The catalogue of cellos is nearly complete. Decades after all this, and only a few years ago, I thought I deserved a proper cello. (I hadn't thought of this before, but was it a case of "like father like son"? Oh dear.) Not of course the kind of instrument Father had bought himself – those are for serious soloists, or museums. And of course they now commanded serious money, laughably far beyond my reach.

I decided I should go to a professional maker, and have one made for me. Which is where all the complications began.

CHAPTER 7

Gainsborough

MONDAY 30 MAY

Warmshowers is a big organisation. It's a community of tens of
thousands of long-distance cyclists, all offering accommodation to
each other on their mad long-distance rides. You can look anywhere
in the world you want to go, and as long as you're on a bike, and
planning to cycle not less than about five thousand miles, you can
find people willing to offer you a bed. The *quid pro quo*, of course,
is you have to offer a bed too. You're allowed one get-out clause:
"currently unavailable – cycling round the world."

I'd been performing at Penrith's monthly Plug and Play – where
you just turn up, and take pot luck, whether you're musician or
audience – when I met Barbara. She introduced me to *Warmshowers*,
and the next day I spent an hour or two exploring its tall tales and
esoteric conventions.

A week or two later I passed her on the way up Hartside and
thanked her. It doesn't always work, she warned me, but when it
does it can be wonderful.

She wasn't wrong about that. I more or less gave up on it in
Italy. But my first experience, in York, was a treat.

Tim was at home that day, he said, so I could come whenever
I liked. So after I'd gently peppered the good city of York with
spontaneous outdoor performances here and there, I pedalled over

to his neat terraced house in a quiet corner of town. It must be one of the world's longest terraces, uncountable front doors opening onto the street. I couldn't help wondering at the resources of a builder who built such a number of dwellings, presumably in one go. Did you, I wondered, build them all together, from the ground up? Or did you start at one end, and just keep going until the market dried up, or some competing builder blocked your way with a street at right angles to yours? York must have been a busy place, and noisy, in those days.

Tim was directing me the half mile or so back to the end of the street, where I could access the alley all these houses back onto.

"I'll meet you at the back gate," he said. "You'll never find it otherwise."

Then he was casting an appraising eye over the bike set-up, while I shifted from one foot to the other, hoping it wouldn't fail the examination. I was to learn that many *Warmshowers* hosts are serious bicycle experts, many of them (though usually politely) surprised at what I didn't know.

He nodded, which I took as approval. I could relax at the neat kitchen table while he plied me with tea and discussed arrangements for dinner.

"I've made a chicken curry, and naan, and an apple pie," he said. "Will that be alright? Then I'll show you my bikes."

Tim's house was neat – did I say that already? It had to be. It was built at a time when workers didn't expect space, and didn't have many possessions to fill it with anyway. They had children instead, of course, and you could imagine the two little bedrooms at one time being very full of those. It was a classic two-up-two-down, with very steep stairs in the middle, and a later extension out the back so you could have a proper bathroom, and kitchen, instead of a yard with a pig or potatoes.

Tim had restored the house himself, and everywhere there were signs of his careful attention to detail, and a very marketable interior design eye. Many people, having realised such a project, would get itchy feet and fingers, and want to move on and do it all again.

"Not me," he said. "Been there; done that. Let's just enjoy it."

Alongside the neatness, in tandem or superimposed on it, were the bicycles. One or two in every room. Fine bicycles, to be admired. I admired them.

We talked about the meaning and purpose of bicycles, and life in general, ate the chicken curry, saved half the apple pie for breakfast, and then I played a couple of tunes in the little front room, the only room without a bicycle. I played quietly, because the room was small, and the neighbours were very close by.

It's fifty-five miles to Gainsborough, and I'm booked to play in All Saints Church at 3.00pm. But it won't be hilly, and Tim has offered to accompany me to the edge of the city so that I don't get lost, which I certainly would do without a native guide, he said. He would set me off on the right road, which was actually a fine cycle path along the line of an old railway, and then pedal himself off to work. I'm going to try without the GPS thingy today, because it sulked and refused to download the route.

Fifty-five miles, and time to allow my wrists to recover from the ride, so that I can play the cello. That should be quite manageable, as long as I don't dawdle. And barring mishaps.

Tim cycled a few miles with me, until we were on the old railway line.

"That way," he said, pointing along the nicely surfaced track, under the road bridge, and a straight line to Selby.

But just the other side of the bridge, and when Tim was out of sight in the other direction, the promised cycle path disappeared.

Actually it was still there, but it was severely cut off, with Heras fencing, concrete blocks, barbed wire and fierce notices. A bridge just ahead, the notices said, was being "dismantled", and so we had to KEEP OUT. I could see the dismantling, a great big hole in the ground. Maybe if I could just find a way, along a road, to the other side of that hole?

I wasted half an hour trying, before I gave up and went on the A19. That was suicidal. Heavy lorries swept past far too close, creating wind tunnel effects that pulled me along swiftly, but often threatened to dump me in a ditch, or worse. A few miles on I looked for the National Cycle Route again, but by then it had degenerated into a narrow and muddy canal path.

It was threatening rain. One of these small towns must have a place for coffee, surely?

Yes, there it is; that's the place. It looks quite posh for this little town, which doesn't itself seem to be posh. It should do nicely.

Sometimes appearances are deceptive. It wasn't posh. It was the kind of place elderly gentlemen come for their lunch at eleven o'clock, where they just sit down at a table and eat whatever's put in front of them, where the staff address them very loudly across the room, and where you feel slightly out of place if you're a visitor. The cheerful local radio was on, loud. The plastic blossom tree by the door stayed rigid in the wind when the door, with its unnecessarily clanging bell, opened. The millionaire's shortbread, with just a bit too much milky chocolate on top, was made by the lady mopping the floor, they told me. Don't get me wrong; I liked it all. I missed a heavy shower. And I was fortified for the twenty-five miles I still had to go.

The road was flat, and every mile it was flatter. So Drax power station, which seemed to have a different number of cooling towers from every angle, dominated the flat (did I already say that?) country for half an hour. Then I remembered that – decades ago – a favourite uncle had moved to the nearby village of Haxey, with some favourite cousins, in order to work there. So I should stop by and see the house they once lived in, and the garden we sometimes played in.

But it was too long ago to remember properly, and I couldn't find it. I didn't have time. I had to abandon the search.

Drax stayed with me for a while, as I pedalled further across the flat landscape. The cooling towers, with their slow-motion release of steam, looked altogether peaceful.

But there's a lot going on behind the scenes, and not just turbines whizzing round at 3000rpm. Drax was built in the late sixties, when the Selby coal field was discovered. Soon it was the biggest coal-fired power station in the UK. Now it hardly uses any coal at all. It's mostly wood fired, like the best pizza ovens, and claims to be almost carbon neutral. With its leading role in carbon-capture technology development it will soon, its owners say, be carbon negative.

Drax has detractors, though, and they aren't so sure. It burns twenty-five million trees a year, they say, nearly all of which are turned into compressed pellets in North America and shipped across the Atlantic. It may produce 6% of the UK's energy requirement, but it is also, according to their calculations, the single biggest producer of greenhouse gas in the UK. Its several biomass storage tanks, each one bigger than the Albert Hall, are, according to the company that runs them, "bomb-proof". But that hasn't stopped the occasional fire – spontaneous combustion according to expert reports, but perhaps sparked by divine displeasure, according to others who have different information.

I was brought up not to wear a hat in church, so wheeling a bicycle across the beautifully tiled floor of All Saints Gainsborough feels like a step too far.

But it is part of the show – the audience have to see how we got here.

All Saints is a lovely Regency building, light and welcoming inside. It shouldn't be, because it stands right next to Gainsborough Old Hall, which dates from about 1460. So there must have been an old church here once. Richard III and Henry VIII are known to have stayed at the Old Hall – though not at the same time, obviously. Henry VIII went so far as to get rid of wife number five (Catherine Howard) there, by accusing her of adulterous behaviour within its walls, while he also went off with the widow of the house, who became wife number six, Catherine Parr. He had a thing for Catherines, didn't he? Half his wives were Catherines.

Yes, said Sue, who was looking after me, Gainsborough, like Lincolnshire in general, was prospering in the eighteenth century, and the medieval church was too small for the growing town. English Heritage wasn't around then to stop them, so they knocked it down, and built new.

Sue, who administered the church without recourse to email, doing it all by post and telephone, had brought me an M&S egg sandwich, just in case.

The Old Hall and the church make a lovely composition in the middle of the town. If you think the church looks remarkably like St. Martin-in-the-Fields, on the corner of Trafalgar Square, in London, you would be right. Its local architect was heavily influenced by James Gibbs' famous design. Would you go so far as to say it was plagiarism? Good question.

Whatever you think of that, you have to admire the interior. It's big, and light, and pillared and galleried, with a magnificent round apse, and a later Burne Jones window. And it was a beautiful place to play. The curved wall at the East end made a perfect amplifying amphitheatre, and Libre's voice filled the big space. Gainsborough supplied an audience that laughed and cried in all the right places. A recently arrived refugee from Ukraine thanked me profusely and tearfully for my playing of *Meditation* by Frank Bridge, and the accompanying poem, dedicated to Ukraine.

The day ended with an unexpected turn. This was the first – though it wouldn't be the last – night on my journey when I didn't have any accommodation. I was planning to be bold, to ask the audience if some kind person would be able to give me a bed for the night, and breakfast me in the morning, before sending me off to Grimsthorpe and Edenham.

But I didn't get that far. Some old friends, not seen for many years, had connections in the town (the story was complicated).

They'd made a trek from the Welsh Borders to spend a few days here, carefully timing their visit to coincide with mine, without telling me. There's a room in our guesthouse, they said, and we've a lot of catching up to do.

So I went with them to the guesthouse, and later out for dinner, to do the catching up. There was a good deal of congratulation all round, and it was late by the time I got to bed, tucked up under the eaves. I need an early start in the morning.

CHAPTER 8

Cellos are *very* complicated

The UK has probably the world's highest concentration of violin and cello makers. They're mostly graduates of the Newark International School of Violin Making, which was set up in the early 1970s. In the eighteenth century, when all the world's most expensive instruments were being made, the international centre of violin and cello making was in Cremona in Italy. Now it's in Newark, not a cosmopolitan and exotically exciting city, but a small and (sorry, but it's true) insignificant town in Lincolnshire. So there are lots of cello makers to choose from.

And the makers and graduates of Newark have an advantage that the makers of Cremona didn't have. The Cremonese relied on sound, and tradition, and instinct, and the feel of the instrument as it took shape under their hands. But they didn't have an advanced scientific knowledge of acoustics, or know very much about the physics of vibration, or possess three-dimensional laser measuring devices. Having a combination of all these things means that good modern makers build beautiful and magnificent instruments.

Their only problem is they can't make the instruments three hundred years old.

(Unlike antique carpets, which can be made for tourists in places where they make carpets, just by leaving them out on the street for a week or two and have the buses drive over them. Preferably in the rainy season. You can't do that with a cello.)

Traditionally, everyone knows that cellos and violins improve with age and with playing. So a three-hundred-year-old cello, leaving aside its rarity, is always going to be better than a brand new one. But there's a growing feeling that after three hundred years some instruments are perhaps beginning to wear out. Maybe they don't sound quite so good as they did, say, a hundred years ago.

So apart from issues of cost, and insurance, and everything else – not to mention who should be entitled to play them – many players now opt for new out of choice, rather than necessity. It's a good time to buy new.

I visited lots of makers. I tried out lots of cellos. And – whisper it quietly – I fell in love.

I fell in love with a beautiful, petite and flame-backed cello I met at an exhibition in Manchester.

The maker, Kai-Thomas Roth, a quiet German with untamed Beethoven hair, wanted me to know all the technical details. I tried to listen, to distract myself from the factors I wasn't telling him had already completely sold it to me. The gleaming new ancient-recipe varnish had a warmth of colour you couldn't describe. It smelled like heaven.

The ribs, made from the same piece of flamed sycamore as the two-piece back, were so highly figured it had been impossible to make them properly flat. There was an undulation in them like the ripples on a pond stirred by a summer breeze.

There was a small blemish low down on the fine-grained front, an almost black feature you could only call a beauty spot. And it sang divinely.

Then came the blow. It was probably sold. It was just about to go to the Netherlands with someone who'd been playing it for the six months since it was signed off, but who hadn't yet been able to raise the funds. This time, Kai-Thomas said, the funds were practically promised.

Only if it came back in a fortnight's time unsold… Then I could have it.

In the meantime, he said, trying to back both horses at once, I could play it for a week, before it had to go abroad. Then I'd know if I wanted it if it came back, he said.

It wasn't the first time I'd fallen in love, of course, only to be cruelly disappointed. But I'd been happily married for a long time, and I'd forgotten what it was like.

I didn't sleep. I ate erratically. I sweated. My wife noticed and, I'm sure, recognised the symptoms. Think about it – there wasn't anything I could say that wouldn't make it worse, was there?

Kai-Thomas's cello occupied the music room. I didn't want to play it too much, because that would make it worse if it went to the Netherlands and didn't come back, which was very likely. But I wanted to play it. I wanted to play it a lot.

I reminded myself I was supposed to be choosing a maker, not an instrument. The maker was going to understand what I wanted, and then make the cello I could properly say I'd specified in all important respects, made from the pieces of wood I'd chosen in their raw state, coloured to my exact taste. An arranged marriage, as it were, rather than what just happened.

So I went to see some other makers, including one who was also a dealer. I spent a whole day with the dealer, playing several of his cellos, and several more of his stock. I was trying to put a particular flame-backed beauty out of my mind.

This maker's instruments were beautiful, too. He built very precise copies of famous old instruments, by Stradivarius and Guadagnini and Guarnerius. They sounded lovely. They were beautiful to play. But they didn't call to me across the wild.

These cellos were in a way almost too perfect. They were works of art of such precision you felt you should be admiring them under a microscope. The purfling was more exquisitely cornered than the naked eye could properly appreciate. The spruce tops were so straight grained they might have been ironed before being carved into shape. There would be no ripples along the ribs of these

KENNETH WILSON

instruments. They sounded clear, and confident, and masculine.
Rich and warm, classy and comforting, like the most expensive
men's shoes. Thoroughly reliable.

Not like the flame-backed beauty, with her ripples and her
beauty spot. Not a minx like her.

I've hinted that the gendering and naming of cellos is a
complicated, perhaps esoteric, matter, an art more than a science,
and fundamentally a mystery. There are – obviously – no physical
gender characteristics you can identify to distinguish a male from
a female cello. You have to wait for the cello to reveal its gender
to you, which it may or may not do. All those cellos, I realised – at
least as far as I could tell them – in that workshop and showroom
in the Fens, were masculine. As I believe, though without sufficient
authority, are most cellos.

And in that moment, in that fug of masculinity, I realised the
flame-backed beauty wasn't.

That was probably the beginning of the complications.

I was on the rebound. Against my better judgement I took away
with me an instrument that now makes me ashamed to remember.
It was more expensive than I dared try to justify. It was big for
a cello (and I'm only little, so we would always have made an
odd couple). It was French – well, kind of; that's complicated too.
It had belonged most recently to a professional orchestral player,
recently retired.

And it made a noise like the foghorn of the Queen Mary. In a
good way, I mean. It was the loudest cello I've ever met.

In hindsight maybe I should have bought it. It would have been
a good investment. The maker was one Georges Chanot III. He
was a Frenchman, as were Georges Chanot II and Georges Chanot
I, both of whom were also luthiers. (That's quite a lot of Georges, I
remember thinking.) For many years his workshop was in Wardour
Street, London. So when he exhibited at the Paris Exhibition of
1878, he was described as "English".

He was a sought-after maker. He made a violin, for instance, for the then famous virtuoso Joseph Joachim. He was a rake by reputation, and not averse to putting fake labels on instruments in order to inflate their prices. After all, he had a lavish lifestyle to fund. (He wasn't, of course, the first or the last dealer whose authentications could be suspect, was he?) In court he justified this by claiming it was "common practice".

The name Georges Chanot III features on all lists of known and investable nineteenth-century French instrument makers.

The following week I was due to be at Higham Hall in the lovely Lake District, to play for a few days with a little chamber orchestra. Part of the programme was Vivaldi's concerto for two cellos. The other solo cello was Mary, who plays the second oldest cello I've ever seen, in or out of a museum. It's English, almost black with age and experience, and with the richest voice imaginable. In the upper registers it's perhaps fading a bit, but its lower strings are layered and complex and deeply beautiful. Mary plays it as though they've been friends, and possibly lovers, for a hundred years.

Which cello to take? Why is everything so complicated?

There was a good reason, apart from the obvious one, for having to make a decision. The Chanot was a big instrument, while the Kai-Thomas Roth was, as you know, petite. This means there was a difference of about 20mm between the string lengths of the two instruments – nearly 3%.

So what?

If I played in tune on one, and then played with the same finger spacing on the other, it would be noticeably out of tune. It's not easy to make an instant adjustment for that.

In the end I took both. We played the Vivaldi with one, and then with the other.

The opinion of the orchestra was unanimous. Why would you buy the Kai-Thomas if you could have the commanding power of the Chanot?

That undivided consensus decided me. They were all wrong.

Of course the Chanot was powerful. But that's really all it was. Yes, it would be the instrument to have if orchestras were queuing up to ask me to play the Dvořák Cello Concerto with them. But no-one's ever done that. And no-one ever will. I can't play the Dvořák, and I'll never be able to play it. It's not a question.

And at 120 years old the Chanot's a mature beast, grown-up. In another fifty years it will sound just as it sounds now. It's confident, certainly, but it's got nowhere else to go.

Kai-Thomas's beautiful cello, on the other hand, is a baby. Six months of playing and she'll be out of nappies, beginning to develop her voice. In ten years' time who can say what riches of tone she might acquire? That's a wonderful thing about cellos – they mature. That's why people buy old instruments. And that's why I wanted a new one – to nurture it and hold its hand as it grew.

At the end of the week I'm on a train down to London. To deliver the flame-backed beauty to the cad and possible ravisher who's going to take her away, probably for ever. And to take the Chanot on up to Ely and give it back too. Because I'm not going to buy the Chanot now, am I?

It's a rush hour train, and the ticket inspector is loudly unhappy about two cellos occupying two seats. Sue me, I tell him, nearly loud enough to be heard.

This is all a bit of a blow. I'm pining, and not sleeping, and eating erratically, and I'm by now sure my wife suspects something, and there's nothing I can say that won't make it worse, is there?

I'm picking myself up off the floor, and thinking about ringing Kai-Thomas Roth, to arrange to see him and ask him to make me a cello. We'll go through all the possibilities, all the nuances, and debate them at length. I'll pretend to consider them all most carefully. And then I'll say, make it just like the flame-backed beauty. I won't say "her" of course; I'll just say "it".

Only I didn't ring Kai-Thomas. He rang me. He sounded unhappy. But he was unhappy because he'd lost a sale, and he wasn't all that hopeful of getting another one quickly. Was I still interested in the "Batta" Stradivarius model I'd played in Manchester? Did I remember? Well, it's come back. It's for sale.

He trailed off, that lovely half-question hanging in the air for a moment. Only for a moment, though.

As I said, that's where the complications really began.

CHAPTER 9

What have the Romans ever done for us?

TUESDAY 31 MAY

I'd spent a bit of time, I realised, organising a pretty full-scale tour, by which I mean a series of concerts that you could put on a poster, or print on a T-shirt and sell to the masses – or just wear yourself if there weren't any masses.

It was a difficult and delicate matter. How to approach somewhere out of the blue? How to find the contact? What introduction to give? What to propose, to offer, to ask? And all in the context of the main enterprise, the cycling from here to there. So likely places had to be en route, and at the right distance, and on the right day.

In retrospect that was a rather tall order; a tad ambitious. So every time I got a positive response it was a major boost to the morale, and a big step forward in the planning, I thought. Finding a suitable place, and getting a gig there, between Gainsborough and Cambridge was one of the headaches – and eventually one of the major achievements, I thought – of the whole thing. If you're a bigger outfit, of course, you have an agent, or a booking manager, or a tour organiser, or just a queue of people begging you to come. I didn't have any of that.

So when a stately home in approximately the right place said yes, why not, come and do a concert here, and we'll promote it to our Friends and visitors, I was well pleased. But then there was a mix-up about their opening times, and then another about Half Terms, and Jubilees, and things like that, and in the end they thought it was maybe too much trouble. Something about dead horses, and floggings, came to mind, and we agreed "another time".

Did it remind me of Ogden Nash? *A child need not be very clever, to learn that "Later, dear" means "Never".*

They suggested I ask a nearby Castle.

Lucie, at Grimsthorpe, thought it an altogether splendid idea, something so totally bonkers how could you not love it? She watched the clips, and we spoke on the phone, and it was all set up. Until more commercial voices intervened, and asked lots of difficult questions, and in the end it seemed like maybe too much trouble, and might be better another time. Did it remind me of Ogden Nash? A little bit.

Lucie wasn't defeated, though. Well, she said, there's Edenham Church just down the road. She was on the committee of a Christmas pensioners' lunch, and why didn't we do a fundraiser for that? Why not? I echoed. And if I get there in time, what about a little *pop-up* in the Castle gardens, among the roses and the *parterre* – wouldn't that be nice? And so these things go.

But it's sixty miles to Grimsthorpe Castle, not counting the mile or two up the Castle drive, so there really isn't time to dawdle over breakfast, to continue and conclude last night's overdue conversation. And it's almost certainly going to rain.

It more or less didn't, though, for the first twenty flat and straightforward miles to Lincoln, where the trouble started. If it had been further on in the day's journey I would have stopped at Lincoln's fabulous cathedral, which sits on a little tussock that passes for a hill in these parts. But I should get on if I'm to feel that Grimsthorpe can be reached in time. Some pretty tow path, followed by a maze of unmapped paths going in approximately the right direction, a little bridge over the river and its flanking swamps, before total confusion, and a complete failure of navigation.

65

The roads here are small. They take you miles, to an isolated house, where someone looks at you quizzically from their garden, wondering why you've come to see them, because you couldn't be going anywhere else. What the map shows as a continuous road ends here, in a convincing ditch. And when it starts again the other side, it isn't a road at all, just a half-hearted path across a field.

The worst indignity is when you come to "Ermine Way Roman Road".

Yes, you think, almost in triumph. You know Ermine Way, or Ermine Street, is a straight road, all the way from here to London (or York, if you go the wrong way, so don't do that). So it will be direct, navigable, stress free. You'd be wrong. Of course, mostly it *is* all those things – straight, direct, navigable, stress free, as I was to see later – but not here. Here it's a muddy track at the edge of a field.

When I say muddy, that's definitely the mildest of the many words that came to mind in that moment. Some tracks can be cycled, if you've got a suitable bike, which isn't a Dawes Galaxy with a cello strapped to the back. This one couldn't. It's so deeply rutted if you put the wheels in a rut, you can't turn the pedals. They just get stuck. In the rut. If you try to ride on the ridges between the ruts you fall off into the ruts – where you can't pedal.

So this is what a Roman road looks like? "What have the Romans ever done for us?" seems like a very reasonable question just now. On either side of the ruts it's knee high in grass, or a light brown quagmire. The quagmire of course is because the day's intermittent rain became, half an hour ago, more like a tropical storm. Without the tropical temperature.

But the map shows what must be a real road not more than a mile further along, and there isn't really a viable alternative, and I did say I was going to ride some Roman roads from the Edge of Empire to its Heart, so I grit my teeth, gird everything that needs girding, and push.

At least where there are real, non-Roman, roads, they're

pretty flat. That's a big difference from the roads nearer home in Cumbria. There's another big difference, here among seriously big and productive arable fields. There are no insects. The wraparound glasses I've been wearing are redundant here.

I arrived at Grimsthorpe Castle more or less in time, in another cloudburst. The rain was so heavy I couldn't see the castle itself from the gate. The drive is every bit as grand and straight as a grand drive should be, but I was soaked, and freezing, and beyond caring.

Jolie, in the hut that controls everything – except the rain – welcomed me profusely, sympathetically, and damply.

Go and meet Sam at the tea tent, and have a cup of tea, she said, and radioed ahead. She must have told them the state I was in – the tea was ready and waiting, and so was Sam.

I put up a marquee for you, Sam said, slightly sheepishly. But it's blown away. It was the first time we'd put it up. It's destroyed. So would you mind playing in the tea tent itself?

I wouldn't mind at all. There's a tightly packed and steaming audience here, sheltering from the wind and the rain. The only problem is, my hands are blocks of ice, and I can't feel a thing – much less put my fingers delicately and precisely on the fingerboard and play a tune. I'm soaked through, as is all my stuff, and even if I had a few dry clothes, you can't get undressed, and re-dressed, in a crowded tea tent, can you?

The show must go on, of course, so stop making a fuss. Eat that rather splendid caramel apple pie slowly, to allow a tiny bit of thawing out, but not so slowly they think you're taking the mickey, and then get on with it.

Grimsthorpe Castle isn't really any such thing, though it might once have been. What you see now, as you approach it through the three-thousand-acre Capability Brown park, along the grandest drive (I'm speculating here) north of Windsor Great Park, is an un-warlike but definitely austere Vanbrugh façade. There's a Tudor house behind the facade, and bits of an older castle. In 1516, Henry VIII – yes, he's been here too – took it from someone he didn't like and gave it to someone he did, the Eleventh Baron Willoughby. The present owner is the twenty-eighth in that dynasty, and a Baroness.

I wonder if Jane Austen visited. She must at least have had it in mind when she started writing *Sense and Sensibility* – the Eleventh Baron Willoughby's daughter (see above) married one Charles Brandon. I think Jane Austen only took the names, though; the story is entirely her own.

I played the kind of tunes I thought would bring the sun out, which they did. The audience drifted away, out into the new sunshine, and I went to walk around the rose garden and the *parterre*, which had suffered a bit in the storm, but not too much, and then went back into the tea tent as they were closing up, to thank them for the tea and splendidly wonderful pie. They gave me a *panini* to take away for later because, they said, the only pub in Edenham shut down last week.

The Vicarage at Edenham isn't hard to find – it's one of those rather few remaining real vicarages occupied by real vicars – so it's hard by the church, practically part of the churchyard, and a splendidly rambling affair. Quite, of course, unlike the vicar himself, Fr. Ed, who although he rides a bicycle straight out of Grantchester, is succinct, to the point, and never loose with words. Never.

My accommodation is a converted stable block, next to a small space recently converted into a lovely chapel. I had to put the heating on, to dry out all the soaked stuff. The cardboard box keeping the CDs in shape won't ever recover. It should probably be abandoned.

Lucie couldn't come to the fundraiser in the Church of St. Michael and All Angels – complicated story – but Lynda, who was deputed to look after me in her absence, gave a full, and apparently satisfactory, report. Like most of my concert audiences, the good people of Edenham expressed lots of interest and equal amounts of disbelief, in the bicycle, its set-up, and the journey in general. After Gainsborough I wasn't quite so diffident about wheeling the bike into a sacred space and allowing it to block an aisle. Once they get talking about the bicycle, the audience also generally confesses they really didn't know what to expect, but since they had nothing better to do... and really it wasn't bad. At all. Thank you; I'll take that.

I began the performance with a loud and brash rendering of the *James Bond* theme tune – very suitable, I thought, for a quiet country parish church. I can't look at the music when I play this, or I'd miss the look that comes over people's faces, a look that sweeps in a wave through the audience, as they realise they're listening to *James Bond*. It breaks the ice.

And then, I tell them, this is a poem called *My Lonely Heart*. It's about how much the poet's life is like the life of James Bond. At which they laugh, even before they've heard it.

My Lonely Heart

Psychosomatic
paranoic
hyperventilatic
intolerantic
episodic fanatic
ditto kleptomanic
sofa-slobbic
pedantic
ingrowing tonalic
tonal moronic
arrythmic
self-centric
olfactric
illiteratic
repetatatic tic tic tic tic – toc
flatulentic

thyroidic overactic
lifestylic inactic – hic
dipsomanic
dyspeptic
depressic
invertebratic
male...
WLTM
(would like to meet)
attractive female
with none
of these
issues.

We got off to a good start, and went on quite late, in the quiet and beautiful little church in Edenham.

CHAPTER 10

Libre and The Lady

"You love that cello more than me," she accused me quietly, not looking at me. And I knew there wasn't anything I could say that wouldn't make it worse.

Of course I loved the cello. Of course I loved her. And of course I loved *her* too. You can't make a comparison. It's a completely different category. Be serious. (I'm not saying this to her, but I'm thinking it quite loud.)

The cello I took home from Kai-Thomas Roth was both new and old. It was his cello number 83 – which is to say he'd made eighty-two before he started on this one. That's a lot of cellos for one person to make. All cellos have a label inside them, which you can see through the F-hole (that's not a rude word – it's a sound hole that's shaped like an F) on the C string side. The label tells you who built it, and when, and usually where. Unless it's a fake, of course.

That's how we know this cello began in 1714. That's the year Stradivarius put his label in the cello now known as the "Batta", or "Batta-Piatigorsky" cello. Kai-Thomas is especially fond of the Batta cello, and he has the carefully-made moulds and cramps to turn out very exact copies of it.

Before the Batta, most cellos were significantly larger. Stradivarius himself made about sixty cellos, and two-thirds of them are bigger. But the invention of a different kind of string at the end of the seventeenth century made smaller and less unwieldy

– and cheaper – instruments feasible.

Strings were traditionally made of animal gut (not necessarily from cats, though they're often called "cat-gut"). Then it was discovered that if you wound some very tight fine wire around the gut you could make the strings shorter, and the instrument therefore smaller. Easier to play, too.

Stradivarius was possibly trying to see how small he could make a cello, because the Batta is definitely petite. Most modern cellos are a bit bigger. Size does matter.

It's called the Batta because in about 1836 a Dutch cellist called Alexandre Batta acquired it. He was only twenty, and he played it until 1893 when he was forced to sell it. And it's called the Batta-Piatigorsky because – you guessed it – a very important cellist called Gregor Piatigorsky had it for nearly fifty years from 1956.

If you think I'm the only person whose head has been turned by a cello, read what Piatigorsky wrote in his autobiography about this instrument:

"I played the 'Batta' for a long time before appearing in concert with it. In solitude, as is befitting honeymooners, we avoided interfering company until then. From that day on, when I proudly carried the 'Batta' across the stage for all to greet, a new challenge entered into my life. While all other instruments I had played prior to the 'Batta' differed one from the other in character and range, I knew their qualities, shortcomings, or their capriciousness enough to exploit their good capabilities to full advantage. Not so with the 'Batta', whose prowess had no limitations. Bottomless in its resources, it spurred me on to try to reach its depths, and I have never worked harder or desired anything more fervently than to draw out of this superior instrument all it has to give."

Exactly. And when you make a perfect copy of something it tends to sound quite similar. With the important difference, of course, that Gregor Piatigorsky was playing the original Batta, and Kenneth Wilson is playing the perfect copy.

You can't age a cello three hundred years except by playing it for three hundred years. But the perfect copy does, on the other hand, have the beauty of youth. Did I mention that she's also a little minx?

So you can understand the trouble I was in. Though in my defence I didn't ask for a female cello. That was just accident. Maybe, too, the feelings were a bit one-sided (I wouldn't go so far as to say unrequited). I'm not, after all, in quite the same league as Mr. Piatigorsky.

She's never told me her name. She's just Lady Cello, or The Lady. Just goes to show.

"You love that cello more than me," is hard to forget hearing. It was also hard to forget saying. And feeling. It might have been another beginning – the beginning of an end. It was complicated.

It did mean, though, that I recognised the feeling instantly when I saw it again. The Luis and Clark had been out of its case for a couple of hours. I'd checked it out carefully, discovered its childhood trauma, and was wondering what to do about that. I'd played some careful scales on it, testing every note from the open C to well over the end of the fingerboard. The whole of the first Bach *Suite*, and quite a few other things.

The perfect copy of the Batta, Lady Cello, was on the floor beside the cello chair, so I could make the occasional comparison. Suddenly I was hit with a wave of jealous resentment, a tsunami of passive-aggressive sulk. The little minx was expressing her feelings, and they weren't happy ones.

Perhaps she knew – or feared – more than me. How could a carbon fibre cello, bought only to save the perfect and delicate Batta from going out in the wind and the rain, and being put on a rack sticking out behind a bicycle... How could such a thing possibly, *possibly*, displace that Batta from the centre of my affections?

You can't make a comparison. It's a completely different

category. Be serious. (I'm not saying this to her, but I'm thinking it quite loud.)

Sometimes I think I don't learn. I've been here before. And I really do know what complicated means.

Other times of course I just think what you're thinking: *Is this guy for real? These are cellos you're talking about.* There's nothing wrong with a bit of mild anthropomorphising – people do it with their dogs all the time. But there's a difference between that and being just plain loopy. Is there?

Well, what about this, then? In the night – or maybe it was the next night, it's all a bit of a blur – I learned the Luis and Clark cello's name. It's Libre. Pronounced Spanishly, not Frenchly, so something like LEE-bray. Put that in your pipe, eh? Don't talk to me about complicated. I *told* you it's complicated.

But – since somehow I still feel some need to justify all this, to feel, as I may have said, less of an impostor – Libre's gender was by no means a clear issue. At least to me.

You would think it might be obvious. The instrument is made from carbon fibre, not from centuries-old wood that was once living and growing on three different continents. It – the cello – isn't in itself complicated. You'd think.

It wears a little black dress. It's shiny. It's curvy. Totally without corners. There's a slinky iridescence about its surface. And it's unfeasibly thin. Still not obvious? Yes, ok, it must be female.

Yes, but it's not uncomplicatedly so. It has quite a masculine voice, and quite a masculine heart. Maybe – this is serious – it's gender non-specific, non-binary. It isn't at all clear to me what are its preferred pronouns. On the few occasions, guided by looks and feel, I've felt that "she" would do, I've felt a mild rebuke.

Until anything happens to change the order of things, Libre will have to be an "it". I can tell the relationship between us is going to be complicated, even without The Lady having anything to do with it.

I've got one cello with a gender but no proper name, and another with a name but no proper gender. I don't learn. Is it any wonder I'm a bit close to the edge?

What was I thinking? Less than two days later I was laughing at myself. And, I suspect, being slightly mocked by Libre herself. How could her gender have been the slightest bit in doubt? Just look at her! Those beautiful hips, narrowing seamlessly into the most delicate waist. Widening into her voluptuous upper torso.

You don't know the assumptions you make, the prejudices you carry, until something or someone else points them out to you.

What did I mean, she had a "masculine" voice? And a "masculine" heart? Did I just mean loud, or strong, or clear, or opinionated? Dear me; I didn't realise I was so unreconstructed. I've got a lot to learn.

There's a whole industry dedicated to the sound of string instruments. It's like the wine industry. There are really only two questions though. First, what words do you use to describe what you mean? And second, why do you pay a thousand times more for this bottle than for that one?

It's the same with cellos. Only here you have the added dimension that it rather depends who's playing it.

So why *do* the best players have the best instruments? If you can make such a good sound on an old orange-box, why fork out for a Strad? Why not drink Domaine Leroy Richebourg Grand Cru with your chips, instead? Or drive the orange-box around in a fleet of Ferraris, colour-coded to the days of the week?

It's partly prestige, and rarity, and tradition, and expectation – and money, of course. But it's also the ease of playing a good instrument over a poor one. And as with the fine wine, there are subtleties of flavour and tone, which I'm sure I couldn't taste if given the chance, but which the connoisseur would certainly claim to.

Wood is such an amazing material. Like the grape's *terroir*, it acquires subtle characteristics from a process that can't be replicated in a laboratory. Every piece is different; in its growth patterns, its grain and its shading of density, laying down a lifetime of weather and climate and soil.

You can't make a cello out of just any kind of wood. The front (the "top") is always spruce – fine-grained, but not too fine-grained. The back and the ribs are traditionally sycamore or, very occasionally, maple. The back is nearly always made from a wedge-shaped piece of wastefully cut "quarter sawn" timber which is then cut down the flat plane and joined so that the two sides are mirror images.

Then it's laid down – seasoned – ideally for about twenty years, of which at least ten should be in the workshop. Then it's carved to shape.

The result is a fearsomely complex resonance, a bouquet of sound, in which the bowed note is overlain with harmonics, and overtones, and sympathetic noises. It's impossible to describe, except in an esoteric vocabulary like an oenophile's.

If you can't quite hear it, as you may not quite be able to get the "cherry" in the wine that's made from grapes, you can be sure the professional player is thinking of little else.

If you're lucky enough to have a favourite fine wine you'll see why a player can spend a long time choosing an instrument. You'll appreciate there's room for debate over the "best". And why we all have slightly different preferences. Even, perhaps, why one player just can't get the same beauty from someone else's prized cello.

And why, therefore, the relationship between a player and her cello can be intense, and complicated. And why, therefore, too, cellos are so often named and gendered. You thought I was just not quite right in the head, didn't you?

So what happens then when you make a cello out of carbon fibre, instead of sycamore and spruce (and ebony for the fingerboard, and rosewood for the pegs)? Good question.

It turns out there are more things in heaven and earth, Horatio, than are dreamt of in your philosophy.

It was the hum of his catamaran's hull in the water – its resonance – that first set Luis Leguia on his path towards making a carbon fibre cello.

Traditionally – though it's not a long tradition, because it was only invented in 1958, and didn't become a practical material until 1963 – carbon fibre has been used in aeroplanes, rockets, and high-speed boats. It's stronger than steel, and five times lighter. It's actually made of the same stuff as wood – when dry, wood is about 50% carbon; carbon fibre is nearly 100% carbon.

There are basically two elements to carbon fibre, that combined make it suitable for all these high-end high-speed construction uses – the carbon fibres themselves, usually twisted and moulded into a mat, and the resin that binds them together to make a strong and usable shape.

Which is really the same structure as wood. Wood has very strong cellulose polymer fibres, held together with lignin, a hard resin.

Carbon fibre is a much more uniform material than natural wood, which of course you want it to be if you're making rockets and things. Because of that, and its lower elasticity, the sound it supports when it vibrates is purer than anything you can get from wood.

If you use a word like "pure", it sounds like a good thing.

Well, it is and it isn't. When you're playing a cello you want a pure sound – a beautiful note that will carry over a long distance. But you also want a rich sound. That means a sound that's complex, with all the harmonics and overtones, and deep sensual suggestions. To a materials scientist, or a physicist, that's an impure sound. To a musician, a sound that's too pure is boring.

Without going into the physics and the product development, which I couldn't begin to understand anyway, clever people can now make carbon fibre that's a lot more like wood. They've "tweaked the viscoelasticity", they tell me.

The end result is that my new carbon fibre cello has a rich, full, projecting, warm, subtle, complex, round, earthy, strong and free sound, with after-tones of cherry, and vanilla, and bird-song, and polar bear. It's not a wooden sound. She's called Libre for a reason.

CHAPTER 11

Cello on a punt

THURSDAY 2 JUNE

The Book of Common Prayer – the BCP, or just the Prayer Book – ranks alongside the King James Bible and the works of Shakespeare as one of the founding documents of – well, I'm not sure what exactly, but there's no doubt it's very important. It's where we get the phrase "miserable sinners" from.

Thomas Cranmer became Archbishop of Canterbury in 1532, a reward from our old friend Henry VIII for his very considerable assistance in the matter of a divorce from the first Catherine. He began work on his Prayer Book, an important part of establishing the identity of a Reformed Church of England, more or less straightaway. But progress was slow, because the inconsistent Henry was stubbornly conservative in such matters. The Reformation was collateral damage in the divorce, and he wasn't – deep down – as convinced about it as he might have been.

So it wasn't until 1549 that the Prayer Book was published. It survived the ups and downs of Counter-Reformation, re-Reformation, and abolition and restoration of the monarchy, and underwent some revision and tidying-up in 1662. If you're a Prayer Book sort of person, 1662 is the important date. "I'm 1662," is the kind of handshake introduction you might get in a deeply serious Anglican convocation.

But 1662, like *thee* and *thou*, and knowing when to end verbs with -eth and -est, has gone out of fashion. When the Church of England decided in the 1960s, along with everyone else, that it was time to modernise, it began issuing a series of "Alternative Services", to try to get with it. This being the Church of England, what, a lot of people got very hot under their collars. The Prayer Book Society was founded in 1972, dedicated to the earlier status quo.

It has had a modest success. Eighty Church of England parish churches are members – though about 12,400 aren't.

St. Michael and All Angels, Edenham, is one of those eighty, a Prayer Book church.

"Oh yes, everything is BCP here," Fr. Ed told me, almost modestly.

So I was looking forward to an old-fashioned Morning Prayer in the dimly lit stable chapel next door to my room, when I could imagine myself a brave moderniser nearly five hundred years ago, with the frisson in the back of my mind that if discovered I might face burning at the stake. Which was Archbishop Cranmer's fate when Henry was no longer around to look after him.

But Wednesday was Fr. Ed's day off, and he didn't Morning Pray on his days off, so it wasn't to be. He came out in his pyjamas, and without his wraparound clerical collar, to wave me off and invite me to come back and play for their Festival. I liked Fr. Ed very much. I think with more time we would have had a lot to talk about.

Day six, and I upset a speed camera today. Being told off by a speed camera when you're on a bicycle is a matter for wild celebration. I admit, it was a 20mph zone, but still, over the limit is over the limit.

And the GPS thingy, which sulked all day yesterday, and just refused to download the agreed route, has been trying to restore the relationship. It's been very well behaved.

Plus I've been on a Roman road that was not just a proper road, but wide and straight, and almost devoid of traffic, and felt downhill all the way. This was the Old Great North Road, once the A1, and before that the Great North Road, and before that Ermine Street/Way. Now it's just a local B-road, more or less abandoned since the A1(M) opened. The motorway roars beside it, audible but unseen behind a thick screen of trees.

So altogether it's been a good day of biking. And made better by a bit of sunshine and a complete absence of deadlines. There was also an absence, however, of possible coffee halts, so it was forty miles and lunchtime before I stopped in St. Ives for a bistro and a bit of busking.

I hadn't planned the busking, but there, in the middle of the highway, looking stern, all-conquering, and all-abandoned, was Oliver Cromwell. And being the day before the Jubilee, I thought I should at least give him a little bit of consolation.

So I leant the bike up against him, got the cello out, and played some Irish laments. OK, so maybe the choice of music was rubbing it in a bit.

Then, feeling as though suddenly I was on a proper holiday, I walked down to the Great Ouse, and across St. Ives' famous bridge, before setting off for Cambridge.

The road to Cambridge is the flattest fourteen miles I've ridden in my life. A railway line has been taken up, and replaced with a "guided bus", whatever that is, and a bicycle super-highway along which commuters race between their work in Cambridge and their dormitories in St. Ives.

Down Castle Hill, across Magdalene Bridge, and into town. Pedalling slowly along the middle of Trinity Street, where the tourists don't confine themselves to the narrow pavements, as though I own the whole place. Which I think is a not uncommon feeling if you were a student here a hundred years ago, and you're returning generations later, incognito among the tourists.

Incognito, anyway, apart from a cello on a bike, of course.

And because I wasn't working to a timetable, and the sun was shining, I stopped outside Great St. Mary's, the University church, smiled at the welcomer who said I couldn't leave my bike there, and played for an hour.

I think I featured on about a hundred tourist videos. A young man from Poland, studying Economics at Anglia University, sat and vaped and watched for half an hour. I've never seen a more relaxed and contented looking person. What was his secret, I asked?

He worked as a chef besides learning economics, he said, and that paid all his expenses, and there was no work today, and the sun was shining, and this was Cambridge, and could you possibly want anything more?

An American, who played the cello himself, he said, thought a carbon fibre cello was "just the sweetest little thing you ever saw". He wanted to talk, when I just wanted to play. Eventually I sold him a CD and he allowed me to carry on.

There are ups and downs on this journey – though not of course on the roads and paths here in Cambridge, where the biggest hill is Garrett Hostel Lane – and that's only a bridge over the river.

Everyone comes to Cambridge to see the river, and the College Backs, which back onto it. It's very beautiful. The best thing to do, of course, is to admire the Backs from the river itself, in a punt. Today, being Jubilee bank holiday, half the world has come out punting, and the river is chaotic.

Koenraad, a PhD researcher from King's College, whose academic interest is the restoration of Italian antiquities, has agreed to punt me and the cello. The assignation was brokered by the Domus Bursar (now *that's* a job title) of King's College, with whom I'd been negotiating to play on the forbidden cobbles outside the College's main gate, and we are to meet at that same gate. Koenraad is the President of the King's College Punting Society, so I feel we'll be in good hands. I've seen a Luis and Clark carbon fibre cello being played up to its lower bouts (the curved part) in seawater, but I'm not convinced total immersion following a capsize would be good for Libre.

I like breaking rules. I especially like doing so having negotiated exceptions and exemptions with inflexible authorities. As I tell them, this is so exceptional that no-one could ever think it was establishing a precedent. So, wheeling a bicycle through King's, which even College Fellows are not allowed to do, has to be done ostentatiously and magnificently. Well how else am I going to get the cello down to the river and the punts?

Suzette, also Dutch like Koenraad, and also a Medievalist, like Koenraad, and celebrating the very recent award of her Doctorate, met us by Garrett Hostel Lane Bridge. The bridge has recently acquired a new, and less formal, name. It's now the Orgasm Bridge. So named, Suzette explains, because Cambridge cyclists don't know what a real hill is, and the noises they make as they struggle up one side, and whoosh down the other, are, well, suggestive. She looked at Koenraad, but it was me who went slightly pink.

So here I am, sitting on my folding stool, a bit precariously because it's a boat and of course it wobbles, playing *The Swan*, and Debussy's *Syrinx*, and other watery things, and being videoed by a million tourists. Only once did a sudden collision threaten to capsize the enterprise.

That was an up. It was followed by a down.

We had a quick lunch together in the beautifully re-purposed fourteenth-century St. Michael's Church, and afterwards I went straight to play on the sacred and forbidden cobbles outside King's, as negotiated with the Domus Bursar, above, who'd told the Porters he'd allowed it, so they shouldn't rough me up or move me on, and I expected a crowd.

There were indeed crowds, but they weren't interested in a cello. Except for one small child, whose parent thought it was fun to film it trying to dismantle my set-up while I played.

But when four shirtless and shoeless fellows put up a loudly amplified beatbox in the middle of the road, and began dancing to it, they attracted a big crowd in an instant. Ah well.

It was also a bit of a disappointment in that Covid had undone a lot of the rules that would otherwise probably have lasted forever. The grass outside King's, once so hallowed and pristine and empty, was now piled high with tourists, variously lounging, picnicking, and sunbathing. And the cobbles, where loitering was so firmly discouraged, no longer have that exclusive feeling of privileged empty space. Ah well.

I was a student in this lovely city, at Selwyn College, a very long time ago, and ex-students can occasionally invite themselves to take dinner at High Table with the College Fellows. Tonight, after a special Jubilee Evensong in the soaring red-brick chapel, there's a very special Jubilee dinner.

Would I be allowed to go? It wasn't certain. Of course I could, if I had a tie, an ironed shirt, a suit and proper black shoes. Those weren't rules with the Covid flexibility of King's College's open spaces. But I wasn't going to be carrying those things, on a bike. And although James, who I'm staying with, would certainly have lent them to me, he's a foot taller than me, and with the shoulders of an ox, so it wouldn't work.

We found a way round that difficulty (I'd sent it on ahead, to await my arrival) and I cycled over to Selwyn, in my suit, in good time for the Jubilee Evensong. It wouldn't be BCP, like yesterday's missed Morning Prayer, but it wouldn't be far off, and it would be sung, and not just said, by Selwyn's lovely choir under the direction of Sarah McDonald.

Sarah's was, as I told her once, the most important appointment the College had made since it appointed Owen Chadwick, OM, KBE, FRSE, PPBA, etc., Master in 1956.

First I had to play in Selwyn's Old Court, on the once billiard-table grass that was now not quite recovered from the enforced anarchy of Covid. The duty Porter said she would have to ask the Bursar. The Bursar gave consent, as long as the Chapel Choir were not disturbed in their rehearsal. It was a tribute to the College I loved with a fierce loyalty, a love and loyalty that were gradually being monetised by the College as it expanded into the twenty-first century.

I sat between a theoretical physicist, and the retired University Librarian – eight million books – opposite a professor of medicine, and a lecturer in Italian. We ate Coronation Cauliflower. We clapped the Jubilee Pudding as it was carried in like a haggis. And with our cheese we drank 1952 Madeira and 1977 Port. If I'd known a retired University Librarian was going to be there I might have made sure to remember a poem I once wrote. Perhaps just as well; who wants an uninvited poetry recitation? It was called *Song of the Books*, and it was full of real historical references...

Song of the Books

How many books have you read?
How many books do you have, unread?

There are eight million in the Cambridge
University Library.

You could read one a day there
for twenty-two thousand years.

That's a lot of books;
and you know what the prophet says:

Of making many books there is no end,
and much study is a weariness of the flesh.

But I find I have a worse weariness;
I rowed my currach slow across

from Portmagee too late before the storm

85

and all my books were lost.

I am set adrift, bookless,
and very far away

from that beautiful
library.

I had to get up early after the Jubilee Madeira. Rutherfords Punting had heard about my river adventure and wanted to offer me a photoshoot on quieter water.

That meant being river- and performance-ready, on the other side of town, before the tourists would be wanting to engage the punts. It was worth it though. The Cam was empty, and as I was playing *The Swan* we punted past seven little cygnets, six of them swimming, and one peeping out from under the parental wing.

The sun was shining in Cambridge – which it nearly always does – and the tourists were coming out. Sitting on the wall opposite the locust clock (which I think is ugly, but is important for reasons I can't remember) a Japanese lady insisted I play *Amazing Grace* for her to sing to. Her husband was instructed to record it so she could send it to her singing teacher, along with a photograph of her almost sitting on my lap.

I was in no hurry to leave Cambridge. It hadn't been possible to space everything out perfectly on this journey, and I only had a couple of hours' cycling to get to the village of Buntingford. So I parked the bike, with Libre locked onto it, and wandered.

I put my head round the door of my favourite little Cambridge church, a Grade 1 listed building almost exactly seven hundred years old, and – coincidentally – another Prayer Book church, like Edenham. But I didn't go in. I'd been due to give a lunchtime concert there, but the arrangements had fallen apart without explanation, and I couldn't guarantee not to be slightly cross. It seemed best just to pass on, and not to wonder.

There are so many places. Which to choose? The rugby ground, where I once watched the All Blacks – yes really – from a suicidal perch on the unguarded edge of Selwyn's Cripps Court roof? The Senate House, where I'd spent a few nights looking up at the "leap" across to Caius College, failure at which would have meant a four-storey tumble onto the flagstones (if you were lucky) or the spiked railing, below? The University Library, with its eight million books, and its mysterious and always out of bounds brutal phallic tower? Grantchester Meadows, where you punted to impress, or swam to forget?

No, none of those. Nor any of the hundreds of other corners and moments that made me part of this ancient, magical, place. Let's go somewhere even older, that didn't exist when I lived here – at least, not in its present incarnation: the Museum of Classical Archaeology.

You could traipse all over the ancient Greek and Roman world, and visit the planet's most important museums, to see a fraction of what's here. It's probably the most comprehensive introduction to Roman art and history anywhere. And it's all housed in an anonymous building on the University's Sidgwick site, West of the main drag, built the year after I left.

It's all fake, of course. What you're looking at isn't ancient marble. These are plaster casts. Many of them are still old, though not Roman-old. It was a fashion, two or three hundred years ago, if you were a young man with a lot of money, to go on a Grand Tour, and then to decorate your principal houses with plaster cast replicas of the Greek and Roman statuary that had most impressed you. There was a whole industry dedicated to it.

Most of those plaster casts are long gone. But Cambridge made a collection. Do you want to see the Kritios Boy, the Dying Warrior, the Discobolus that so impressed Mr. Adolf Hitler, a dozen Aphrodites too beautiful for words? Do you want to know what every Roman Emperor looked like, at least in his public image? Do you want to see Hadrian's young lover, Antinous, and understand why Oscar Wilde was so smitten?

All of that, and much more. It won't tell you how Antinous met a mysterious end before he was twenty, perhaps when he was only fourteen, because nobody knows. But it will tell you all about Hadrian's making of Antinous – officially – into a god thereafter, and why Hadrian's marriage was not spectacularly successful.

Talking of marriages, I forgot to tell you I was married in that chapel, in Selwyn College, where I went for Evensong last night, under the gaze of Karin Jonzen's 1958 sculpture of the ascending Christ and a pair of adoring angels. A long time ago. It was all a long time ago.

CHAPTER 12

Edinburgh Fringe

TWO YEARS AGO

I was thinking about those people who claim ancestry from the famous – Lloyd George, say, or Florence Nightingale, or Genghis Khan. They always seem to do it in a way that suggests they're the *only* living descendant of said famous person.

Which is most unlikely to be true. It's like the grains of rice on the chess board. One on the first square, two on the next, then four, then eight, and so on. By the time you get to the 64th square, the 64th generation, you've rather lost count.

In particular, claiming Genghis Khan as an ancestor is no big deal. About one in two hundred of the world's population can truthfully do that. But then he did have a reputation as a stud – if you can really call it that when it's mostly rape and pillage – so he may be slightly in a class of his own.

Nevertheless, the point is anyone might end up with lots of great-great-great-grandchildren, through not much fault of their own; at least not specifically. Equally, every one of us will have had approximately thirty-two great-great-great-grandparents. (I say *approximately* in order to allow for wife-swapping, incest, and other ancestral irregularities.)

Even of our four grandparents it isn't really fair just to claim descent from the famous one.

So when I defined the beginning of *Highway Cello* as that

Damascene moment on a Saturday morning on the A69 I was maybe being hasty. Only telling a quarter of the story. Maybe this is another beginning…

I was in Edinburgh, one of thousands hoping to get themselves noticed as part of the annual Edinburgh Fringe, EdFringe as its fat website calls it. I was performing as *The Poetical Cellist*, and I was having a ball.

I was also chronically short of sleep, frazzled, confused, disappointed, and quite close to tears. EdFringe is *hard*. It's a tough world out there, and no-one's going to give you a break unless you rear your horse up in their face, swirl your black cloak, point your blunderbuss in their face and from behind your pantomime mask demand their money or their life. Even that might not work.

What I mean is you have to work hard to get an audience. So you print ten thousand fliers, spend half the day trying to press them into passing hands, and try not to feel that little death when you see them immediately dropped on the pavement, or put in a bin, or politely added to the bundle already in the passing hand.

You book short slots on the open stages on The Mile and try, when the officials aren't looking, to turn your own amplification up to match that of the mime artist or the screaming slapstick on the next stage. You sell yourself with all kinds of hyperbole and dramatic embarrassment.

It was windy in Edinburgh. There was no possibility of playing from music. I didn't even put the stand up. I just had to play what I thought I could play without it, which wasn't much. When I stood up to perform a witty poem, my chair blew away. I thought, maybe I need to be able to do *all* of this without the music in front of me.

When it wasn't quite so windy, I went to play on the street. I put my placards up, to tell passers-by they should experience the whole show. A few of them, I think, might have done. But I'd registered for the Fringe on the last day of registrations, more in answer to a childish dare (I mean, by one of my children – why am I trying to impress *them*?) than anything else, and the only slot I could get was ten o'clock in the morning.

Ten o'clock in the morning? At EdFringe? They must have laughed when they took *your* money.

That was my first time busking. I found I liked it. A lot more than playing to a sleepy and *very* small audience in a blacked-out room in some sweaty and labyrinthine fringe-fest factory.

A plumber's mate leapt out of the passenger side of a white van stopped in the traffic in front of me. Waving his arms and shouting, I thought he was going to do me some violence. I didn't think my playing was *that* bad. But instead he dropped a fistful of coins in my open cello case, then ran off, still shouting, up the road – the traffic had set off again and the plumber wasn't waiting.

The very friendly administrator of the Russian orchestra, who I'd already met a couple of times because they were performing somewhere in the same building, was giving out leaflets close by, and occasionally threw me an encouraging smile. If my mother hadn't warned me about pretty Russians and their encouraging smiles, it might have distracted me.

The best moment of all was the approach of a young French woman. (I didn't know she was French, of course, until later; she wasn't wearing a badge proclaiming *Je suis Française*.)

She listened carefully for a bit. Then she began to dance – not very extrovertly, but quite definitely. I finished what I was playing, and she asked – timidly – if I minded. *Au contraire*, I said. *Au contraire*. I might even have said it a third time for luck. So we played and danced for ten minutes. And then, cruel fate, I had to wind it up because I had a date at the Festival Theatre bar. Who knows what otherwise might have happened?

When I say a date, I mean an actual date. It was the first I'd been on since that other beginning I mentioned before, the beginning of an end, had played itself out, and it was allowable and appropriate (and by my many admirers – haha – expected) that I should go on dates. It was so long since I'd been on one, I was totally clueless. But it wasn't me who suggested gin and tonics (in the plural) in the Festival Theatre bar, before lunch.

The date went well, I thought. I charmed, I extroverted, I laughed, I bought several gins. How many children did I have, she queried? Two, I told her, and I told her their ages.

"Ah," she said; she also had two, aged two and twenty-two. Both of them mistakes, she said. And we giggled over our glasses at the mistakes we make. I almost, but not quite, stopped myself from repeating my mother's characterisation of me – "wrong decisions and missed opportunities".

A man who talks about his mother on a first date? What a cliché. Honestly, though, I didn't *talk* about her. That was the only time she was mentioned. By either of us.

But afterwards she didn't answer the phone – the date, that is. My mother always answered the phone.

So whether or not I was consciously thinking about the administrator of the Russian String Orchestra, as I took a seat for their performance that evening, I couldn't absolutely say, m'lud. Though it was very nice when she smiled at me again.

The Russian String Orchestra is a dazzling performance machine. A collection of young and very talented players from Moscow, under the baton of an apparently strict and definitely not young conductor, they come to Edinburgh every year and work very hard. For a month they perform every night, and often during the day as well. They pack a hall, and presumably take home some decent winnings.

They play a jaunty and virtuosic repertoire, at breakneck speed. And they have a couple of little tricks, which involve audience participation.

Every single member of the orchestra has to be prepared to

react to this one at a moment's notice. The not-so-young conductor asks for an audience volunteer – and there are always a few, even though they've no idea what they're volunteering for.

He asks them to choose a member of the orchestra – any one of them – to play a movement of a concerto. Which the chosen player does immediately, without hesitation, accompanied by the rest of the orchestra. It's the double bass player who's picked on most, apparently. Cruel world.

But the other trick! I had my cello with me – I'd been carrying it around all day, it being a long way back to my lodgings. The conductor – I've remembered his name; it's Misha Rachlevsky – stopped the performance and turned crossly to the audience.

"I don't like it," he said, "when I see unopened musical instrument cases in my audiences. It's lazy. One of you must come and play with us. A solo."

He was looking at me. I froze. If you can be frozen when you've gone the colour of a beetroot. This can't be for real, I thought, and shrank into my seat. But my cello case is bright pink too (I bought it on the internet promise it was red, but it wasn't) so there was no hiding.

The seats around me were agitating and drawing attention to me.

Then I saw the same thing was happening elsewhere in the hall, and eventually a violinist stepped forward. Nervously. After a brief exchange – she declining to play his suggestions, and he declining to conduct hers – they settled on something, and she played it.

Again I thought, this can't possibly be real.

Then – this was Edinburgh, remember, and you had to do anything you could – anything – to promote yourself – I realised it was a now or never moment.

It was a set-up. It had to be. After the concert, when Misha Rachlevsky tried to slip out through a side door, I accosted him, still carrying my cello of course.

I accosted him and I accused him.

Well, that's not quite right; I said something about how fabulous it was, but that he must have set it up, right? Was it rehearsed? I asked, not sure if in translation he would quite understand the leading nature of the question.

"Well, OK, we had a run-through," he confessed. And I barred his way – subtly, but the cello case is a handy doorway-blocker – until he asked me if I'd like to do it tomorrow.

Set-up. His was transparent, but mine was masterful. I'd just got myself a gig with the Russian String Orchestra, who've played 2500 concerts in twenty-six countries on four continents, made over thirty discs, and every one of whose members can stand up and play a concerto on ten seconds' notice (OK, not the cellos; they play their concertos sitting down).

We agreed what I should play – Casals' *Song of the Birds*. He called over his librarian to ask if they had the orchestral parts. Yes, in the archive in Moscow. He'd get them sent over. He'd ring me later to confirm they'd arrived.

He rang at half past midnight, when I'd already done a lot of practice, and was beginning to think it wasn't going to happen. But it was.

We had some crack – by which I mean craic, in case you get the wrong idea – in front of the audience. I used to be a vicar, so stand-up's practically second nature. I accused him of giving me music in Russian, which of course I couldn't play. And then sheepishly I turned it the right way up and apologised. The audience seemed to like it – this was Edinburgh, remember.

I haven't quite forgiven him that we didn't get a run-through beforehand like the violinist from the Shanghai Symphony Orchestra had. But, hey, this was Edinburgh. And what does it now say on my CV? "Has performed an impromptu solo with the Russian String Orchestra in Edinburgh." Or at least it would, if I ever had a CV that anyone ever wanted to look at.

I thought of my mother's description of me – wrong decisions and missed opportunities. She lived the last two years of her life in a care home near me, and we saw each other nearly every day. We had some crack (you know what I mean). She'd say it nearly every time. I used to reply, "No, worse than that – missed decisions and wrong opportunities."

And we'd cackle like two old people together, as though it was the *mot juste*, and the first time it had ever been said.

Well, I didn't miss *that* opportunity, did I?

So why exactly can this also claim to be a beginning? Because I found *The Poetical Cellist's* performance unconvincing – his solo performance of music and poetry, I mean; not his triumph with the Russian String Orchestra. If you read that word – *unconvincing* – in a review, you'd cry, wouldn't you?

Well, it was. It wasn't a polished enough performance to put before an Edinburgh crowd that had too much choice anyway. It was nervous. It was pedestrian.

Most of all, there was something about having a music stand between me and the audience that just wasn't right. Like playing behind a curtain. Or with my back to them. Or with the TV on in the background. Or eating my lunch at the same time. Or sight-reading. Whatever it was, it lacked conviction. Something had to be done about that.

CHAPTER 13

The Swan in Buntingford

FRIDAY 3 JUNE

I biked the twenty or so miles to Buntingford, through pretty villages with thatched roofs and flint churches. I found myself, for the third time, on a section of Ermine Street. It runs straight through Buntingford, a beautiful small town with a real library and a High Street full of ancient pubs.

The High Street, as you would expect of a section of Ermine Street, is straight as a hard stare. It's historic, and pretty, and tidy as well as straight. The kind of place where accountants, actuaries and once-famous cricketers would live, in expensive and discreet houses. Behind the pretty High Street, and its excess of pretty pubs, there are plenty of such houses. Plus a fair smattering of quite passable bungalows.

Buntingford, just to clarify, isn't named after the streams of beautiful little flags that now festoon the place, Jubilee-wise. As you would expect of a town that houses mainly accountants and actuaries and once-famous cricketers, the bunting is refined. There's no plastic here. It's all knitted – or crocheted, I'm not sure of the difference – in tasteful little squares, strung together to make fine displays on lampposts, flower boxes, facades, and everything else.

No, the town is so named because it had a ford over the river Rib, and it commemorates a Saxon chieftain, Mr. Bunta. You can still see the ford, though Chief Bunta has now passed over.

I'm going to stay with one of those actuaries, in one of those bungalows. Colin is my bridge-playing, garden-cultivating, dog-walking brother. He's a very good and quite important actuary, actually. He used to be the Chief Wallah in the actual Institute (and Faculty) of Actuaries and had to go all over the world talking about it; explaining (presumably) that actuaries aren't just a well-paid and boring sub-set of accountants.

If you Google *actuaries*, to find out what they actually do, one of Google's first suggested questions (don't you just love those?) is "Are actuaries boring?" It must be an uphill battle. But Colin will explain patiently. Actuaries are mathematicians who analyse and quantify risk, and then turn that into financial, economic, and fiscal modelling. There. It's a good time to be an actuary, in a world that's facing up to a lot of risks it didn't really know about before, and when you don't want to make your economic and fiscal policies on the back of an envelope, following a hunch.

Colin has arranged a concert at the little church down the road, the Church of St. Mary the Virgin, Westmill. It's one of the lovely flint churches that pepper the countryside hereabouts. It's got a solid – might you almost say *squat*? – tower, and a rather wide nave which makes it look a tad short and fat from the outside. Though only in a certain light, and from a certain angle, obviously.

My brother has a leading role in the organisation of the churches here, as well as in many other social and educational causes and ventures. I think he must be a good man to have on your committee, if you value efficiency, straightforwardness, thoughtfulness and an unfussy approach to Getting Things Done.

My sister-in-law has a role too, being ordained in the Anglican Church, but she can't come this evening, owing to the recent arrival in the world of a pretty, and tiring, granddaughter, whom I hope to see tomorrow.

I like the arrangement of notices on the ancient door of Westmill Parish Church. There's Her Jubilee Majesty – of course – and next to her one Kenneth Wilson, with his bike and his cello. That's the second time I've been placed next to the Queen – though the first time is part of a different story.

Colin has warned me the audience will be small. It turns out to be two-and-a-half times the size of his forecast – which is gratifying for me, but possibly not something he might want to put on his actuarial CV. And they are the loveliest of audiences, engaged and appreciative, and happy to see two brothers treating each other as brothers should.

And the church has a most magnificent acoustic, with just the right amount of reverberating echo, which allows for the occasional dramatic flourish, and long fade away. I liked playing in Westmill Parish Church. If Colin was surprised, he was far too diplomatic to say so.

What are the three most famous works for solo cello, I ask them? There's a short pause, and a little looking around for moral support, before the answers. I know what the answers will be, and usually in what order they'll come.

Elgar's *Cello Concerto*.

I play the opening chords of the Elgar, with a bit of pantomime. And?

Bach. I play the first few bars of the *Prelude* of the *First Suite*, and make it look as though it's a roundabout I can't get off. Nods of recognition.

And? *The Swan*. Yes, of course, *The Swan*.

Camille Saint-Saëns was not a spectacularly happy man. He was very successful, in a slightly pedestrian, and possibly actuarial, way. He lamented that people thought him more "competent" than inspired.

He was perhaps a bit touchy, though. He'd been a child prodigy, which is a difficult calling to follow through on. Rossini, Berlioz and Liszt were known to have thought very highly of him, and Gabriel Fauré called him a genius. He'd been written about as the best church organist France had ever had. That, I suppose, was the problem; he didn't think church organist a very high calling.

And he never quite forgave Berlioz for a jocular remark that maybe went too close to the bone. Saint-Saëns, said Berlioz, "lacked inexperience".

He had reason, too, to be unhappy. Of his two children the elder died in an accident – for which he blamed his wife – at the age of two. The younger died shortly afterwards. He walked out of his marriage a few years after that, without, apparently, even a farewell to his much younger spouse.

Saint-Saëns became wildly famous in France and in England. But it didn't seem to be quite enough. And when he wrote what is now his most famous work, he decreed that it should not be published, or publicly performed, in his lifetime, because it wasn't serious enough. He did not want to be thought of as not serious enough.

He wrote the *Carnival of the Animals* in 1886. It wasn't published until just after his death in 1921. Apart, that is, from one of the fourteen movements.

The only movement allowed out of his private circle was *The Swan*.

Saint-Saëns wrote it originally for cello and two pianos. Normally it's played in the version for cello and a single piano. The piano plays a bar of rippling broken chords before the cello comes in with that wonderful tune. Normally you wouldn't play it without the piano, but I saw a video of Yo-Yo Ma doing just that, out in the open air, accompanying – or being accompanied by – a flowing, though not classically conventional, dancer.

On the *Highway Cello* album, this is the only piece which isn't entirely solo cello. But it doesn't have the piano accompaniment. It has just the backing of a little burbling stream. On the road, or on the stage, I play it without even that.

I love it. We've had the jokes about the famous pieces, and the mood is light. The first three notes of *The Swan* are enough to cast its spell. Immediately there's absolute stillness. Breaths are held. Here is the swan, gliding before our eyes. And we glide with it.

There are other pieces of music where the opening notes grab your attention. Beethoven's Fifth Symphony *(da-da-da-daa! da-da-da-daa!)* Tchaikowsky. Even the Elgar Cello Concerto we just heard. But usually that's music of high drama, declamatory, loud, even violent. *The Swan* is none of those things. Three quiet notes – that falling semitone, and that gliding fifth. That's all it takes.

I play it for couples. I did it often in Rome, that most romantic of cities. A hand loosely, apparently lazily, holding another on the table outside the Cafe Tartarughe there. She glances up at me, with a look that asks silently for something romantic – perhaps this is going to be the moment – and then a little smile of thanks before she turns her attention to the matter in hand.

A little wedding party at the same place, on the same afternoon, come to take a few pictures by the Tartarughe fountain. The bowl of the fountain, with its four turtles, is held up by four young bronze men, dramatically splaying their legs. In times when Rome has been more puritan than it is now there have been temporary fig leaves here. Not that day.

Another couple, on the steps in another piazza, her head in his lap, his bent low to kiss her slowly. She knows I've noticed them. She's wondering if *The Swan* is reaching a more passionate climax than usual. She doesn't mind at all. She whispers something in his ear, smiling, and he glances at me and smiles too. I try to look away.

Yes, that was a specially tender rendering of the tune.

I play it in places that are a bit too noisy, too busy. You'd think it would be lost. An unamplified cello is a feeble thing in a big public space. Often of course it is lost. The traffic doesn't take any notice. The football doesn't stop. But sometimes it seems to have a quietening effect. Even if that's only in my imagination.

Remember that early morning as Rutherfords punted me along the Cam, and that family of swans glided by, six cygnets following a parent, with the seventh hitching a ride under the raised wing?

I played it on an orphan bridge over the Marne canal, where I could see the hardly-moving water for miles in both directions. There were no swans there. There was no audience at all except a few vigilant herons, and they weren't interested. I was playing it for the water.

Sometimes, when they're identifying it, people call it *The Dying Swan*. For a long time I thought that was just a mistake, turning the beautiful gliding on the water into a desperate failure to hold onto life. Or thinking about the legend of the Mute Swan – that it's silent all its life, until its final hours, when it sings sublimely. Its swansong.

In fact it's because they're more widely cultured than I am. *The Dying Swan* is a short ballet movement premiered in 1907 (and allegedly danced four thousand times after that) by Anna Pavlova, to Saint-Saëns' music. I didn't know that. I still think it's a bit of a hijack. Saint-Saëns' swan is definitely alive.

And I played it now, in the wide-naved country parish church of St. Mary the Virgin, Westmill, where the audience was bigger than it should have been. They nodded; they murmured. Then they applauded. I liked that. They looked over at Colin and raised an eyebrow – though I've no idea what that meant.

Afterwards – when the bike had been admired, and interrogated, and Colin had driven and I'd cycled back – we sat at the kitchen table, in the bungalow's handsome kitchen, and ate fine cheese, until it was time for the dogs to go to bed there, and the day ended.

CHAPTER 14

History of the bicycle

I'm in flat country these days. Cambridge, Buntingford, London – these Southerners don't know what a hill is. The Pennines, the Yorkshire Dales and all that, they're far behind. But I'm thinking ahead, and reflecting on the uphillness of things. They're a way off yet, but the route promises Alps, and things like that. Big challenges; big ideas, those goals in the distance. So I'm thinking how much our outlook on life is built around the idea of goal-achievement; pass these exams, get that job, buy the house, get to the top of this hill, win that fight. Then it's the living happily ever afterwards.

You've been trained all your life for this, the achieving of goals – one after another in ever-ascending glory – until you reach the happily ever after. Where – and this is something you're not in the least prepared for – there are no more goals. Nothing more to achieve. I wonder if the happily-ever-after marriage, which is always the end of the fairytale, could ever actually be happy? You wouldn't know what to do, would you? (Well maybe for a bit; but you might get tired of it. I don't know.)

It's an episodic view of life. Like the bike ride that's a series of difficult hills. The only bits that count are the summits. The ride consists of so many summits, with nothing in between them except the goal of reaching them.

It all derives – this is what I'm thinking, wondering, as I'm mentally sweating and weaving my way up this monster of a slope, telling myself I'll just get to *that* point there in the distance before I stop, again – it all derives from the biggest happily-ever-after story of them all. The whole point – the only point – of this life is to get the happily-ever-after prize in the next. Fairytale.

It's a difficult narrative to change. But I've seen some clues. What if it isn't *goal* at all? What if it's just *process*? Hear me out. Short sentences. Not much breath. Uphill. Lungs. Legs. Hurting.

Gardening. That's not goal, is it? That's all process. Every weekend, weather, nature, growth, decay, means there's something more to do. It's never finished.

Children. They're not goal, are they? It'll be alright when they start school, when they leave school, when they go out to work, when they leave home, when they've got children of their own. Will it? I don't think so.

Mindfulness – though it's full of hokum, and I don't like the word itself – is maybe nearer the mark. In *this* moment, *this* turning of the pedals, *this* feeling – of comfort, or discomfort – this everything. It deserves full attention in its own right, and not just as a stage on the way to *that* achievement, the summit over there.

Which, when you reach it, doesn't have quite the significance you wanted it to have when you were striving for it.

Maybe it would be easier if I had a background of Eastern, rather than Western, religions; religions where mostly everything just goes round, and round, and round and round. Like the wheels on the bus, or the pedals on a very long bike ride. Eastern religions aren't completely goalless, of course. But for most of us the goal is so far distant – a million lifetimes, perhaps – it's not really in the picture.

Process. Not goal.

Am I onto something, I'm wondering? Or is it just sunstroke, or dehydration, or exhaustion, or the complete elimination of all calories from my body and the consequent disintegration of muscle and non-vital organs? And why am I going down this road? (The metaphorical one, not the hard and painful one under my wheels, which is very definitely up, not down.)

Well, partly in order to make sense of this journey. And perhaps then to explain why journeys figure so strongly in our collective mythologies and subconsciouses. Because if I'd just wanted to get to Rome, I'd have gone on a train, wouldn't I?

And to some extent I *am* making sense of the journey. It's process, the mindful inhabiting of the moment. It's not about getting to Rome – something which just now I can't even think about.

The trouble with this approach is it doesn't really make a very good story. If it's all process, then where's the end, the goal? And where's the beginning? You know already I haven't had resounding success locating and identifying a convincing beginning. I tried. But you can tell what's coming. I'm going to backtrack and try another one.

I suppose – though I don't know this yet – I must have fudged some kind of ending, though, unless I just stopped when I'd had enough. Or there wouldn't be a book to read, would there? But whether that's Rome, as per the original plan, or whether I'm stuck in some depopulated *cul-de-sac* in (presumably) France, which is where *culs-de-sac* live, or whether by then I just carried on to Timbuktu, how can I tell?

How odd that you – because you've read the back cover – know more about my story than I do. Because I'm still in the middle of it.

At last. The top of the hill. One more goal attained. Just clear this byzantine speculation out of your head and freewheel a bit!

Despite what you may think, I'm a very disciplined person. Productive, even, sometimes. Though I haven't had a proper job for a very long time.

I used to dread the stock question of the assiduous introducer: "So what do you do?" It's taken me until about now to have a good answer to that question: "I get up early, and I work hard. What do you do?"

"Oh, I'm an accountant with X and Y and Z in the City."

"That sounds interesting. Tell me about it."

Yes, disciplined. So I promise I'm only going to try one more beginning. After that I'm just going to get on with the story.

This beginning doesn't involve cellos at all. It's about bikes, and other mechanisms of conveyance.

I've had my bike since I was thirteen. It's not just a bike. It's a Dawes Galaxy. Reynolds 531 tubing, and a frame number stamped into the underside of the bottom bracket – J2584. I don't even have to check that number.

I wasn't nearly big enough for it when I got it, and I could have been in a circus with the contortions I went through to balance on it, with half a toe almost on the ground to convince my dubious mother that I was. She was looking quizzically at the salesman, and whether it was the look I was giving him when she couldn't see, or the thought of a sale he might otherwise not get, but he was assuring her I'd grow into it in a month.

Two years I'd waited for it, and I was *not* going to wait any longer, even if I was the smallest boy in the class, and still sang treble in the church choir.

There'd been another bike before the Galaxy, an unspeakable orange thing with – the shame of it – straight handlebars. In the summer before I went to secondary school I'd gone on that orange bike on an organised week's cycle tour in Wales. All the other boys were older teenagers, and they all had proper racing handlebars, except for one youngster – I think he was called Simon – who was just a couple of years older than me. The bigger boys bullied Simon. And occasionally me as well. That cycle tour blighted my life for years, which is one reason – though not the only reason – I hated the orange bike. It was under the auspices of a highly respectable youth organisation. But the leader was a man called Alan who was as unsuited to having charge of children as were the paedophile music teachers. At the age of eleven he had me, with all the other boys, in the pub, drinking beer, smoking Senior Service, and listening to his filthy jokes. We thought it was wonderful.

Only then something happened to Simon – something that went beyond ordinary bullying (as if that wasn't bad enough). Whether that was before or after I came off my bike going down a steep hill in the rain, and had to go to hospital with a great gash on my leg, and wished I'd stayed at home, I can't remember. Simon's father made a complaint to the highly respectable youth organisation, and threatened to go to court. Alan came to visit my parents to talk about it. To see, I realised later, what story I would tell, and therefore how much trouble he was really in.

He should have been in a lot of trouble. He should have been in jail. But somehow, at the age of eleven, it all turned out to be my fault. Not the fault of the man who egged us all on. I couldn't defend myself, because I couldn't remember what had happened. I'd been drunk.

My mother wanted to buy me the Dawes Galaxy almost as much as I wanted her to buy it for me. The episode with the orange bike had been traumatic for Father. To a man for whom even an income tax form carried the threat of jail and humiliation, it was more than he could bear. He needed all his emotional energy for himself, and I would sink or swim as best I could. To my mother the dark green Galaxy would be a kind of catharsis for both of us, her and me, when the awful orange thing and all it signified could be consigned to a forgotten history of childhood. It almost worked.

On a Saturday I still had to do my practice, of course, before I could go out on it. But by the time I really was big enough for it I was getting up early, so that my friend Roger didn't have to witness the embarrassment of that practice before we both set off for a day's adventure.

I don't think we ever told anyone where we were going. Sometimes we'd pedal through the traffic to Richmond Park, telling each other this would be the week we'd get three times round its seven-mile perimeter in an hour. Which we never did, of course. If we got round twice in that time without injury to any of the park's perambulating population it was an achievement.

Then we'd go further afield. Box Hill. All over the South Downs. Even, eventually, on one forever memorable day, the sixty miles to the coast. And the sixty miles back again. Just. I don't think anyone ever knew where we were or when we'd be back.

I took the bike to school every day, keeping records – and trying to break them – of the time taken. I risked my life every day. Crossing the A3, the Portsmouth Road, without losing time, was a particular hazard. My poor mother.

Lots of boys biked to school then. Now the bike sheds are gone – which isn't just about the smoking. Bikes are for sport now, not for getting from A to B.

After the orange bike incident there wasn't another long – more than an overnight – trip until the summer at the end of school. By then there were notebooks full of reports and mileages. No boasting, though; just times and figures, accumulating. A new biking friend, John, and I set off for a month's meticulously planned, Youth Hostel-accommodated, journey around the coastline of England.

The following summer there was a long cycle through France with Avril, drinking a bottle of wine with our baguette and cheese at lunchtime, and stealing maize from the fields for our dinner. I was eighteen, and she was twenty-three.

I'd gone back to school because – unlike my three effortlessly clever brothers – I'd failed to get the grades for Cambridge, and I really wanted to go. I did an extra term, and then had time to spare. I worked for Her Majesty's Geological Survey in London, and then did three months' field work with them in Scotland. Which is where I met Avril.

She was a Geology graduate, and looking for a proper job, while I was just playing at it. Why she agreed to cycle round Brittany with me I don't know. She laughed at me often, I realised much later – when, for instance, in the *auberge* they asked if we wanted *la même chambre*, and I said *non, merci*. I was very religious and proper and rule-bound in those days. I had a lot to learn. Talk about a wasted youth.

Afterwards, she was going to Cambridge too, as a post-graduate student. I was callow and callous – if only carelessly – and she cried when I said I expected we wouldn't see much of each other in Cambridge. A wasted youth indeed.

After that, when I was freshly married, there were tandem journeys round the Greek Islands. Not quite a honeymoon journey, but within a year or two of that actual honeymoon in an unfinished and unfurnished house miles from anywhere in Scotland.

The tandem didn't last. Bicycles made for two, we discovered, are really only for those who've had a lot of practice at being married, or who want something to expedite a divorce.

I don't think there were any more proper long bike rides after that. Even so, I'm sure this was a kind of beginning too.

We moved to Cumbria and settled in a beautiful place at the bottom of Hartside Pass, one of the highest roads across the Pennines, and the most anticipated part of the year-round C2C cycle fest. Thousands of cyclists every year passed our door on that adventure.

The Dawes Galaxy came out of its child-rearing-and-work-induced rest. A teenage daughter and I used to get our bikes out late on a Saturday afternoon, and race the four miles and thirteen-hundred-foot climb to the top of Hartside, seeing how many Coast to Coasters we could overtake. It was cruel sport, because of course they'd been cycling all day and carried luggage. We were daisy-fresh. Cruel, but such fun.

Then the daughters left home, and the Dawes Galaxy went back into a kind of hibernation again. Until now.

That's a tiny exaggeration. I got the bike out, for what I tried to call "training", a little while ago. I got to the top of Hartside, stopping on the way to chat (in very short sentences) to Steve, who'd parked his white van in the lay-by off the hairpin bend near the top. Steve was pointing a very long-lensed camera at me, which immediately made me think I was in trouble, though I knew it wasn't for speeding.

No, he said, you're not in trouble. I take pictures of bikes and motorbikes, and they go on my website and buy them. Everyone likes an action shot of themselves on Hartside. And you can't take a selfie on a bike, can you?

It seemed an auspicious start to the "training", though I didn't buy any of the photos. Who wants to see me looking like *that*? Not me, anyway.

I tried to take the training seriously, as people do, but it was always going to be a bit haphazard. I'm no longer that young fellow, I thought, who promised a girl he'd do the Cambridge Boundary Run (twenty-six miles round the boundary of the City of Cambridge) and then – as young men do – forgot the promise. She reminded me a week before the event, and I had to run (is that the right word?) a marathon on four days' training and two days off.

The city boundary ran through quite a lot of fields, many of them recently ploughed. You can't run with twenty kilos of Fenland mud stuck to each elephantine foot.

So a bit of training would be in order. Then, the following sleepless night, I was idly calculating how many circuits of Hartside would be an equivalent climb from sea level to the top of Everest (twenty-two, since you ask, and 176 miles of road). I told myself not to be completely stupid, and turned my attention to Mont Blanc. 4809m, so only about twelve times up and down Hartside, which is 96 miles of road. Maybe I could work up to that? Or maybe not. Actually, not "maybe".

Go to sleep.

But before we leave Cambridge where, I think, I must have seen

109

Avril twice – she lived a long way out of town, and by the time I'd grown up a bit, she'd already moved on – I should say something about those three effortlessly clever brothers. And the cello. I know this was supposed to be all about the bike, but we can't have a whole chapter without mention of the cello.

They'd all got scholarships to Trinity, and I'd scraped into a College no-one had heard of, and then only on my second attempt. And perhaps only because the College would have felt guilty turning down someone who'd gone to all the trouble of trying twice. So the younger brothers – twins, and three years younger than me – were only just behind, and Elder Brother was doing a PhD, so we were all there at the same time. We played a concert – well, an item in a concert – as the Wilson Quartet. Four brothers, all playing instruments made by their father. It wasn't very good (apart from the mathematical and musical genius, the Elder Brother), but it was one of Father's proudest moments – and perhaps the moment when he almost forgave the shame of the orange bike.

OK. I promise we're done with beginnings. No more beginnings. Onwards. Upwards. South. Process. Lungs. Legs. Hurting.

CHAPTER 15

Not at home

SATURDAY 4 JUNE

On the way to London – going up to town – today. Which I presume a proportion of Buntingford's good residents (though probably not the once-famous cricketers) do regularly, maybe three or four times a week. It's not a convenient journey by train. There was a station in Buntingford for a hundred years, but it closed in the great railway purge, and the efforts to get it re-opened are faltering. Perhaps Colin should be on the committee.

No, you have to drive eleven miles to Stevenage first (if you want to get to St. Pancras), or the same distance to Ware if you want to go to Liverpool Street. I don't suppose many commuters go by bike.

I'm nervous of London Town, even though I lived there – Streatham Hill, Tulse Hill, and Walthamstow, in that order – and worked there – Westminster, Ealing, Norbury, and Walthamstow, in that order – for years. But I'm going to be on an unwieldy and unbalanced bicycle. I have a feeling today is going to be the day I have to answer to some law-enforcement officer. *Do you have a licence for this thing? Is it roadworthy? Can you ride in a straight line while looking over your shoulder?* The answer to all three of which is *No*. Three strikes and you're out. The last question in particular – look to see where the traffic is behind you, and you lose all control of the beast. You just have to guess. But today is Saturday, and it's the Jubilee weekend, so London's roads should be as clear as Christmas. I hope so.

I diverted five minutes off route to visit the newly arrived great-niece. But it's early, and they probably shouldn't be disturbed. So I just passed the end of the road, sending love and best wishes through the ether. More flint churches, more thatch, more rain, less flat. I crept quietly through the village of Nasty. I didn't look down Gore Lane a mile or two further on.

I'm looking forward to this evening. There's a lot of personal history in these three days – yesterday, today and tomorrow – and I've known Henry for a very long time. When I first knew him, he was a loud and scary political activist, whose daily discourse was peppered with placards and protests, and words like proletariat and Palestine, and power, and bourgeoisie. At least, that's what I remember; I didn't know him well then; he was scary.

But I've got to know him better since. He rides a bike, and he's been to visit a couple of times, to ride up Hartside, and suchlike. But he rides too fast, and falls off. So if you make an arrangement it's quite likely to be cancelled, via a short message – *fell off bike broken shoulder another time sorry.*

It's nice sometimes to tell people I knew him before he was famous. He's the founder, and Chief Happiness Officer, of a company called Happy. He wrote *The Happy Manifesto*. He's a manifestly happy man. Quite like the Dalai Lama. His concern for social equality and justice has not diminished in forty years. But now he channels that considerable energy into demonstrating it, living it, and proving to others they can do it too. He's a social saint. He said there might be some music tonight. It will be fun.

A bit of Roman road. A bit of cycle track beside the railway. Down the Lea Valley, past a family cricket match at the entrance to the park.

"Is there a body in that case?" the batsman distracted himself by asking, and turned back to find himself bowled out.

There's such a maze of cycle paths here you couldn't possibly follow a map. You just have to keep an eye on where the sun is, and go in the general direction. Fortunately it's now quite sunny, after some heavy showers earlier.

The river – though I don't know if it's properly river, or canal – is crammed with houseboats, sometimes two deep along the bank. How much of this is lifestyle choice, and how much dysfunctional housing markets? It's very pretty just now, but what about the winter?

I stopped to send a message to Henry – what time should I arrive at his house in Stoke Newington? He rang straight back. *You didn't get my email? Oh dear; I'm not there.*

Ten minutes later, while I was riding slowly along the canal – I think it's a canal – slowly so that I could think what to do, he rang again.

"Solved!" he proclaimed in a happy voice. "My daughter will let you in; make yourself at home."

That sounds like an inconvenience, and I don't want to be a nuisance… "No, no, she lives round the corner; it's no trouble. Just tell her what time."

Yes, it was a solution, of sorts. But I was really looking forward to seeing Henry. We had a lot to talk about. We'll have to make another arrangement.

Later, there was a restoration. After two hours around the kitchen table, on one of the lower floors of Henry's narrow house built on about nineteen different levels, debating politics with Miri, I felt I'd been with Henry all along. Not, I hasten to point out, that the daughter is any kind of clone of the father (what kind of biology would *that* be?) But the tradition was clearly strong, and I liked it.

We haven't got there yet, though. Walthamstow. Pronounce it with more of an "f" than a "th". I was a curate here years and years ago, so I ought to visit some old haunts. I wheeled the bike up the mile-long market, stopping for a little busking where it widens out a bit.

Walthamstow market used to be the place for jellied eels. I mean *the* place. The eels ran up the Thames in their millions, and a good living could be made by netting them and bringing them up to the East End, to feed the masses.

But the eel is a fish, and it goes off very quickly. It keeps a bit longer if you jelly it. Then the Thames got too dirty, and the eel became an endangered species. Some people still ate jellied eels – old habits die hard, they explained – but it wasn't approved of. It may even have been illegal.

Now the Thames is clean again, and eels are coming back, and you can eat them openly in Walthamstow market. There are better things to eat, though, in my opinion, like the Jamaican red bean soup and dumpling I had from a busy stall. Oh yes!

There was a man there, taking two small daughters out to lunch. The girls fidgeted, and giggled, and occasionally ate a small mouthful of patty, while they competed to ask him the most profound, unanswerable and silly questions. Most of us would just have told our children to be quiet and eat their dinners. Not him; with the straight-faced panache of a Michael Rosen or a Benjamin Zephaniah he answered every one, and marvelled with them at the silliness of nature. I couldn't help overhearing, and it was a happy lunch for all of us.

I remembered how I enjoyed the multicultural nature of Walthamstow (briefly, for instance, taking sitar lessons in the Cultural Centre). Now the market seems even more wonderfully diverse than it was then. I lost count of the languages I heard. And the eccentric essentials I could have bought, if I wasn't travelling by bike, and on my way to Rome.

I said something silly to the little girls, then staggered off to look for the church of St. Peter-in-the-Forest. It really is in the forest, and you have to walk under ancient trees, across ancient leaf litter, to get there. It's had some renovation and alteration since I was its curate, but it's still very recognisable.

As was Frances, the person who opened the door to me, though I had to be reminded of her name. She didn't need any reminding about me though (apparently I look just the same). At least it was nice of her to say so.

St. Peter-in-the-Forest is a special church – by which I mean congregationally, not architecturally. Architecturally, despite its being listed for its "pleasing Italianate Romanesque" design, I think it just looks Industrial Revolution. And it was built on London Clay without proper foundations, so when I knew it, it was cracked and crumbling and always looked in danger of collapse.

Congregationally it had a reputation for being liturgically wayward, theologically argumentative, socially adventurous, and generally unpredictable. The curate's job description – I paraphrase – was to do what he liked, when he liked, if he liked. Naturally it suited me very well, and I worked very hard there. I lived, recently married, in a tiny curate's house, on the edge of Epping Forest, drove an old yellow Mini with a furred-up radiator, and watched the free-roaming cattle of the Forest periodically invade and destroy the garden.

Frances showed me everything that was different in the building. They had made very good use of a modest Lottery grant to re-order it and make it exciting and functional. And a beautiful place to play a cello. I played a Bach *Sarabande*, a requiem for all the lovely people I'd known there who were now buried in the churchyard, or scattered in the forest.

Then I hurried on to Stoke Newington, to be there at the appointed time to be let into Henry's empty house. Later I went out to get a pizza, counting the days until – with any luck – I'd be over the Alps and into Italy, eating real Italian pizza. So I passed up a takeaway that proclaimed itself a bit too wide-ranging in its offering, and therefore unlikely to be expert in anything particular, pushing open the door of the very Italian-looking place a bit further on.

Good choice, I thought, as I admired out loud the way the chef whirled the dough in the air and dropped it neatly on the counter.

Thanks, she said, with a flashing smile.

But you're not Italian yourself? I ventured, thinking I detected something in that one-word answer, or in her look.

No. She was, she said, Persian, though she'd lived in Italy a long time, and most people thought she was very properly Italian.

I visited that beautiful country, once, I said. Am I allowed to ask why you call yourself Persian, not Iranian?

So we had the kind of conversation you couldn't legally have in Iran, as I counted out the coins from the Walthamstow market busking, and she didn't bother to count them in. But pizza cooks very quickly, and the conversation was brief.

I went home and ate it in front of Henry's television, though I couldn't work out how to switch it on, remembering the ruins of Persepolis, and the bridges of Isfahan, and the rugs of Shiraz, and the traffic and watchfulness of Tehran.

I even thought about those people who said, why stop in Rome? Carry on, on the *Via Francigena* to Jerusalem. Or turn left and go to India. The old route to India goes through some of those wonderful places in Iran.

But it also goes through Afghanistan and Pakistan, I'd said, and a few other places Western cyclists might not feel especially welcome. And Rome will be far enough.

CHAPTER 16

What's the worst that could happen?

LAST JANUARY

It's halfway through that nervous, waiting, time when you know it's going to happen but it isn't happening yet. If you're a military person it's called "build-up", "war-footing" or – less judgementally – just "preparation". If like me you're a panicker, it's called "panic".

I'm definitely not sleeping well. I make lists at the beginning of the day, and more lists at the end of the day – as much as anything trying to forestall the waking up in the night in order to make more lists. Which, because of the nature of the night, are always headed PANIC.

I'm a rational person. I reason with myself. And I listen carefully when other people reason with me. It doesn't matter, they say, whether you succeed or fail. What's the worst that could happen, anyway?

No, I agree, it doesn't matter in the slightest. And oddly I'm not all that afraid of failure. I keep a list of my memorable failures, starting with scoring less than the Elder Brother at the Cycling Proficiency Test, when I was maybe seven. I could ride a bike, and he couldn't. So I was cocky, and the examiner shifted the balance by not giving me the emergency stop command until he knew I was going to run into him anyway. It's unfairness I can't bear, not

117

failure. The failure list is far too long for one more entry to make any difference to it. Success is over-rated. Though I suppose, if pressed, I have to say I do prefer success to failure.

There is a possible failure that's weighing on my mind a bit. I had carpal tunnel syndrome. In my bowing hand. Brought on by playing the cello. When it became almost impossible to play, I had it operated.

One of the most traumatic days of my life. Quite unlike the two or three other minor operations I've put myself through, even though one of those involved not being able to sit down for three days. Whether it was imagination or an anaesthetic not working very well, I don't know; but I felt every cut, and pull, and tear, and drop of surgeon's sweat. He told me I had to calm down, because I wasn't helping him. I told him I wasn't expecting it to hurt so much.

Six weeks, he said, and I'd be right as rain. You can probably play the cello again in a couple of days; just don't overdo it.

Eighteen months later I still couldn't play more than an hour.

Cycling aggravates it. And it seems to be starting in the other wrist, too. There's no way I'm having an operation like that again.

I've padded my handlebars until they look like a toddler's play pen. What if it's not enough? A week into the journey, and I can't cycle *or* play the cello? Surely God wouldn't let that happen to someone on pilgrimage?

But as for "what's the worst that could happen?" – well, that's a completely different question. It's not just that I might get a puncture and fail to repair it because I bought cheap patches that didn't stick, and I couldn't use the tyre levers properly and I made more holes in the inner tube, and so I couldn't get to a destination in time, and missed the performance that a cathedral full of people was waiting for me to give. Is it?

No. It's not even that the cello might not be quite as indestructible as it's billed, and somehow it cracks under the strain, and I can't call myself *Highway Cello* if there's no cello, can I?

So how about this for just one of many scenarios that play through my head in the middle of the night: I get caught in a snow storm going over the Alps, but I don't freeze to death (which is what a sensible person would do) because instead of taking shelter I press on, and skid off the road and plunge to my destruction in an alpine forest where no-one ever finds me?

It's not *failure* that's the issue. It's loss of life, or something like that. I wouldn't like that.

I don't know if thoughts like these count as preparation. I suppose they do, in a way. In recent years I've taken many religious-interest groups to India, and I recognise this feeling from those trips. The weeks beforehand are always dreadful. The Buddha had something wise to say about it (not specifically about biking to Rome with a cello, you understand, just something that can be extrapolated, I mean). He said there's no help to be found in this life, this universe. We live on the edge of a cliff, with our toes over the nothingness, and all that's in front of us is void – infinite, empty, emptiness. And our eyes are closed.

We should, he said, open our eyes, and face the void.

If there's nothing there, we need to face that nothingness. Nobody gains anything by imagining the void full of goodies, or divine protectors, or even just soft fluffy clouds to land on.

I think he had a point. The point being that it's pointless.

Perhaps surprisingly, this helps, at least a little. My journey is unnecessary. Fundamentally, it's meaningless. I'm not doing something no-one's ever done before. I'm not compelled by some evolutionary force that can't be denied. I just decided to do it, and now I'm going to do it. So what? Big yawn. Face the void. The journey is insignificant because it can't be significant. I'm a microbe blindly moving a small fraction of the way over a speck in the insignificant glow of a small light in a forgotten backwater of a

119

rather dusty emptiness.

That viewpoint might not be everyone's cup of tea. I do see that. So here's another. One of the five "pillars of Islam", the holy religious duties incumbent on Muslims, is the pilgrimage to Mecca, the *Haj*. When you've been to Mecca you ever afterwards wear the title of *Hajji*, the person who has fulfilled the *Haj*. The title marks you. It also makes it known that a pilgrimage is of such importance that it changes you. The afterwards cannot be the same as the before.

The Buddha tells me the journey is not significant. The Islamic *hadith* tells me it's of the utmost significance. It's both, of course. A comforting thought to lie awake to.

Hang on. Did I say this was a pilgrimage?

That's a complicated question. Actually it's a *very* complicated question. But since there are still three months until I get on the bike and point in the direction of Rome, I'd better try and answer it.

I used to be a vicar, as I think I may already have confessed, in the Church of England. I used to wear a dog collar, and a cassock on Sundays, and some really spectacular gold finery when the Queen came to visit. I baptised people, and married them, and buried them, and preached at them twice a week. I did all the things I was supposed to do (and maybe a few I wasn't). It was fun, and I loved it.

Then one day – long story, and not totally out of the blue, and maybe I'll tell it if we do get to Rome – I woke up with the realisation it had all gone.

Those stories on which I'd staked my life, because they were, after all, different in *kind* from every other story, and somehow *true*, had become, as if by magic, *not* different in kind from every other story.

The reaction was nearly always the same, if I told anyone. They said, *oh, you mean you've lost your faith?* That's what they said, but they didn't all mean the same thing. Sometimes they meant, as if slightly raising an eyebrow, that that was a careless thing to do. Sometimes they implied a degree of moral reprehensibility. And some went into immediate mourning for the loss of my immortal soul.

No, I wanted to say, I haven't lost it. I know exactly where it went. I can see it – just over there. Like the story Jesus told of the rich man in hell, looking up and seeing heaven, and there being a "great gulf fixed" between them, which he could never cross.

OK, maybe not a helpful picture in this case.

I'm trying to answer the question of whether this is a pilgrimage. I lost many things when I gave up being a vicar. I served out my contract, telling anyone who would listen that the stories hadn't become less important just because they'd lost their special uniqueness. If anything, they'd become more important – because you still wanted to live your life by something that was a *story* rather than a mandate from God in his heaven.

But when that contract came to an end I couldn't in all conscience apply for another job in the C of E. As G.K. Chesterton (I think it was him) pointed out, a long time ago, we pay the vicar to believe the things we can't, or won't, believe. That's the job description. And I failed it.

I lost a job that I rather liked. I lost a great big vicarage. I lost a kind of status – everyone recognised the vicar in a place like All Saints, Wolverhampton, and the vicar had a kind of unspoken permission to knock on any door, to stop anyone in the street, to pat any baby on the head, to enquire into any unhappiness, to play anyone at pool in the pub. I lost quite a few friends. Maybe I lost my way.

But one thing I didn't lose was my sense of the importance – the sacredness – of place.

Even when I was a vicar, I was taking people to India, asking them to remove their shoes and walk on other people's holy ground, and examine how it felt, what it did to them. Don't decide beforehand what you think, I said. You don't know until you do it. Holy ground is special.

Not just in India, of course. We revived an ancient tradition, and "beat the bounds" of the parish, walking right round the limits of the church's patch with crosses and prayers and holy water. I took a Sunday service outside into a playground, and blessed the playground, and incidentally invited the TV cameras to shame the local authority into spending some money on it. (That worked a treat, though the Chief Executive asked me, slightly aggrieved, why I hadn't just asked him for the money.)

What is a pilgrimage? In a religious sense, isn't it just a special journey to a special place? So when I stopped being a vicar, when I was no longer conventionally religious, I was left stranded with this anomaly. I'd become almost more religious than the religious in respect of this one thing. Places, and journeys, remain sacred. Geography is sacred. Maybe I need a better word than sacred, but sacred will have to do for now.

Why – why this specialness of place? Of journey? Two reasons, I think. When heaven lost its meaning for me, all that meaning descended to earth. We are creatures of earth, and the earth is special, and precious. It defines us, and gives us not just our context, but our meaning, and our life. There's a reason she's called Mother Earth. Perhaps people have to worship something, and when I stopped worshipping God, maybe I started worshipping Earth?

Well, hang on. I'm no longer religious, so *worship* can't be the right word, can it? And even in this new and enlightened age I don't want you putting a New Age label on me, OK?

The other reason is to do with stories. When I stopped believing in them in the way everyone assumed I should, the stories became more important, not less. And so often stories attach to places. *It was in Cana of Galilee that Jesus… On the Mount of Olives… In the Temple at Jerusalem…* And so on.

Places have significance because we locate our stories in them.

Unrooted, disembodied stories just don't do it for us in the same way.

What makes us human, as opposed to just animal, is culture and language. In other words, the stories we tell – about ourselves, about the universe. About the places that host us and our stories.

So a journey to Rome couldn't be anything other than pilgrimage. Rome sinks under the weight of its stories. So many stories. Such a library, and museum, and cornucopia, and mess, of culture and history and language.

That's where I'm going. That's my journey, my story, my pilgrimage.

It's important for me to write this down, halfway through the stage of preparation, when I feel so completely unprepared, and in a state mostly of panic. Because I want to say I'm with both the Buddha *and* with the Islamic *hadith*. This journey is both perfectly meaningless, and utterly meaningful.

I was corresponding with the Dean of a cathedral, asking if I could perform there as part of my journey. The Dean asked me if the journey was a pilgrimage. He didn't – as perhaps he should have done – ask me if I could actually play the cello. I struggled to give the Dean a proper answer. No, I said, it wasn't exactly a pilgrimage. But yes, I said, of course it's a pilgrimage.

That's a good answer, he said. Yes, come and play the cello for us.

CHAPTER 17

Not expected

SUNDAY 5 JUNE

I dropped Henry's house key through the daughter's letter box, as arranged, and set off for proper London. I'm very glad it's Jubilee Sunday, a good day for a ride down Shaftesbury Avenue, round Piccadilly Circus and such-like. I wouldn't like to do this on a Monday morning.

The cycling-route-finding app doesn't know, of course, that it's Sunday. The route it proposes is an idiotically convoluted and tortuous one, keeping to speed-bumped roads with parked cars on both sides, avoiding all big roads. Yes, on Monday that might be a good idea, safer than leapfrogging the buses along arterial routes. But speed bumps aren't good for bikes laden with cellos, and I can feel Libre's discomfort and displeasure. And of course it's slow – I have to brake for every speed bump, and every little junction.

I went twice round Piccadilly Circus, just because I could, parked Libre and the bike at Eros's feet where I thought she'd feel at home, and reappraised. I abandoned the downloaded route and decided to follow signs, the general direction, and what I thought I knew of the capital, in that order.

But it's Jubilee Sunday, and it seemed the Queen was having a party, *another* party, quite a big affair in Hyde Park, and most of the main roads were closed. I didn't get very far.

I stopped to pass the time with a couple of uniformed and hi-vis

124

security who were blocking one of the closed roads and looking bored. I thought momentarily of just speeding past them while they looked the other way, until Libre made it clear that was a bad idea. What would they think was in the cello case? And how do the security forces respond to a suspected suicide bomber? Not a good idea to be shot first and have the questions asked afterwards. I'm sure I would answer questions better if I wasn't shot first. So I negotiated. It usually worked.

Over Vauxhall Bridge, and I began to feel almost at home. Most Londoners regard *South of the river* as beyond the pale, the outback, the badlands, where the Tube doesn't go (which isn't quite true) and where you wouldn't admit to going yourself except under duress. But I like it. I moved by accident to Streatham Hill, when I had my first job, in Westminster, and it's felt like home ever since.

So I'm relaxed. I stop at a Portuguese café, which already had quite a few customers, including some brave souls outside. Most of them were speaking Portuguese, which I've always thought a most peculiar language, like a very drunken kind of Spanish. But then I suppose if I'd learned Portuguese instead of Spanish I'd think Spanish was a drunken kind of Portuguese, wouldn't I? That's the way wars start.

I'm following the A3, which used to be the road home, the road I risked my life on so many times going to school, unwilling to sacrifice a second to the traffic, which I somehow always managed to dodge. It's quiet today, and mostly it has a very serviceable cycle track. Sometimes I'm sharing that with a couple of buses, which is quite satisfying because there are just enough passengers waiting at the stops that I'm slowly winning the leapfrog.

Then on a whim I decided I would go home. Not, of course, that it's home any more. But I lived in Esher for nearly the first twenty years of my life, and my parents lived there all their long marriage. The house was only sold quite recently, after it became too much for an elderly widow, and it stayed empty a year or so while I tried and failed to get agreement from the owners of the adjoining back gardens for an infill development. That infill had been on the cards when the house was first built, but all the new purchasers along the street lobbied for a tennis court instead, and then someone built a house – by accident, I presume – where the access was going to be. The tennis court never got built, and the developer sold off his now-useless land so everyone could have a long thin garden instead.

Over the years every other house in the street had been enlarged beyond recognition and, when it was sold, no. 7 looked like a very poor thing in comparison. I expected the purchaser to bulldoze it and start again. In an idle moment I looked at the planning application and was disappointed to see nothing more radical than an industrial-sized single-storey extension taking up half the long thin garden.

I cycled past the school, where a cabal of sadistic – and worse – teachers made life uncomfortable for their charges. I stopped off at All Saints Church, where as a small boy I'd sung in the choir, and where the service was just ending so I'd timed it perfectly for coffee and Jubilee cake.

Then I found myself going slower as I approached, not sure if I really want to see the house, which had been home for so long, but might no longer be recognisable. I think I intended just a slow cycle past, just a nod and a little bit of sadness. But the sun was shining on it, and with its new windows it really looked very pretty, and quite happy in its new lease of life. There was a skip by the gate.

On a whim I knocked on the door. I was shown the garden, where I told them all the varieties of apple. I was shown over the house, still recognisable – though much upgraded – upstairs. And downstairs. Downstairs was transformed, and it was hard to relate the new and very expansive spaces to the little rooms that had been there before.

I didn't feel sad for the house, after all. I didn't feel sad at all for what was gone. Here was a house and garden doing what they should be doing, looking after a young family fully occupied with its growing up and its bright future. Doing again what it had done before, and with a new strength, and new bathrooms.

The elder daughter played the violin, just as all that other family had done, so long ago. She was preparing her Grade VI. So I got the cello out, and sat down with her, and played one of her Grade VI pieces with her – some very sprightly Handel – while the rest of the family looked on and admired. It was a very happy interlude. Why do we care if our old homes are in good hands? But we do.

Somehow it's then further than I expect along the A3 to the wrong side of Guildford. This is a road I used to cycle often, going to Wisley, or the ponds in the woods on the way. But you wouldn't cycle it now, if you had any other choice. More than the enlargement and alteration of all the houses I used to know, this really underlined how the world changes between the time of our growing up, and our nostalgia for that time.

When I first opened my mouth to demand attention from the world, there were five million cars in the UK. There are now thirty-three million. And each one of those cars drives three times as far and – I'm guessing – twice as fast, as those old Cortinas, and Rovers, and Minis and Austins.

The A3 South of Esher is now truly terrifying if you're on a bicycle. You couldn't share the road space with the traffic. There's a little cycle track just to the side, separated by an overgrown verge and an intermittent steel barrier. When it's a choice between certain injury and likely death, you have to choose the injury, don't you? The path is narrow, underpinned with tree roots, and overgrown with nettles, brambles and hawthorn. I was stung, and scratched, and thrashed, and cross. But at least I was alive.

I navigated around Guildford, very relieved to be off the A3, towards Christopher and Susan's house, in a very salubrious village of private roads and shiny cars. They were expecting me.

But they weren't.

If I thought the communication gap with Henry might have been down to him – he meant to write the email, I'm guessing, and then thought he had, when he hadn't – then this one was definitely down to me. The arrangement was made, warmly, and I'd signed off with something like *plenty of time to sort out the detail nearer the time*. By which I meant – *obviously* – the concert in their beautiful drawing room with the grand piano that plays jazz every day, but which they thought meant the actual date, and fundamentals like that. And since there had been no subsequent email they assumed I'd thought better of the whole thing, and they didn't want to rub it in by raising the issue, did they?

Susan and Christopher are very old friends, from South London days, so it didn't matter too much. And Christopher is a very expensive lawyer, so we've got more important things to argue about if we wanted to argue. And if you want something organising then you ask Susan, anyway, and within a couple of hours it was all fixed and here's the list of people coming to the concert this evening.

It was, as I should have expected, an intimidating list. Half the audience would be proper professional musicians, and by the way there will be an ex-Tour de France cyclist and his family…

I try not to be intimidated. It's a rule of life. So I locked the bike to one of the beautiful oak piers of the clay tiled porch, and carried Libre across the medieval styled hall of the house a builder had built for himself twenty or thirty years ago, into the music room with the grand piano, determined not to be intimidated.

Then the Tour de France cyclist rang to say they couldn't come after all, which he was very sorry about because he really wanted to see this bicycle and talk about the Col de l'Iseran, but maybe another time. Why was I relieved? I shouldn't have to be; as I may have said before, in another context, it's a completely different *category*.

I recognised one of the names on the list. I used to know someone with that uncommon surname, I said; he was called Paddy. Yes, they said, that's her husband. But he can't come, because he's stuck in Israel.

Well, well. Talk about history. Paddy had been the assistant minister at a Baptist Church I went to when I was at school. He became an Anglican vicar, and then he retired, and now he does something I didn't want to enquire too deeply into because the organisation had *Jesus* and *Jews* in its title, and I didn't want to put my foot in it.

Ann was exactly as I remembered, even down to the youth and sprightliness. We laughed as we talked about that old Baptist Church, and Paddy's formidably larger than life boss there, of whom we were all in awe, and the convoluted trajectories we take in life.

Then I played my set, performed my poems, and told everyone to buy the book because there were much better poems in the book. Besides, I said, I didn't have an import licence to take them across the Channel into France and they were heavy. Thomas played a couple of beautiful jazz numbers on the grand piano, and as he played I felt loved and supported. There were professional musicians in the audience, but they'd hardly made me nervous at all.

Everyone was reluctant to go. Ann bought the poetry (writing very fulsomely about it to me when she'd read it), and there was a bit of clearing up to do. Susan said how much trouble had been saved by not knowing about it in advance, so not being able to spend time planning and preparing. And of course it was another late night.

Thomas says he'll try to get up in the morning, get his bike out and ride a few miles with me, along the way up into the Surrey Hills and the High Weald, and the little art gallery at Melford. But that's not until tomorrow.

CHAPTER 18

Poets, Pennines and pilgrimages

So what else have I done by way of preparation, at this halfway review, apart from rambling and panicking? Well, quite a lot, and almost nothing.

There are the lists, of course. The things I need, and the things I need to do. I haven't been on the bike much, I confess, because I'm a fair-weather cyclist, and the winters in Cumbria are wet and windy and filthy. So there's still all that – "training", I might call it if I were young – to do. I've got panniers ready, and a few spares, a couple of tools.

There's been more cello prep than bike prep. Playing a cello is more difficult than riding a bike, after all. I booked a few gigs – mostly, I feel, under false pretences. I recorded an album and sent it off for manufacture; it should be back in a fortnight. That was a big thing,

The lists are still intimidating, and growing. I don't understand how there can be so much to do. I thought it was just a matter of getting on a bike and setting off.

There's nothing new under the sun, is there? Remember my idea of biking up and down Hartside until I'd climbed the height of Everest? I mentioned it to Ian, outside the van where he lives, in a field.

"You mean Everesting," he said. "I know a couple of people who've done that."

Turns out it's quite a thing. Which should have been obvious, if I'd thought about it. There's a website, and a whole community, and rules, and procedures, and verification, and T-shirts to buy, and a hall of fame, and of course a few arcane disputes about what really counts.

So I'm obviously not going to do that now then, am I? Maybe the height of Mont Blanc instead. Perhaps I'll set up a more modest European alternative, for the old and infirm like me. I'll start by copyrighting the name: Montblancing.

And idiotically long-distance cycling. How many people have cycled round the world? Or from Greenland to Morocco, or through every state in the USA? Quite a few, it seems. Thousands, actually. Hadrian's Wall to Rome? Hardly counts.

I already had more than an inkling of this from the *Warmshowers* website. Everyone there has a bit of a biography; an introduction so they're not a total surprise when you meet them. A significant proportion relate seriously epic adventures.

Then I came across the *Crazyguyonabike* website (I think "guy" is a gender non-specific designation). It's an online collection – a whole catalogued library and archive – of these epic adventurers' blogs and stories. So if, for instance, you want to know what the road is like from Timbuktu to Bamako, you just look it up, and find accounts from several people who know, complete with photos of every pothole. Perhaps this isn't the most popular route, though; *Warmshowers* can only put you in touch with one willing host along that particular road.

Lots of crazy people on bikes, cycling crazy routes and distances. But, as far as I can see, not many who do it with a cello. In fact, I can only find one. She's called Ida. She's Danish, and she cycled down the Rhine (by which, presumably, she means beside it – I'm not competing with someone who cycles on water, that's not fair). Six hundred miles, and concerts every day. *Vidunderlig*! (I think that's Danish for *wonderful*). Though I suppose there aren't that many hills along the Rhine.

The pictures show Ida riding a Danish sit-up-and-beg bike, wearing the cello on her back. And, perhaps most amazing of all, she plays a cello she made herself! I think she's altogether *vidunderlig*. I hope to meet her one day. Perhaps we could do a concert tour by tandem. *Daisy, Daisy, give me your answer, do. I'm half crazy*, etc., etc.

Preparation. I've been reading some long-distance travelogues – bikers, walkers, skateboarders, pilgrims. The cyclists write matter-of-factly. The longdistance walkers are another breed altogether, and far more literary. I read *The Crossway*, by Guy Stagg, as well as *Walking Home*, by the Poet Laureate, Simon Armitage. Guy Stagg describes a pilgrimage from Canterbury to Jerusalem, via – of course – Rome. Hiking the ancient pilgrim route, the *Via Francigena*, and staying in its monasteries and religious guesthouses, he enters the heart and mind of the medieval traveller looking for salvation.

He's looking for salvation, too; though not for him exactly a religious kind. Stagg isn't a believer. So quite like me, then – a pilgrimage and not a pilgrimage. A pilgrim and not a pilgrim. This, after all, is one of the axes that brought me to this point – the way language changes through time. You can't know you mean the same thing as someone in a different context, just because you use the same words.

Guy Stagg's pilgrim intent is clear. After years of mental fragility, and sometimes breakdown, he's hoping for at least a measure of healing through ritual. I'm not sure mine's as clear as that. Maybe it will become clear along the way.

The Crossway is a totally absorbing read. Beautifully written, too. I feel Guy Stagg would perfectly understand my answer to the cathedral Dean: no, it's not exactly a pilgrimage, but yes, of course it's a pilgrimage.

Simon Armitage is a Poet Laureate. So you'd expect him to write beautiful prose too. Even if not in complete sentences. He's writing about a walk down the Pennine Way – *down* meaning from

North to South, of course. And every night, wherever he stop, he gives a performance. Just poetry, though; no cello. I don't know if he plays the cello, but it wouldn't be any fun carrying one the length of the Pennine Way.

I live at the foot of the Pennines. Hartside Pass is the route over them and into Alston, where you can pick up the Pennine Way. And there, on page ninety-four, is Simon Armitage, meeting my friend Josephine, magnificent and wonderful Pennine Poet, who once showed me a poem that made me blush. It was about an abandoned mistress, and most indelicate, I thought. No, she said, when she'd stopped laughing; it's about a vacuum cleaner that doesn't work anymore. Such is the nature of poetry.

I've played my cello in Alston, in St. Augustine's old and beautiful church. Josephine said she would be there, and would it be alright if she played the church bells beforehand – a sort of announcement, and welcome, and summons? I don't know what I expected – I mean, how much can one person do on a set of church bells? – but this was incredible. A complicated and intricate and confident peal rang out over the town and the moor. I was afraid it announced more than I could deliver. And I'd never heard of carillon bells before – where via a "baton keyboard" and a secret mechanism one person can play a belfry-load of bells. Josephine is a real musician as well as a real poet.

Do I feel overwhelmed, discouraged, belittled, or redundant by these discoveries – that everyone else has already done it, that there's nothing new under the sun, that as you read this there are – right now – tens of thousands of travellers criss-crossing the globe on foot or on two pedalled wheels, in an endless merry-go-round of pointless journeys, looking for something that isn't to be found?

Well, yes, of course, I do. And, no, why would I? No, it's not exactly a pilgrimage, and, yes, of course it's a pilgrimage. I'm with the Buddha, and also with the *hadith*. This is my meaning, and my story, everything and nothing, and it doesn't matter a jot.

And then, one afternoon, round about this halfway point in the preparations, I was playing a gig in Castle Carrock, ten miles from home in the other direction from Alston, in the beautiful little church of St. Peter. Three Met-office-named storms in a week, and I drove through eight floods across the road, and skirted one fallen tree. It would be an exaggeration to say I considered cycling there. As the concert promoter said, I would have ended up in Kansas.

I introduced them to Libre and told them about the cycling. And afterwards four members of the audience, separately, told me about Richard Durrant. You know Richard Durrant, of course, they said. He's been here a few times. He's the cycling guitarist. Goes everywhere on a bike, with his guitar in a trailer.

Then I remembered. Yes, I had met Richard Durrant, not so far from here, at the eccentrically wonderful Upfront Puppet Theatre, about four or five years ago. I didn't remember the bicycle. Though I did remember the bare feet. And exquisite – though of course stolen – Bach *Cello Suites* played on the ukulele. Richard's a proper guitarist, a graduate of the Royal College of Music, with six or seven albums under his belt.

So I found an online video of his 2014 tour – forty-six days, thirty-six concerts, 1470 miles. Two of them, carrying not just the guitar, but amplifier, speakers, projector, lights, and all the other paraphernalia of a proper roadie-accompanied band tour. He had an album, too. Called *Cycling Music*. One of the numbers on it was *J.S Bike*. I wish I'd thought of that. I should give him a ring.

This is about the halfway point of the preparation.

CHAPTER 19

Full house in Mayfield

MONDAY 6 JUNE

You can gauge the age of an oak tree by measuring its girth. The Woodland Trust has a handy table on its website. That's how I know the big oak at home was probably planted in about 1700, a generation after the house was built. But here's a truly great specimen, a few miles from setting off. I've nothing to measure it with, but I'm guessing it's at least five hundred years old.

I'm waiting for Thomas, who was indeed out of bed and keen to cycle, despite the threat of rain. He keeps apologising for holding me up, but I tell him he needn't at all. I'm just happy that after these months of training, and ten days of the journey, I can go faster than a man half my age who isn't carrying any baggage. He doesn't realise what a moral support he's being.

This oak tree is as far as he's coming. He can see the hills ahead, and they look rained upon. Like me, he prefers to be dry. I enjoyed his company, and I enjoyed his piano playing last night. I'm sad to see him turn around.

I pass a signpost, *Gateway to the Surrey Hills*. A bit of marketing hyperbole, I decide; the hills I'm encountering are negligible. They weren't so negligible when I crossed the county boundary into West Sussex, though. It wasn't so much the fact they were big – in the scheme of things they were modest – but they were definitely steep. It still surprises me how quickly a steep hill can bring a heavy bike almost to a standstill. But I can't stop, because it's too heavy to push, and too unstable to start again unless I can get a bit of momentum.

This is a completely different ride from yesterday. The roaring and terrifying A3 might have been another country. The biggest place I went through today was Horsham – not really somewhere you would go if you were looking for a crowd. This is England's green and pleasant land – narrow high-banked roads, little villages and big houses, views that roll around you. And trees.

There are lots of beautiful and wonderful trees today, and they make for a dark ride. Mile after mile of green tunnel, where the trees on either side meet in the middle. Magical, but not a good time for the rear red light to point out it needs charging occasionally.

It rains a good deal, and when it isn't raining it's always threatening to. I cycle through the village of Ardingly, not seeing any reason to stop, until I smelled the bakery. *L. Fellows Ltd., Bakers*, said a little sign in the window you would have shot straight past if the door hadn't been open. What a heavenly smell.

But then it's a bit cold and wet to stop anywhere to eat the sausage roll and calorie slice I bought in Ardingly. Until I come to Ludwell Spring, on the Bluebell Railway side of Horsted Keynes. I didn't know it was historically important, and could cure the Plague, until I read its notice, which I didn't do at first because I couldn't sit on its bench under the thick sheltering oak and read the notice at the same time.

It was a splendid oak, and I could see beyond its shelter a very sharp shower. The bike, propped up on the metal railing, was getting wet; but the bench and I weren't.

A lot of things on a long bike ride are just not quite right. So when you come across something that is exactly right, in exactly the right place, and more than you could expect or deserve, you look around for some local deity to give thanks to. I wouldn't have drunk the spring water, whatever it could do in the time of the Plague, because it looked as though now it would have the opposite of a curative effect. But I was grateful for its bench, and its oak tree, and I said so, out loud, for the benefit of any Sprite or Nymph to whom credit might be due.

I haven't mastered the art of keeping warm when I stop cycling, though, so a lunch break has to be swift. I'm eagerly anticipating more leisurely lunches, and longer digestion time, when I get to warmer parts.

Ashdown Forest, across the top of the High Weald, has uninterrupted views without any sign of human habitation. Perfect country for filming a Thomas Hardy novel in. It's a sandy heath, with a few trees; the kind of place you'd expect to see kings hunting their deer. I did see a few deer – though they looked more cultivated than wild – but no kings I recognised.

After all the steep hills , I'm quite tired when I get to Melford House and Gallery, just outside Mayfield. It's a beautiful and quirky arts centre, with a sculpture garden, marquees, and a performance space filled with ancient and plush red theatre seats.

I first came across it by chance, when I was scouring the map for a suitable stopping-off point between Guildford and Canterbury, and it's everything its website promises. It kind of jumps out at you as you pedal up the hill – those coloured flags that are neither Jubilee celebration, nor Buddhist prayers, but something quite different. And the monumental sculpture in its garden. It looks like a work in progress, where almost anything might happen next.

Richard, who runs it, welcomed me with open arms. He was in a bit of a flap (hence the open arms) because he was sold out for tonight, and was wondering about a rearrangement of the chairs, in case more people came, and what did I think? Well, just arrived, and not knowing anything about it, I didn't know what to think. Except, of course, that I'd sold out his little venue. OK, it's not the O2 Arena, but little acorns, you know.

I stood in front of the great stainless-steel sphere in the garden. It stands nearly as high as me. It reflects, and distorts. All the trees lean into its North Pole. It has an expansive belt around its middle, made of different things depending on where you view it from. It seems to hold the place within itself. It's part of the garden, and yet it's like an alien spacecraft.

There's more adventurous sculpture scattered about, but I shouldn't distract myself from a bit of preparation. I hadn't properly appreciated that when you're on the road all the time and staying in other people's spaces when you stop, there's no opportunity for practice. The careful scales that get played every morning at home, that keep us from straying too far out of tune, just don't get played. But here, facing the silent and expectant red theatre seats, I can have half an hour of private time with Libre. We've both missed those intimate moments.

There's just enough space for a hurried dinner, with Richard and his partner David who has to go off and do a night shift in a hospital, before show-time.

It's nice to play to a full house, where the front row is within touching distance. Richard said we should have two intervals, for the charging of glasses, so I quickly re-jigged two sets into three, and sat down to the full house, everyone with a full glass. I thought of the difference between the feel of this performance, where I could whack the front row with my bow if they misbehaved, and the concert in Westmill Church, three days ago, where the audience was so far away I had no idea what they were up to.

I refused all the kind offers of a drink in the glass-charging intervals. I know that trombonists and the like traditionally think a hefty dose of alcohol makes the second half go better, but I'm not sure, and I've never been brave enough to try. Best stay sober. I'm trying to pay attention to an elderly lady telling me about some of the concerts she's been to, in a long life, while not being too distracted by the thought of the tango I'm about to play, when suddenly the tango goes right out of my head.

She's telling me that she once, in her youth, went to see a performance by the greatest cellist ever, Mr. Pablo Casals. I'm pretty sure the hairs on my neck stood on end. This is the closest

I'll ever be. Closer than those people who say well this is what my teacher says, and when he was young he was a pupil of so-and-so whose teacher was you-know-who who sat at the feet of Liszt who was taught by Czerny who had it from *Beethoven himself.*

She had been in the presence of Casals. She couldn't remember what he'd played, of course, but I could tell her one thing he would definitely have played. And I said I would play it for her now, straight after the interval, postponing the tango, which would have to wait.

Casals, who had performed for Queen Victoria, went into exile from Franco's Spain in 1938. Franco outlived him by two years, so he never went back. For years he seemed adrift and lost. Slowly he recovered a will to live, to play, and eventually he settled in Puerto Rico. But it wasn't the same.

He remained a thorn in Franco's side, though. He kept his resolve to open every one of his concerts with a performance of the traditional Catalan tune, *El Cant dels Ocells, The Song of the Birds.* This had been an old Christmas song, but Casals turned it into music of protest and resistance and freedom. It made Mr. Franco cross.

So when she heard Casals in London, in the 1950s or 60s, she would have heard this. I told the plushly-seated audience about the change of plan. I told them the story, and I played *The Song of the Birds* with everything I had – and as much Casals as I could muster. The hairs on my neck stood on end again.

Afterwards, sitting in the empty theatre, on the plush red chairs, I had that drink with Richard. There was a bottle, he said, that really needed finishing, so it would have been churlish not to. We talked about many things – Art as Protest, garden sculptures, future plans for the lovely Melford House and Gallery – and he hoped I would come back next year to see some of it come to pass.

Then he told me of a fierce injustice he had suffered at the hands of an inhuman officialdom. I raged inwardly. Sometimes we run up against a system that seems to have no other intent towards us than an implacable desire to destroy. All we can do is hope to escape with our lives, abandoning everything that's precious, and protest impotently from exile. And it's worse when you can't shout it from the rooftops, but only tell one other person quietly behind closed doors.

Will the system change? Will it relent? Will it recognise the injustice, and right it? Or will the system and the injustice outlive us? I hoped for Richard it wouldn't be that. I went to bed angry. The next time I played *The Song of the Birds*, it would be for Richard.

CHAPTER 20

Is it Art?

There's a very big book on my bookshelf at home. It's an awkward book, because there's no shelf quite big enough for it and wherever you put it, it sticks out, drawing attention to itself as you go past, or threatening to cause a fracas.

I don't mind, because it's one of my favourite books. I've had it for nearly twenty years. Richard Long's *Walking the Line*.

It's an Art book, with very definitely a capital A. If you have a book like this on the shelf you can pretend you know what Art is, and what it does. In this case it threatens to cause a fracas.

Richard Long was nominated for the Turner Prize in 1984, and actually won it in 1989 (a year in which Lucian Freud was only "commended" in that august competition). His work is often called *Land Art*. He prefers to call it *Sculpture*. Which some people think is odd, and some people think is ground-breaking.

Often it is literally ground-breaking. Richard Long makes many of his works of art by interfering in the landscape, or interacting with it, or just looking at it in unusual ways. He walks a lot, and sometimes his walks are of rather epic proportions – "a walk of 80 miles in 24 hours", for example, or "a thirty-hour walk". Sometimes he only walks when he can see his shadow. Sometimes he takes a stone from here to there. Sometimes he walks within the imaginary confines of a random circle.

In some contexts I imagine this would be called *Performance Art*. But Long is clear. It's sculpture. He makes a lot of circles, usually out of stone, but also out of found wood, or grass, or water, or snow. So they last a short while, but not very long. He takes a photograph, or writes a sentence or two of description, or traces some lines on a map, to record it. Most of his outdoor work is in locations where not many people would ever see it.

In *Walking the Line*, Richard Long uses the word pilgrimage, but I think only once. He's writing about different possible ways of connecting with landscape: some people made pilgrimage in it, or out of it – I made sculpture in it, and out of it, he says.

I've been thinking about my answer to the pilgrimage question. And about Guy Stagg's *The Crossway*, and Simon Armitage's *Walking Home*, and now Richard Long. When my head hurt too much with it, I wrote a poem:

Pilgrimage

Going to a holy place
to have a cup of tea
wash my sins away
wear a white shift
token of a new innocence.

God will be pleased
his favour rests
thick and warm
at that holy place
and I'll be free.

By what bargain?
How is there merit in it,
this indulgence?
Does God want this for atonement?
Is God held to place, or journey?

Why do I tell this story –
of a God like this?
By what bargain
what indulgence
what deceit?

I want a proper answer for people who ask the pilgrimage question: *is it a pilgrimage?* Nobody, of course, would argue if I said confidently that yes, it is. Mostly they'd nod approvingly (or at least noncommittally), and probably put a little bit more in the collection than they'd first thought of. But I once – by mistake, obviously – read some Wittgenstein. And so I know that language only works properly if the person you're talking to is walking in approximately the same field of meaning as you are.

I shouldn't have had to read the Wittgenstein to know that, should I? Lewis Carroll's conversation between Alice and Humpty Dumpty already explained it much more succinctly. "When I use a word, it means just what I choose it to mean", Humpty Dumpty claimed, to Alice's considerable discombobulation. She knew that would get them nowhere.

Pilgrimage, then. Yes, and no. As you already know. I'm Humpty Dumpty, and the word can mean whatever I choose it to mean. But even if I don't inhabit quite the same field of meaning as the medieval, or even today's truly religious, person, still I think we need some overlap. In my private language, then, *pilgrimage* will still do, (and the word will probably sometimes leak out, for which I apologise in advance). But helped by Richard Long I'm going to try another definition, too. This journey is going to be a Work of Art.

A Work of Art? Yes, a Work of Art. Maybe I should drop the capitals. A work of art.

I'm going to be moving through the landscape, modifying it

ever so slightly, and ever so ephemerally. Yes, small tyre tracks on the road, beads of sweat, disturbances in the air, swooshing past, slicing through it. And the music.

Because of course it's not just music. It's music in a place, as a journey, as way markers on that journey. If I perform a Bach *Sarabande* in Masham Town Hall, near the beginning, it won't be the same as that *Sarabande* played halfway up the Alps, or in the shadow of the Leaning Tower of Pisa, or on a bridge over the foaming Tiber. Hopefully the notes will be pretty similar – *haha* – but the performance will be the moment, the place, the flow of the journey, the mental exhaustion, the sunburn, the *polizia* wondering if they should move me on, and everything, everything, else. Everything. Everything. Else.

How about that, then? In just a few pages, and all because I was a bit squeamish about *pilgrimage*, I turned the whole thing into a Work of Art. (Actually we agreed to drop the capitals; this isn't the Turner Prize.)

But let's not be hasty, or they'll just label us *Postmodernists*, and not take us seriously. All I'm saying is fixed meaning is a bit last century, and everything – from knitting, to space exploration, to forestry, to internal monologue, and including travels with a cello – has to be undertaken just a little bit ironically and apologetically, and under the label of *performance*.

Maybe it's not just a postmodern discovery though. Didn't Shakespeare have something to say about all this strutting and fretting about the stage? It signifies nothing. Oh, he meant something slightly different, did he?

Everybloodything is performance. Pilgrimage is no exception.

And here's another word then that's grown out of its clothes: *performance*. Medievals *performed* their pilgrimages, and meant something quite different from anything I can ever mean. Complicated.

These were my thoughts, in some shape or form, before I set off. But the pilgrimage question of course didn't go away. It kept reappearing, in all kinds of ways; some that were perhaps – or at least should have been – expected. And some that weren't.

CHAPTER 21

Blessed by a Bishop

WEDNESDAY 8 JUNE

Canterbury has two Bishops, which is maybe a bit confusing. One, of course, is an Archbishop, so perhaps doesn't count. And the other is actually the Bishop of Dover. So maybe Canterbury doesn't really have any Bishops at all.

I've never met the Archbishop, though I did shake hands once with one very retired, big-eyebrowed Archbishop of Canterbury. And I sat opposite another, with a Charles Dickens beard, on a train once. I pretended not to recognise him. He seemed to appreciate that, because he nodded to me very warmly when we got off at the same station.

Being the Bishop of Dover – she's also, and more confusingly, called the Bishop in Canterbury – is a complicated business. Bishops preside over cathedrals. But of course they don't really, because there are Deans, and Chapters, and possibly whole Books, devoted to that, and you would be in serious trouble if you trod on their toes.

Bishops are in charge of a diocese, but the boundaries of that oversight are a bit fuzzy. All those parishes are looked after by vicars, who aren't actual employees. In law they're *ecclesiastical office holders*. Some of them are on contracts, but some aren't. Some have a *freehold* and can do just whatever the hell they like. The Bishop is certainly in charge, in some sense, but the

146

Church of England's official website lists thirty-two frequently-asked-questions about what that means in practice. Exactly how frequently they are asked I wouldn't like to guess. Suffice it to say, the matter is complicated.

And that's before you factor in the silly theological difficulty that the present Bishop is a woman, and some people – yes, really, in the twenty-first century – think that being a Bishop isn't a woman's job and God wouldn't like it and so she isn't a real Bishop and they need to find a *Flying Bishop* to tell them what to do when they need telling what to do. Oh dear.

I'm on my way to see Rose, the Bishop of Dover, in Canterbury, who I've known for a very long time, since long before she even could have been a Bishop in the Church of England, and we should be prepared.

If anyone can get through the arcane muddles of being a Bishop in the Church of England, it's Rose. In 2007 she was appointed Chaplain to HM the Queen, which I think means she uses the back door at Buckingham Palace. And three years later she became the seventy-ninth Chaplain to the Speaker of the House of Commons, which I think means she uses the front door there.

I've seen her straighten the Speaker's tie before he goes on public display. Imagine.

But Canterbury is fifty miles away yet. I waved goodbye to Richard at the lovely Melford Gallery and set off uphill. The legs always feel very heavy on first setting off, and it's worse on a hill. Six miles of bottom gear, uphill, or fierce braking, downhill, and nothing gently in between.

The last hill is School Hill, and there's a crocodile of children going up it, closely guarded by their teachers because there's no footway here. I give them a little wave, and in return I get clapping and cheering until I get to the top. Wasn't that nice?

A front gate with a neat written sign, *Dog Please Close the Gate*. Someone's got a very clever dog, I thought.

I have a prejudice against large and unnecessary cars. So when a Range Rover refuses to drive a foot onto a grass verge so that we can pass each other on a narrow road, the commentary in my head is not polite.

And when another sees me on a roundabout, going the same speed as the cars – because that's the only safe way to go round a roundabout on a bicycle – and cuts me up with three feet of clearance, I wave my hand at it as though I'm swatting a fly.

These were minor annoyances on an otherwise beautiful day. I don't mean weather-wise. The weather was mostly appalling. But there were tea shops in all the right places, quiet roads, and beautiful places to see.

I stopped at Goudhurst for a bacon baguette, and told the lady she was a genius for suggesting – when I said it was maybe a bit big – I could eat half of it now, and take the rest for lunch. (It really was too big to eat in one go.) And she went straight to tell the boss – that she was a genius, I mean.

When you're in Goudhurst you can't not take a picture of the Star and Eagle pub sign. You pedal determinedly up the hill, and there it is, in front of you all the way. Bang in front of the church. There's absolutely no doubt; the church is claiming to be a pub. Not until you get up close can you see the pub is actually off to one side, and the church has its own little noticeboard, clarifying that it is actually a church, and not a licensed public house. So then I looked inside the church, which turned out to be the first of many today, each more lovely than the last.

And I'm notching up the counties, too. Over the last two days I've cycled through Surrey, the Sussexes (that's West and East) and Kent. And I've made a few comparisons. The steepest hills are in West Sussex. The worst drivers are in East Sussex. The best tea shops are in Kent. And the least modest house names are in Surrey – things like *Ten Acres*, and *The Manor*.

This isn't prejudice; this is careful observation. I'm telling you.

Just before Pluckley – St. Nicholas, another fine flint church – a road called Lewd Lane. England used to have lots of road names like these – you can imagine what might have gone on there – but there aren't many left, owing to the sensitivities of house-buyers, mostly. So when you pass a Lewd Lane, you want to take a picture, in case next time you come this way it's called Babbington Crescent, or something.

I propped my bike against the wall of the Archbishop's Palace. There was no Archbishop to object, and it's no longer much of a Palace, Henry VIII having seen to that. Sorry, I should have said, this was the Palace in Charing, not in Canterbury. Henry may have taken the Palace, but he left the lovely flint church. At one time the Archbishops had seventeen palaces between Canterbury and London – presumably to allow for a choice of routes. Even if Henry hadn't taken most of them they would be a bit redundant now, wouldn't they, when you can just hop on the train. Which is where I met an actual modern Archbishop once.

A few miles further on, and Chilham is also a very handsome place – Agatha Christie films are sometimes made here. You can't visit the Castle, though you can see it through a firmly locked gate. Admire instead the huge *Pilgrim Milestone* oak carving just outside the Castle gates. It makes you think of Chaucer, and reminds you you're on the Pilgrims' Way, and Canterbury is only a few miles off.

Canterbury. I've ridden 544 miles since I left home.

From here there's a proper pilgrim route to Rome, the *Via Francigena*. So everyone understands the concept of an arduous journey South to the Mother Church. *Francigena* is a bit of a tongue-twister, so let's clear the air before we start. Be sober. Be vigilant. The "c" is pronounced "ch". The "i" is long. The "g" is pronounced "j". The stress is on the "ci", so *chee*. Fran-*chee*-jena. Why am I telling you this? Because nobody told me I was saying it wrong through two countries, which makes me suspect it's maybe one of those words people read, but don't say, so no-one knows how to say it. Fran-*chee*-jena.

The usual story told about the *Via Francigena* involves Archbishop Siguric the Serious. He wasn't the first Archbishop – that was Augustine, remember? – he was number twenty-eight, or thereabouts. But he wrote a book, and that made him famous, at least in this context. He went to Rome, in the year 990, to collect his signs of office from the Pope, and wrote about the eighty places he stayed on the way home.

So that's the pilgrimage route to Rome. Only it isn't.

The Romans themselves were in Canterbury, weren't they? They called the place Durovernum Cantiacorum, at least officially. But it was the same place. And they must have gone home sometimes on holiday, or sent home for pizza, or reinforcements, or whatever, so there must have been a Roman route between Canterbury and Rome. Of course there was. And when the Romans packed up and went home for good that didn't mean there was no travel between the cities for five hundred years until Siguric came along.

But of course there wasn't really a *single Via Francigena* – the word just means *going through France* – and there wasn't much in the way of maps. You just pointed more or less South, and hoped for the best, and that the natives wouldn't mislead you too much on the way.

No, the *Via Francigena* owes as much to modern invention as it does to Siguric, however Serious he was.

Let's not be cynical about it though. It's not entirely a commercial enterprise, for which you buy a *Pilgrim Pass*, to prove you're a pilgrim, and then get discounts at tourist facilities en route. It wasn't just about using European money to open up some neglected areas to visitors. Or to invent some history, and tell a story of European integration, or anything like that.

The point is, rather, that the *Via Francigena* is an Idea, a loose scrapbook of historical and religious mistakes and adventures. It's kind of a bit like religion itself. So if anyone tells you you've strayed from the true path, you can be a bit agnostic, and a bit inclusive, and say you're taking a slightly different route, but that you hope to get to the same place in the end. They may look doubtful. They may offer to pray for your soul. But you don't have to respond in kind.

You can't, I realise, set off from Canterbury on the *Via Francigena* to Rome without therefore asking yourself the question – are you a pilgrim? Am I a pilgrim? Am I a *proper* pilgrim? They make a big thing of the *Via Francigena* here. Perhaps not quite as big a thing as they did before the Reformation, and all the bloody anti-Rome stuff that entailed, but it's important history, and shouldn't be ignored. And it's undergoing a bit of a revival as more and more people want to make their travels more symbolic, more significant, less frivolous, less guilt-inducing.

Just up the hill from the ruins of St. Augustine's Abbey, pillaged by Henry VIII because he didn't like the Pope and he needed the money, is St. Martin's Church. Like most people, I didn't know it was there. But it's older, and in some ways more important, than the church we all go to see in Canterbury, the Cathedral. It's recognised as the oldest church in England that still functions as a church. It's also the oldest *parish* church in England. It has real Roman elements in its construction.

It's where King Aethelred was baptised, after he gave up arguing with his Christian wife, Queen Bertha, about it, and stopped being a pagan. It was where St. Augustine first set up shop when he arrived from Rome in 597, and before he built his ruined Abbey, and started on a cathedral, and became its Archbishop, and then a Saint. I could go on. It's that important.

It's so important that if you want a certificate that says you're a proper pilgrim, on your way to Rome, and entitled to stay in pilgrim hostels in France at slightly less than commercial prices, and can go straight to heaven without passing Go, etc., etc., if you die on the way – this is where you have to go to get it.

Might be useful, I thought. And what harm could it do? Like the diplomatic passport you keep in an inside pocket but only show in emergency because you're actually on holiday.

Only St. Martin's Church was locked, and they weren't issuing pilgrim passes that day.

I walked round the outside, to see if I could identify the remaining patches of Roman brickwork, and stepped over a bicycle belonging to one of the boredly-smoking boys artistically draped under the lychgate. One or two of them looked at me indulgently as I stopped to read the notice about the *Via Francigena*.

"You could come back in the morning; it's usually open in the morning," one of them offered.

I thanked him. In the morning I would be pedalling to Dover, anxious about a ferry, and without leisure to be concerned about anything like a pilgrim's papers.

I've known Rose and Ken for a long time, ever since they were newly arrived from Jamaica. Rose is a daughter of Jamaica, and a hero of that country, and her house is full of the glass and silver awards to prove it. We lived in the same house, in Tulse Hill. We went to the same church, Holy Trinity and St. Matthias, where the vicar was John Sentamu, later the second black Bishop, and then the first black Archbishop, in England. There are still only a handful of black Bishops in England, and Rose is one of them.

I've known them for a very long time. And it's lovely, really lovely, to be here with them, in a Bishop's house that isn't quite a palace. Where there's a framed copy of a Parliamentary Bill on the hall wall – *The Rose Hudson-Wilkin (Farewell) (Appreciation) (Amendment) (No. 2) Bill*. So I'm going to stay an extra day – to be with them, to take stock, to pause, and to panic about crossing the Channel and cycling on the wrong side of the road and playing the cello in a Foreign Country.

This is a journey in three Movements – like a Sonata, or a short Symphony – England, France, and Italy. The First Movement set out the themes, the mood and the structure. The Second Movement is going to introduce some variations on those themes. And if we get to it, the Third Movement is going to be, how shall we say, a bit improvised.

Some proper ceremonies and good omens should therefore accompany the setting off from here. A proper *rallentando*, a perfect cadence, and a bit of coughing and foot-shuffling to mark the end of the First Movement.

So with the Bishop's permission I've wheeled the bike into the Cathedral and propped it against a pillar. *Have you cleared this with Security?* they want to know. I reassure them, without telling any untruths.

I'm due to play during the midday service, which I will take as a suitable blessing on me and Libre, before we sail across the Channel tomorrow. *Meditation*, by Frank Bridge, seems appropriate. This is a big place; a seriously big place. It's overwhelming and awe-inspiring. You could play football in here, perhaps even cricket if the windows weren't so precious and expensive. It's big, but the acoustic for playing a cello is magnificent. "Do you want a microphone?" the Canon asks. I do not. I'll show you what Libre can do.

There are about thirteen thousand square feet of stained glass in Canterbury Cathedral. A lot of it is twelfth-century. The Cathedral even has a Director of Stained Glass to oversee it all and organise its maintenance. One of the Director's favourite windows depicts Methuselah, grandfather of Noah. In another hundred years that window will be as old as the Bible tells us Methuselah was when he died – nine hundred and sixty-nine. That's old, even for a window. You need big adjectives to describe a Cathedral like Canterbury.

And here I am, playing my cello. If you look at the pictures, you can hardly see me, a tiny dot in the middle of it all. But you could hear Libre. I'm sure she was taller when we finished.

After the short service the congregation transforms. It becomes an audience. There are a few of those rolling hand gestures that normally mean *And...?* We've paid and we want our money's worth. Play on, Macduff.

I look round for the Canon, but he's gone. He can't say yes, but he can't say no, either. So I play. *El Cant dels Ocells, The Song of the Birds*. For Canterbury Cathedral. For Richard in Melford, as I promised you. For the end of the First Movement.

I moved into the Cloisters to play some Bach to an appreciative but itinerant audience. There's a school party in fancy dress. I'm not sure if they're being monks, or if they meant to be at a Harry Potter do and got lost.

Then some more Bach outside the South door. A kind member of the Cathedral staff says I have to sign the *Via Francigena* pilgrims' book. So he goes off to fetch it but returns empty handed and apologetic. He can't find it. Perhaps it's gone for a walk itself.

Back through the town, past the bookshop with the seriously wonky doorway, and three upper storeys each cantilevered above the one below. Charles Dickens above the door: *A very old house bulging out over the road… leaning forward, trying to see who was passing on the narrow pavement below*.

And then the most extraordinary encounter, sending the day in a quite unexpected direction. Here is another cellist, carrying his cello on a bike! It's parked up outside a restaurant, and when I stop to take a photo Christian emerges, in a sharp three-piece suit.

He's been busking like this for twenty years, he says, and making a respectable living. He kindly told me all the things I was doing wrong, and why my hat was empty, and his tin was full.

After his lunch, we pedalled off in tandem and set up in the Butter Market, where I'd played solo earlier in the day when it was sunny, to play a few things together. We improvised a little tune, which I thought wasn't bad at all, to get the measure of each other. We were just about to embark on *The Swan*, to the accompaniment of his backing track, when the heavens opened, and curtailed it all. A short Coda to end the music of the First Movement.

Surely an auspicious beginning to the *Via Francigena*, which starts tomorrow…

CHAPTER 22

The Second Movement

THURSDAY 9 JUNE

I don't know why I'm doing this. I'm not a good traveller. I'm not completely sure what it is, though I think the question people often ask, thinking they're being helpful – *what's the worst that could happen?* – has something to do with it.

When I don't know what's ahead, round the next corner, over the brow of the hill, I imagine the worst. Not always consciously, but it's always there. The worst that could happen – that's a bad thing to think about. It could be very bad.

Is it worse when I'm entirely relying on myself, or when there are other people, and other factors, involved? Have I got the strength to get to the top of this hill? That's almost a straightforward question. But when it's a matter of staying in someone else's house, meeting their dog in the kitchen in the morning, getting to the port in time, finding the right ferry, not losing a passport, etc., etc., well, you see the state I'm in. Anything involving a passport is always going to be a major trauma. Don't ask how many times I checked it was in the right pocket. Then I put it in a better pocket, and have to check all over again, several times.

Ken and Rose don't have a dog, and the kitchen is really quite safe in the morning. No-one else is up (Rose works very late) so there's time for a cup of tea, and some deep breaths. I didn't sleep well. I'd rather stay.

Then Bishop Rose comes down, smiling and bishoply, and then Ken, and I'm being looked after, and fed, and asked helpful and solicitous questions, and everything's going to be alright.

And when Bishop Rose sends me off with a proper Bishop's blessing I take it, even if I believe a lot less than her these days, and pretend a confidence I don't feel.

It's not far from Canterbury to Dover, though oddly it's uphill most of the way, until you get to the dramatic plunge down the cliffs at the end. I'm on the Pilgrim's Way a good deal, mostly bridleways, narrow and straight and paved, with the occasional local car doing a ton and raising a cloud of dust. It's sunny and warm.

Exactly halfway – and you would miss it if you didn't know it was there – is Barfrestone. Hard by the road, on what looks like a specially raised platform, is the most exquisite, and tiny, Norman church. It's so striking because it's completely Norman. This isn't a little bit of Norman re-used and tucked into a newer idea.

You know I like old churches, but you should believe me this is something special. At first sight you think it's flint, like so many in and around the Chalk of the North and South Downs. In part it is. But you don't recognise the stone of the upper part. Then you read somewhere that it's a kind of stone called ashlar, and that it had to be imported from Normandy. Imported from Normandy. What would that have cost, in the twelfth century?

The ashlar is carved, magnificently and exotically, over doorways, around windows and corbels, inside and out. St. Nicholas fell into disrepair following a landslide, and there's a Victorian drawing showing it roofless and neglected. But in the 1830s it was restored with a dedication unusual for the period. Only some twelfth-century wall paintings were lost, and repainted. When you've seen the Cathedral, come the ten miles to Barfrestone, and see which you prefer. I want to play some music for St. Nicholas, Barfrestone, but somehow I feel self-conscious. And perhaps it was this that made the passport panic re-surface, even though I've got at least two hours to spare.

Then suddenly I'm freewheeling into Dover. From the main road at the foot of the hill I can turn round and see those famous white cliffs, backdrop to the ferry port and a thousand Polish lorries. There's a red line through the port directing bicycles in a convoluted maze.

In a ferry port, bicycles aren't like cars. They're a kind of exotic beast requiring much checking and paperwork. But eventually it's done, and I can sit down, drink some plastic coffee, and relax.

I haven't finished the coffee, sitting inside, keeping an eye on the bike propped up by the window, when another coffee buyer asks, smiling, if that's my cello?

Catherine plays cello with the Lausanne Chamber Orchestra, and she wants to know all about a carbon fibre cello on a bike. So after we've finished our coffees, we get it out in the car park, and she plays Haydn and Bach – beautifully – and expresses much approval of the instrument.

There follows an invitation to Lausanne, to play a concert of two cellos. I'll have to look at a map and see how far off route that is. After all, in this Second Movement there is supposed to be improvisation on the themes of the First...

Bicycles are allowed to skip to the front of the car queue for embarkation, and I find myself next to a young Brazilian, on a well-laden but suspiciously clean, fat-tyred bike. I don't speak Portuguese, and he doesn't speak English, but we make do in Spanish. When a roll-on-roll-off ferry is empty the car deck looks like a cathedral. I think the traffic-wallah is indicating I should get off and walk, but I refuse to understand such an instruction – it's a long way to the front of the boat. And you don't see any car drivers getting out and pushing their cars, do you?

Lunch. A little lie-down in the nearly empty lounge. A meet-up with Catherine again, and a repeat of the invitation to Lausanne. As I'm queuing for the exit in Calais, I'm pondering the nature of these invitations, these promises, these expectations of return and

157

re-meeting, these obligations we express to ourselves and others. Some of them – many of them – don't mean much. *A bientôt. Next year in Jerusalem. Come and see us some time. Maybe at Christmas.*

It's only polite. Sometimes it's a gentle way of dissembling to ourselves, trying to avoid thinking that we generally only pass this way once. Occasionally it's a way of getting rid of someone you would cross the street to avoid if you saw them again. I'm wondering how many people we're going to meet once in this life and never see again. So what is the nature of our relationships with them? Should they be forgotten? Facebook-friended? Christmas carded?

I'm thinking there may be a lot of such meetings in the next month. As indeed there have been in the last fortnight. So I haven't overdone the glib promises to come back next year, do it again, come and stay, or whatever. But this one, this invitation from Catherine? Yes, there was something about it. Yes, I'm going to try and make it work. Maybe not this time – though maybe – but some time. I don't think I've made a mistake, but you can never really tell, can you?

Roll off at Calais. Here there's no red line to guide a lonely bike out of the concrete chaos. Instead there's an electric van waiting. *Follow me*, he says to the two of us, and takes us on a sightseeing tour of the port, slowly and convolutedly approaching the high security perimeter fence until, suddenly, he's accelerating three hundred and sixty degrees the wrong way round a French roundabout, and waving a cheery goodbye out of his window. The Brazilian cyclist, who was just behind me, has fallen by the wayside.

The sense of abandonment is brutal.

In England most of the itinerary – performances and places to stay – was organised ahead. Here I plan a more extempore, improvised, uncertain version of the same thing. And I'm in an enormous panic about it. I realise I've been putting it off, and pushing it aside, all day. All that stuff about passports and ferries was no more than a diversion. *This* is what really scares me. How did I ever think I could do this in a foreign country, in a foreign language?

The further I pedal, the more impossible it seems. It's only twenty-five miles from Calais to St. Omer, but the side wind is strong and relentless. I'm exhausted, and for the first time since I left home, properly lonely.

There's an abandoned chateau by the road. It's a beautiful silver grey, with a lovely roof. Five floor-to-ceiling windows in the central bay, and three more in each wing, repeated on two fine storeys. It's a handsome building, but it lies open to the road, set back a bit, but unprotected. Alone on the edge of a French town. I relate to it.

I found a place to stay in St. Omer, through the cyclists' website *Warmshowers.org*, but I can't locate it. Even a French address is a foreign thing. This is just a road name he's given me, I now realise, and there are forty houses along the *cul-de-sac*. He didn't give me a house number, or a phone number.

OK, all the houses have post boxes out the front, and half of those have got names on them. Once up and down the street, and that's twenty houses eliminated. There's a man in a front garden, washing a car. I'll ask him if he knows. That's three more eliminated – him and two neighbours. Knock on a door halfway along the street from him – three more down. Ah, a woman walking up the street, looking at me suspiciously, who gives the impression of being a long-term resident. Approach carefully so as not to frighten her off. *Oui, oui, oui, number eleven!*

Yves doesn't speak much English, and I speak less French, and communication isn't easy, falling down the gaps between two languages. He's in his rear garden, with a heavily laden bike. *I've just come back myself*, I think he said, which can't have been right, because I've been up and down his road for nearly an hour. It seems his wife lives here, and he lives mainly by the sea in Dunkirk, and has come to the house only to see me – which doesn't sound to me like a scenario for a happy evening.

But that must be a misunderstanding, because when she comes home to the spotless bungalow, they're clearly very pleased to see each other. I go back out into the garden for a bit.

Forget all the stories of foreigners happily conversing in sign language, laughing and relaxed without a common tongue. It's hard, plodding, work. I'm remembering more French than I thought I knew, but it's nowhere near enough. It's not until after I decline his invitation to go a couple of miles into town for an aperitif that I work out Yves has gathered a few friends for a performance in a bar. By then it's too late to rescue the situation. What the English call a *faux pas*. I don't know what the French would call it.

But when I get the cello out and play for Yves and Caterina in the lovely bungalow, everything is restored. Then she finds me on YouTube, and puts the videos on the big screen in the sitting room while we eat in the adjoining conservatory, so we don't have to worry about continuous conversation. Caterina is speaking to her daughter on the phone, and the daughter then wants to speak to me: *You're coming to Arras on Saturday, so you will stay with us, please.*

Ten minutes later there's another *Warmshowers.org* email, and I find I've got two places to stay on Saturday. But as yet nowhere on Friday, tomorrow.

Perhaps if I get a good night's sleep it won't all be quite so overwhelming in the morning. At least I'm safely over the water, on French soil, in a real bed, and I didn't fall overboard on the way, or get mangled up with a French lorry going the wrong way round a roundabout, and I've still got my passport, and I think my phone works, and the Hundred Years' War was over a long time ago.

Which pocket did I put the passport in?

CHAPTER 23

The Bach

How much of today's popular music will last three hundred years? Well, all of it, of course, in the sense that nothing can now be totally erased from the historical record. But in the sense that it's still going to be an important part of the culture? Probably very little.

You can't tell what will last and what won't. Plenty of artists and musicians reach fame and fortune very quickly, and then fade away. Some take time to be recognised – sometimes so long they don't see it themselves.

The story of Mozart and Salieri is well-known. In 1979 Peter Shaffer wrote a play about their supposed rivalry, and five years later adapted the play to make a very successful film. He did caution that the work was a "fantasia"; a fictional creation of something that might have been, or might not.

Was there a fierce rivalry between Mozart and Salieri? The idea wasn't new when Shaffer wrote his play. Pushkin had written a dramatic poem on the same theme in 1830, and Rimsky-Korsakov made an opera of it in 1897. There was even an earlier, silent, film, in 1914. So the story had quite a track record.

The rivalry may or may not have existed, but what is true is that in their lifetime it was Salieri who had the fame and fortune, and it was Mozart who died young and poor. Now, conversely, we call Mozart a genius, and most of us say "Salieri who?"

Mozart's music is sublime. There are all kinds of stories about playing it to babies in the womb and turning them into members of MENSA. And what might European history have looked like if Napoleon had listened to Mozart in the bath, instead of commanding marching bands to play under his window? We'll never know.

Maybe the real genius of Mozart, though, is that the manuscripts of his sublime works contain no crossings-out. There are no revisions, no second thoughts. He just wrote them perfect first time.

Beethoven was a genius too; the master of the symphony. Can you imagine a London Proms season without a single Beethoven symphony? Of course not. He wasn't a genius in quite the same way as Mozart – the manuscripts of his music are almost indecipherable with revisions and improvements.

Schubert wrote the loveliest songs you could imagine. Chopin and Liszt produced liquid heaven from clunky keyboards. Wagner wrote operas the cognoscenti listen to in fifteen-hour box sets, that are so harrowing and intense they turn your hair grey and leave you in a permanent state of catatonia.

But ask any cellist, and the answer is Bach. It's the Bach. Johann Sebastian (usually just J.S.) Bach wrote *Six Suites for Solo Cello*, three hundred years ago. Or thereabouts – no-one can be completely sure. Some people aren't even sure Bach did write them. Maybe Mrs. Bach wrote them for him.

The oldest known manuscript is in her handwriting. But that doesn't prove anything. She wrote out most of his music at that time. Without Anna Magdalena Bach's secretarial and management skills, a lot less Bach would have survived the eighteenth century.

It isn't even clear the *Suites* were really written for the cello. The cello was a rather less definite, certainly less definitive, instrument then. It sat alongside *violas da gamba*, and things like that, and was sometimes played in a smaller version, resting on the arm like an overgrown fiddle.

This is my point about knowing which music might survive three hundred years. For a long time the *Suites* were not important (and without Anna might have been lost completely). Lots of not very positive words have been used about them. They're academic, study-like, difficult, devoid of performance markings, without a good tune in the whole thirty-six movements.

They wouldn't have had much of an airing on the radio.

Their genius and magnificence has been slow to prove itself. But now, if you told a cellist you thought the Bach *Suites* were not up to much, he would at the very least not consider your conversation worth the time of day. And she might even accidentally spear your foot with her cello spike.

We all, as I may have suggested before, devote many of our practice hours to them.

But here's a thing. When I was planning *Highway Cello*, and thinking about what music to take, Bach wasn't at the top of the list. For lots of reasons.

Not only those not-very-positive words I just noted. My concerts in the UK would include poetry, and I didn't have much Bach-inspired poetry. My playing on the street, I imagined, should have tunes that you'd want to stop and listen to. And although I do, privately, play through most of the six *Suites*, I need the music in front of me for all except the First. And numbers Two to Six have never been performance-ready in my repertoire.

Once I'd crossed the Channel there was no more poetry in the performances. I found myself on the street quite often playing Bach, either to warm up (cellistically speaking – the weather was nearly always hot, of course) or because I'd run out of more tuneful things to play.

And, to my surprise, it was what I was most often asked for.

So the further South I went, the more Bach I played. Sometimes I played the whole *First Suite*, with all the repeats, and then went back to the *Prelude* and did it all again.

In the little Davidin restaurant in the middle of nowhere, for instance, Luca, whom I'd only met an hour earlier, presented me with a painting and demanded to hear "the *First Suite*, in G Major, the way Yo-Yo Ma plays it."

In Testaccio market, in Rome, a man in yellow trousers listened

163

patiently to an accelerating performance of *The Basso*, a rather exciting gypsy tune, and then said quietly, "My wife says you play Bach." He'd applauded *The Basso* politely. He applauded the Bach loudly. The café behind interrupted their serving to applaud; their customers paused at their tables to do the same.

The *Prelude* to the *First Suite* does have a dramatic ending. It builds quickly and recognisably to a very satisfying resolution. Everyone knows when you've got there. The final G major chord rings nicely on the cello – emphasise the bottom G, so it lasts, then add the B in the middle, and finish with the two top notes singing together.

And everyone recognises the opening bars. Those first broken chords, beginning with that same G major, repeated, feature on TV and film more than any other cello music. Whenever the director says they think a bit of cello would give just the right feeling here, that's what you get. Those notes can sell sliced bread, running shoes, and expensive cruises. They can tell you that this is love; real love. They can make you feel at home on the top of a mountain, or alone in a crowd, or just perfectly in harmony with everything.

Then the second movement, the *Allemande*, is a liquid, wandering, calm and questioning meander, a gentle conversational commentary on the beauty of the world. It's very conventional. Like so much of this music it's in two repeated halves. The first half takes you predictably from the tonic, the key of G, to its related dominant, the key of D. The second half brings you back again, with the merest hint of a more adventurous diversion. And that's all there is to it.

But there are no performance markings. The slurs, or bowings, in the Anna Magdalena manuscript, appear slapdash. You can't say clearly which notes they're meant to include. And you know they aren't Bach's own notation anyway. You can bow it however you like.

There are no dynamic markings. Do you crescendo to this cadence – gradually or abruptly – or do you fade away, diminuendo, suggesting the path is too clear to need anything more? Do you stumble into this diversion, and make a big thing of finding the path again, or do you merely nod to it in passing? Or pause and wonder, and then set off again, wondering?

You can do it however you like. You can do it differently every time. You can do it, as it were, as a conversation with the passers-by. Or a series of not-quite-connected conversations with each of them. I think I like that the best. I like it when someone looks as though they feel they've been addressed directly, just for a moment.

Then there's the *Courante*, with just the same performance questions. To me it seems like a bit of a romp, something exuberant that needs to be played at a gallop and end a little breathlessly.

I don't always play the *Courante*. It needs nimble fingers, and after a few hours on the bike the fingers can be a bit leaden, a bit shaky. On the other hand – I tell myself – this is Renoir's *Dance in the Country*, not in the Town. It doesn't always need sophisticated precision. It needs to be boisterous, alive, even to trip over its own feet perhaps sometimes. To end with everyone collapsed, laughing, in a heap. So I play it boisterously, roughly, trying to sweep the other dancers off their feet, not worrying if they begin to sweat. Libre loves the *Courante*.

Go straight into the *Sarabande*, while we're all still out of breath. This is a stately exhibition dance. You couldn't have those sweaty people here. This is where the pros, immaculate in their fine cravats and shoes, pose and treat their partners like priceless porcelain, while looking down their noses at the rest of us.

It's slow. But again you have all the choice and freedom you could want. Play it too slow and it becomes six in a bar, and you've slightly lost the plot. Play it so that it's clearly three in a bar, without lingering on the semiquavers. Lean just a little on the second beat, so no-one could mistake it for a smoochy, intimate, waltz. Be genteel. Only hint at the passion within, something to be unwrapped privately. Libre loves the *Sarabande*. You can feel her quiver at the end.

Lighten the mood with the *Minuets*, one in the Major, one in the Minor, then back to the Major but without the repeats. The *Minuets* will stand alone if you like, especially if there are children who might dance. Even if you're passing by and not stopping to dance you should be provoked to skip – just a single skip, to say you would dance if you knew how, if your load was a tiny bit lighter. Libre loves the *Minuets*. Sometimes she does too many repeats, just for the hell of it.

End with the *Gigue*. Go straight into it, without pausing after the *Minuets*. Make it feel as though you've just stepped up a gear. Watch the *Courante* dancers back on their feet, clapping and swaying a bit Irishly, stomping and pirouetting in a not-so-gentle mockery of those genteel city dancers who took their place earlier.

Watch them pull the city dancers into the melee, and whirl together to the finish.

Lots of more or less pretentious nonsense has been written about the Bach *Suites*. I've just written some myself. But how else are you to talk about them? Maybe you shouldn't. Maybe you should just play them. Because no-one really knows the circumstances in which Bach wrote them, or what he might have intended, we can interpolate what we like.

Later composers would probably have given them titles, each *Suite* making an organised contribution to an overarching whole. But Bach didn't. So lots of us give them our own – if not exactly titles then themes, which inform the whole. We don't agree, of course. Except perhaps about the *Second Suite*. The Second is in D minor, a key which is often associated with mortality. The Second feels sadder, more introspective. I suspect a lot of us play it when someone has died. It seems to be mournful.

Maybe the *Sixth Suite* is triumphal. Maybe the *Third*, in C Major, the key of innocence, is about birth. The *Fourth* and *Fifth* are more difficult, darker, yearning, searching, stretching.

What shall we say about them? Or should we leave them as questions for now?

CHAPTER 24

Is he a proper pilgrim?

After dinner in their conservatory, much more relaxed, and with my YouTube videos on a loop on the big screen in the living room behind the open window, Yves gets out his maps. He wants to interrogate my route, to involve himself in my journey. I'm hoping he's putting it down to language difficulties, not evasion. But it's hard to plead a language barrier when he's just telling me to trace the route with a finger on his map.

The trouble is, I don't know. And I don't know, and can't explain, why I don't know.

I didn't have time before I came away to plan the route in detail. Perfectly true, though he thinks that's very odd, a strange way to go about bicycle touring in a foreign country. You should at the very least know where you're going.

He does a lot of touring himself. He carries a tent, and doesn't book any accommodation. He pitches his tent somewhere he likes the look of when he gets there, without planning it in advance. But the idea of not knowing which road you're going to cycle on… He shakes his head.

If we had more language in common, we could debate the philosophy of bicycle touring. What should be planned, and what shouldn't be – what should be structure, and what should be open space. The *Highway Cello* journey *is* planned out. To some extent.

HIGHWAY CELLO

There's a map on the website, showing where I intend to be on each of the forty nights of the route. I didn't like to tell Yves that those stopping points weren't picked with any great consistency. Yes, I was following a *Via Francigena* idea (even if I was mispronouncing *Francigena*), but it was only an idea. I wasn't informed by a detailed *Francigena* map, and I didn't trust the Eurovelo 5 to be on proper roads.

It was largely a case of pointing South, and hoping for the best – avoiding Paris, and other big scary cities, going for the highest point over the Alps, gauging approximately fifty miles a day, and stopping off in places that looked about right. And all done in a bit of a hurry, when the main thing on my mind was making the *Highway Cello* CD. Yves would have regarded that as hopelessly haphazard, amateurish, and irresponsible. He was right – I didn't know what I was doing, or where I was going.

How much time and space to allow for the impromptu, the riff, the extempore, the opportunity or the disaster? That, I wanted to tell him, was an important and difficult question on this kind of journey. Plan versus Uncertainty. Programme versus Opportunity. Comfort versus Terror.

He tried to help me. This is the way you want to go to Arras, he said, tracing and explaining lengthily and complicatedly on his unfolded map. I could see him debating with himself whether to lend me the map, to be returned to the daughter in Arras, or whether it was too precious, and I was too untrustworthy. I pretended to be following his explanation, and then took a photograph of the map, to reassure him.

He left early in the morning, returning to Dunkirk by the first train. Catarina sent me off, after a most un-Frenchly fulsome breakfast, in the direction of her daughter in Arras, very happy that I was going to be in good hands, and very pleased with herself for having made the arrangement. I smiled as I remembered what a stranger I'd felt last night, and what friends we now were. Perhaps France will be alright after all.

I set off from St. Omer to follow the general line of the *Via Francigena*, and the dead straight Roman road, down to Arras. I've got a day in hand, because I did two days in one yesterday, to get to St. Omer instead of staying in Calais. Which means there is the small question of where I'm going to stay tonight.

In my cello case there's a laminated sheet, alongside the notice offering CDs for sale, and the other one inviting people to read about the journey, in my best French. *Would you like a concert in your home tonight? And/or can you offer me a bed for the night?* I wasn't going to worry if anyone saw *double entendre* (as we say in English) in the second question – you can't worry about everything. I spent half a day, in between struggling with junctions and roundabouts and things, wondering whether I would be brave enough to deploy it.

I feel like such a foreigner. There are so many basic things I should know, but find I don't. Not very far out of St. Omer, and perhaps not far enough, I'm looking for coffee. How can it be so hard to find? Don't the French drink coffee all day? How was I to know I should be looking for a *bar*? In my book that's a place for after work, not mid-morning. I thought of Yves, who would be rolling his eyes at such ignorance – how could you *not* know?

Un café au lait, s'il vous plait. And what I get is an espresso, with a plastic capsule of artificial cream.

Lillers. A town that looks a lot less French than a proper French town should. I'd pictured myself rolling up into a pretty French square, towards the end of the afternoon, setting up, and putting out the *can you offer me a bed* notice, and going on happily from there. Obviously Lillers, in late morning, is too early, and too close to St. Omer to do that. But here is just the right kind of square, set back from the road, with nice places to sit, a couple of bars, and a church advertising a *Sacred Art Festival*, and a wall round a flower bed at just the right height to sit and play a cello. I should at least practise the idea.

So I parked up, and got Libre out of her case, and played. There

170

wasn't much passing trade, but everyone who passed nodded, or smiled, or came up and said lots of stuff that made no sense to me. OK, it's a start. I was going to drop in on the Sacred Art, but just as I was ready to, someone came out of the church and locked it very decidedly behind her.

Lunch in Bruay? *Pourquoi pas?* It's off route a bit, and downhill into the town, which is unfortunate because then it's uphill to get back on the route, but it will have to do. But there doesn't seem to be anywhere. There are fast-food places, that look like converted shipping containers, but I can't go to one of those on my first full day in France, can I?

I found a bistro eventually. *Grand Opening – two weeks today – please come!* So by default it has to be a kebab at *Le Marrakech*. Don't tell anyone.

But the door is locked. I can see people eating inside, so why is the door locked? I hate this feeling of stupidity, of exclusion, not being able to work out the simplest things. Surely it must be simple. But it isn't; the door is definitely locked.

When I find the open door, round the corner, I can at least be grateful no-one took any notice of me doing a Charlie Chaplin at the locked one.

So now I've had half the biggest kebab I've ever seen, and a ton of chips, and the universe is looking like a better place. And there's half a kebab in my bag for later, if necessary. Rashid and Munir have just closed up and come out into the sun for a smoke. They're admiring the bike set-up, and one thing leads to another, and then I'm getting Libre out and playing *James Bond* for them.

A young man in full black leathers walks between us, oblivious, and playing *Terminator* so loud on his headphones it makes us all laugh. *James Bond* goes down very well in Marrakech, as well as with the substantial group of girls – I hadn't seen them before – who have been gradually approaching, and now come over one by one to press coins into my hand.

Rashid and Munir want a photo, which one of the girls is

persuaded to take, and which amuses the others. Please, says Munir, come back this evening and play for our diners, and we'll give you a good dinner. They would have invited me to stay, but they were both recently married and living in adjoining single rooms. So I'd probably better press on to Arras.

Just before I get back on the Roman road, and the *Via Francigena*, there's the ruined abbey at Mont Saint Eloi. It's a strange monument. Only one section of one wall remains, grand and flamboyant. There used to be a medieval abbey here, with the bones of some saint or other, but it was replaced with a much richer building in the eighteenth century. Rich abbeys didn't fare well in the Revolution, and it was shut, and sold, and its beautiful stone re-used elsewhere. Then in the First World War the Germans did their best to destroy what remained, because its fifty-three metre towers gave the French a useful look-out post.

An unsupported façade of this height doesn't look safe to me, so I stand back a bit, and wonder about the little pyramid of bicycles, four high, that stands by the road. It's intriguing, but there's no explanation. Unlike the *Via Francigena* notices, which are fulsome and precise, and show you the way to Arras, eight miles away. The abbey may have been rather presumptuous in its short heyday, but it wasn't always like that, and the *Via Francigena* reminds me there's a long tradition. It isn't difficult to imagine the numbers of people who have come this way; pilgrims from Canterbury to Rome, over the centuries. Add my name to the list.

Or not. Once in Arras, and admiring the *Grande Place*, and wondering where to set up and play, and display my *can you offer me a bed* notice, and finding myself suddenly tired, and by accident in the Tourist Office, I'm having to prove my *bona fides* as a pilgrim. (We're talking the Roman Catholic Church here, so there's no harm in a bit of Latin, I feel. *Bona fides*. Sounds like a name for a dog.)

Is he a proper pilgrim? the voice on the other end of the phone is asking, in a tone which implied he shouldn't have to ask, that the person phoning on my behalf should know the rules but had shown by his previous behaviour that he didn't, or at best that he didn't apply them rigorously enough.

The building, on one side of a fine square, looked as though it had been built in a kind of competition between two enterprises, one religious and one secular. Was it a church, or was it a courthouse? A seat of temporal authority that wanted to imply a proper divine appointment to that authority, or a place of worship that thought it best to disguise itself a little, or was maybe just cutting corners here and there?

It wasn't clear. The point was that it fronted one side of the square with a nice covered portico that would amplify Libre's voice into the big space (and keep us both out of the sun). And there was an official looking gentleman standing outside who looked as though it was part of his function to forbid things, and so should be properly acknowledged and sought permission from.

When I approached him he stepped back, almost as though I was a visiting leper, and gestured to the office diagonally behind him. That was clearly the office for the dispensation of permissions. Then it turned out to be the Tourist Office. And I was tired. So I just asked him.

He didn't completely understand my question. Either that, or he thought it such a silly question he should answer the question I should have asked. Where, I'd wondered, could he suggest I might begin a search for a room in return for some music? Definitely a silly question. Did I think France was a medieval country criss-crossed by one-eyed troubadours? This is post-Brexit twenty-first century.

So he was calling the Catholic Diocesan Office, and speaking to the Master of Rooms, who had authority to allocate beds to proper pilgrims, for a very slightly less than commercial price. The Tourist Officer looked me up and down, decided I wasn't a proper pilgrim, apologised to the room master, and put the phone down.

Well, hang on, I wanted to say. If you decide, without any kind of debate, that I'm not a proper pilgrim, then obviously I'll want to prove I am. Equally, and perversely, because I'm that sort of person, if you think proceeding slowly and painfully along the *Via Francigena* to Rome *defines* me as a pilgrim, I'll want to demonstrate I'm no such thing. This was an occasion to deploy the first argument. So he rang back, and I was told I could make my way to the pilgrim hostel.

But I haven't got the document, which they stamp at the waypoints, to say I'm genuine, that this endeavour is a divine undertaking.

Well, I want to say, under a new interrogation from a different accommodation officer, who hasn't been told about the telephone exchange, everything I do is fraudulent to a degree, improvised, provisional, agnostic, uncertain, ambivalent. Sometimes it's a pilgrimage, and sometimes it isn't.

But that won't get me a bed for the night, and I'm tired. Yes, I say again, I'm a retired Anglican vicar. I played my cello, an essential part of this undertaking, in Canterbury cathedral, and set off from there with the Bishop's blessing. I just haven't got the booklet for stamping, because St. Martin's Church was shut when I set off.

All of which was perfectly true.

The Diocesan House relent their strict policy that allows only the *bona fide* pilgrim to stay. *Have this room – you're the only person here tonight*. Sometimes there must be more pilgrims – there are four ancient iron beds crammed into the tiny room. The building itself is the size of a city museum, with corridors big enough for the kind of political rallies that can lead to trouble.

But in the entire building there is not a single kettle. I know, because I looked everywhere it was possible to look, and asked everyone it was possible to ask. The thing that is top of the English pilgrim's list of necessities – a cup of tea – cannot be had. That's a privation too far, in my view.

Maybe I should have tried harder to make Rashid and Munir's

invitation in Bruay work. Maybe I should go back to the *Grande Place*, lay out my stall and hope for the offer of a bed. Maybe I should find a shop and buy a litre of juice. Or maybe, the lone guest in the Diocesan Pilgrim Centre without a kettle, and too tired and squeamish to eat an old and fading kebab, I should just go straight to bed.

I suppose, since last night I was a pilgrim, I should call this the Refectory. That's a proper monastic word for a communal eating place. Only this morning there's nothing communal about it. There are tables and chairs for a hundred and fifty. Five places are set, but I think that was only to make me feel not completely alone. A couple of people in priest-collars come in to download coffee from the machine and go swiftly away again; but no-one else came to breakfast.

The GPS thingy isn't working. Its actual GPS function is clearly fine, but it will only show the downloaded route as a line in empty space, which is to say not overlain on a map you can relate to the actual geography. So I've located a bicycle shop, and I'm going to buy one of those little cases you can put on the handlebars to keep your phone in, to see if I can use the map on the phone.

He sold me a case, which turned out not to be very useful, because under a plastic cover the phone screen can't be read in the sunshine anyway, and then told me why I didn't need it. I have to ask the app to download the map of France, he said, because it won't use its own initiative, even though it knows you're in France. It was just as well I didn't tell him – which I nearly did – that he might have given me this information before I bought his expensive phone case which I didn't now need and wasn't any good anyway. Just as well, because half a mile up the road a gear cable seized up, and I had to limp back to the shop and ask for his help.

"It's all rusted up," he said, reproachfully. By which he meant, clearly, *don't you know how to look after your bike?* I wanted to tell him it had rained on me nearly *everybloodyday* since I left home.

But I didn't tell him that either, and just sat down in the rather nice sunshine to wait an hour and a half for his shop to clear of a sudden stream of buyers, so he could fix it for me. It's a good thing I'm not going anywhere today.

By the time that's all finished it's lunchtime. The plan for today was to relax a bit, to begin to feel at home in a foreign country, and to play a lot of music – anywhere that Libre liked the look of. Then later to pedal across town to the warm welcome Catarina had promised me would await at Aline and Gautier's house. Sounds like a good plan to me, and one that's not at all derailed by spending half the morning sorting the bike. In fact I'm feeling really quite on top of things – it happened at a time and place that couldn't have been less inconvenient, and it's sorted. And all the other cables checked, so it shouldn't happen again halfway up the Alps in the middle of nowhere.

The *Grande Place*, which looked so splendid yesterday, is splendid in a different way today. It's full of market, and there are tables and chairs set for lunch here and there. I promised myself more leisured lunches when we reached warmer places, and here we are. I ordered a couple of things, guessing that one was the divine concoction I was looking at on the next table, and not worrying too much what a *museau* was.

The same next table, once they'd finished their *ragoût d'agneau* with noisy relish, turned their attention to my cello-on-a-bike. Would I play it now, they wondered, if they bought me a glass of wine? This was, after all, a French lunch, in the sunshine, on market day, and I really should have a glass of wine, and did I know that *museau* is pig's snout?

So Libre came out of her case, in the French sunshine outside the *Brasserie Georget*. At the first notes a passing dog went berserk, and a couple of tables nearly came to grief. It was generally agreed the object of its attention wasn't the cello though, but another dog quietly bristling under a table further along. Once the dog was safely past, and order restored, there was mild attention, and generous applause. The *museau* arrived, with the wine, and I enjoyed a proper French lunch in the sunshine, in the warm embrace of strangers.

They told me, after recommending the proper dessert to follow the *ragoût d'agneau*,which followed the *museau,* that the *Grande Place* had been full of cars until two years ago, and the decision to pedestrianise it had transformed the life of Arras. While we ate, the market had quietly cleared itself away, and six road sweepers had raced into the square and were performing a complicated ballet, *prestissimo*, to remove every trace.

I sat on a bollard across the square after lunch, to play. But after five minutes I had to move. A wedding party appeared outside the Tourist Office, with a big brass band to serenade them.

I found a quiet street nearby, thinking the *Grande Place* was too big anyway, with a bar diagonally opposite, and a good flow of expensive shoppers. A retired teacher from Antibes (I was trying to remember where that was) bought me a cup of tea, and told me not to worry about the drunk shouting at me to *change the music*. It was other shouting that curtailed the music in the end – a huge Gay Pride march filling the main road at the end of this little street that had been nicely quiet when I began.

Aline and Gautier live in Rue Aristide Briant. But I can't find the house. I should perhaps have guessed there would be more than one Rue Aristide Briant; Monsieur Briant having been Prime Minister of France a rather extraordinary eleven times, and taking home a Nobel Peace Prize in 1926. I suppose there might have been eleven streets called Briant, though I think there were only two – the one I was on, and the other one I should have been on.

I was warmly welcomed to the house. It would be an exaggeration to say it was half-built, but it's clearly going to be quite grand when it's finished. Judging by the energy I encountered in it, from Gautier and Aline, and their two small children, I don't think the building works will take too long. Like so many things, Gautier explained, as we talked about his tree work and woodwork, it's a question of time and money – mostly money.

In preparation for this journey I'd contacted a few local authorities – the Mairie's office – in a few French towns, to ask consent for something in between a busk and a proper concert. A *pop-up concert*, I called it, which translated as *un concert pop-up* or, if you wanted to be strictly Académie Française about it and abjure the English adjective, *un concert éphémère*. Arras had replied, affirmatively, after quite a lot of correspondence, and I was due back in the *Grande Place* at 6.00pm.

I nearly didn't go, having realised the *Grande Place* was far too *grande* for it to work without amplification, but then Aline said their three-year-old daughter was looking forward to the ride into town on the back of Daddy's bicycle, so we went anyway. I had a six-page consent form, which I had to show the police if required, and it would be a pity to waste that, wouldn't it?

No police came, possibly because I wasn't making enough noise for them, or because the *Grande Place* is pedestrianised and they don't like to get out of their cars when on duty. But a million other people came, including the retired teacher from Antibes (which I remembered isn't far from Nice, on the Cote d'Azur) and the *Warmshowers* hosts I'd jilted in order to stay with Catarina's daughter Aline.

It would be nice to have a big amp, to fill this great space with Libre's voice, and to show my six-page consent form to a police officer. But as it is, it's a bit of a damp squib and Libre, despite her best efforts, is overwhelmed.

CHAPTER 25

Four times in one day

SUNDAY 12 JUNE

Next stop St. Quentin, not quite fifty miles away. I want to be there for lunchtime, because I have an afternoon commitment, and an unexpected problem is emerging.

After a very happy stay in Arras, the whole family waved me off in the early morning sunshine. I like it when it's both sunny and cool, the perfect weather for the road. The Roman road goes straight and true, through fields of potatoes, maize, beet, oats and a few exotic things. From time to time it's lined with lime trees, but there are no hedges, fences or walls, so it feels open and free.

This is a striking difference between English and French countryside, it seems. England is all walled and fenced and hedged. On a road you feel enclosed and constrained. The fields around you might be very green and inviting, but they're out of bounds, and private. Here, by contrast, the land is open. Sometimes there's a small ditch, but often not even that. You could roll off the road and into the field, without hindrance. It makes you feel a bit more welcome, less excluded.

No doubt there are good reasons. In France there wasn't all that stone that needed clearing out of the fields before you could use them. This is arable, not pastoral, and wheat doesn't wander in the way cows tend to. But I'm wondering if there might be other, deeper, things, and whether we might, still, be subconsciously affected by them.

I'm idly speculating here, of course, as I cycle through the flat country, making good progress towards St. Quentin. Has French philosophy been more radical and experimental than it was in England because the open landscape somehow encouraged open minds? When, at the end of the eighteenth century, the haves in England became afraid the have-nots might behave as they did in France, and create a bloody revolution, were they needlessly fearful? Could you have a French-style Revolution in a land of walls and hedges, where your path was always laid out for you? As I said, idle speculation.

The wind turbines are either still, or turning so slowly you'd think they'd just woken up and needed to practise their Tai Chi before the day's work.

But I'm in a bit more of a hurry than the turbines. Otherwise I would have followed some of these signs pointing to Commonwealth War Cemeteries. There are lots of them. This is the Haute Somme. The main battlefield of the Somme was to the West, but the whole area was fought over for much of the First World War. No-one knows, to within a couple of million, how many soldiers were killed in that Great War. Six million were just "missing".

So another thought arises, displacing the walls and fences. How important is remembering? What purpose does it serve? It's complicated. It's also very sensitive. I've never been an enthusiastic poppy wearer, but it would take longer than the journey to St. Quentin to explain properly. I don't like the way Remembrance Sunday takes over our churches and seems to require God to support and validate our "war effort".

Remembrance is something different from History. The Great War isn't just History. 1066 is History. Henry VIII is History – so we're allowed to think of him as a bit of a colourful character, rather than a monster, a murderer, a torturer and enslaver. But 1914-18 *isn't* just History.

I have an important family connection. My grandfather was

a PoW, for three years. He lived, according to family history, on cabbage water and the occasional potato. My grandmother nursed him to health afterwards, so that she could marry him. Even battles older than the Somme aren't just History – the same grandmother remembers Mafeking. She didn't hear it on the radio, though; there were no radios.

Why does it matter? All these soldiers would be dead now anyway. When you're dead, nothing matters anymore. I can worry about what legacy I might leave, but I can only worry about it when I'm alive. Why then, when it can't matter to them now, does it matter to us that so many of them died at eighteen, when they might have lived to eighty?

It isn't enough to say it's obvious. That we should never forget a Holocaust, or a World War. It is obvious. But why?

So I've more or less decided I have to follow one of these signs, and visit one of these cemeteries, and mourn the dead, and lament the imbecility of the human race, when suddenly there's one right by the road. Delsaux Farm Cemetery is small, by the standards of these things. There are war cemeteries with ten thousand ordered graves. Delsaux Farm has less than five hundred.

Five hundred dead men. In ordered rows designed by Edwin Lutyens.

Four hundred of them are identified by named headstones I can't bear to read. There are a further sixty-one bodies so mangled they couldn't be identified. And then more than thirty identified only by name tags that couldn't convincingly be paired with scattered body parts. All under neat grass, in pleasant sunshine, with skylarks overhead.

This was H.G. Wells' *War to End War*. Human beings like to remember, and they like to learn their history. But learn *from* history? No. Here we are doing it all over again. And again. And now again.

I've been playing Frank Bridge's *Meditation*, for Ukraine, and thinking how fragile civilisation is. There's no-one to hear it, but that's not the point. I need to play *Meditation* here, too, to these hundreds of neat white gravestones, whose names I can't bear to read. And read a poem.

I saw you dancing

I saw you dancing in the rain once;
you weren't dressed for the rain, or for dancing,
I thought; you were just dancing, wet.

I saw you dancing in the dark once,
alone; I couldn't see your face;
it was too dark, I thought, for dancing.

I saw you dancing when the tanks were there,
and all our homes were gone; I thought
your face blue-bruised, your yellow hair burnt black.

I pedal on, not uplifted by the sunshine, or the larks. I get to St. Quentin in time, following a line of sight to the monstrously large *basilique*. I'm surveying the restaurants round the square, looking for lunch. The last one seems the most promising. One of its customers, a gentleman with white hair and a very smart jacket, hails me. *A cello on a bicycle! Bravo! Haha! Come and play for us!*

So of course I do.

I'm plied with drinks, and a couple of plates of *amuses bouches*. I play *James Bond*, which gets a wider audience, then *The Swan*, which goes down very well, and then Frank Bridge's *Meditation* again. I'm being pressed by the smart-jacketed gentleman to stay in his hotel, but we settle on a lunch there instead so he phones his wife at the hotel to say he's got a guest, and off we go.

The Hotel Des Canonniers, dating mostly from the eighteenth century, is an architectural gem. It's a boutique destination, owned and run by Giles and Marie-Paule, with a real small cannon in the garden, and Giles' splendid Morgan parked in the three-sided courtyard out front. They bought it as a family house decades ago and, when the family grew up and went away they turned it into a hotel.

Giles, before he retired, was an accountant and clearly good with money. He shows me some of their own rooms, on the ground floor of the hotel, full of a lifetime's interesting things. Here's a model sailing boat, a lot more than just a dinghy. The real thing is in a little harbour near Calais. The other two are further South.

Giles is an enthusiast. Before he was an accountant, he was a cyclist. Here are a dozen silver trophies, arranged in descending order of size, and a framed black and white photograph showing him nearly at the front of a very serious looking race. He still has a fine bike or two.

We eat in the garden, which requires an umbrella against the sun. Marie-Paule, operating out of a kitchen that isn't at all to the same scale as the rest of the house, seems not disconcerted that lunch for two had to stretch to three. My coming, they both said, was a gift from God, after they couldn't go to a granddaughter's first communion in the *basilique* this morning.

After *foie gras*, a stew from heaven, and wine and cheese, there's barely time to photograph Giles beside his cycling prizes, and Marie-Paule at the door of the hotel, before he wheels me across town to the *Galerie 115*.

St. Quentin is one of those towns, like Arras, I'd written ahead to. Where in St. Quentin could I play, I'd asked, and they put me in touch with the *Galerie 115*. I didn't know anything more, except that I'd arranged with the *Galerie* to be there at 3.00, and there was a small walled garden I could play in if the weather was fine. I thought probably I would be playing to a few random gallery visitors.

So it's a bit of a surprise, when we pedal up to the front door at five to three, nearly sober, to find a modest crowd assembled by the door, and an organiser looking relieved. There are posters in the glass shop front advertising the Opening of the 90th Anniversary Exhibition. The posters show a photograph of the cellist who would perform the concert to mark the Opening.

I was apologising for being late, Giles was explaining that I was a gift from God, and the audience was in the mood for fun.

It was a local amateur artists' association that ran the *Galerie*, and was celebrating its 90th anniversary. So, in the nature of these things, some of the work was strikingly good, and some of it wasn't. Pride of place was given to a painting by Jean Lallemand, a local artist who'd made good, and who had a letter from Buckingham Palace to prove it, and whose work was once featured on a French postage stamp.

There wasn't time to see any of this yet, though. I wheel the bike through the *Galerie*, and out into the walled garden, guided by Hélène, the prime mover in it all. There are more people waiting in the garden, sitting in the sun or the shade according to their complexions. On with the show.

I race through the first half and in the interval for refreshment and general mayhem, discover that the twelve-year old in the audience played the violin. His father needs little encouragement to run home and get it, so we open the second half with one of his pieces, accompanied on the cello. This was the first time, he said, he'd played in public. And he definitely wants to do it again, he beams.

Half the audience is already on its feet, because there weren't enough chairs, so I get the rest up, and they dance to Bach minuets and Irish jigs, and whatnot, and would have gone on all night, I think. But the carpal tunnel syndrome I had operated on a couple of years ago is being seriously aggravated by the combination of bike and cello, and it hurts to play. This, I feel, might become a serious problem, and I need to be careful.

I should give proper attention to the Exhibition itself. André shadows and chaperones. I admire Hélène's work, which stands out, and a couple of other pieces. Ah yes, says André, that's the teacher.

Everyone pauses to clap me out of the building and back on the bike, to weave my way across town to my *Warmshowers* hosts, Gaetan and Fleure. Hélène and André also invite me to stay, so St. Quentin is officially, by my personal designation, the Most Hospitable Town in France.

That designation is reinforced by an evening with Gaetan and Fleure and their student daughter with a friend. When it comes to the cheese, we jestingly debate England v. France. We know how to do it too, I'm trying to say. Have you ever tried a proper Cheddar, or a real Stilton, or Cornish Yarg, or Shropshire Blue, or Stinking Bishop, or Parlick Fell, or a Red Leicester, or an old Wensleydale? Clearly I'm not going to win this. So I concede that we aren't so good as the French at soft cheeses, but that my *real favourite* is an old Comté.

Equally graciously, they get out their best Comté and add it to an already full cheeseboard. And *this*, says Gaetan triumphantly, opening a half bottle of quite old Vin Jaune, is what you drink with it, before the daughter's friend plays some Chopin on the piano, and I get Libre out for the fourth performance of the day.

CHAPTER 26

A broken bike

MONDAY 13 JUNE

Monday. Empty roads, shuttered houses. Sunny, and getting warm. Skylarks and yellowhammers in full voice. A bit of uphill to warm up and break a sweat. A bit of downhill to cool down and dry off. One of those days when you want there to be a God to be thankful to.

There's only one nagging problem as I ride these near-perfect, nearly straight and easily navigable roads. The carpal tunnel pain in my right wrist is getting worse. Last night at Gaetan's house in St. Quentin I had to hold the bow in a very unorthodox way, to control the discomfort, and to get enough pressure to make a sound. Playing the cello is not good for the condition. Cycling is worse. The combination of biking and bowing is too much.

I'm finding this very depressing. The sun's shining, and the road is good, and I didn't waste time getting started this morning, and somehow that makes it worse. All those reasons to be happy, and all I can think of is whether the whole thing will have to be abandoned. Whether I will have to give up cycling, or playing the cello, or both. Life without Libre is almost unthinkable. Does it need another operation? Would that help? Is it even possible? The first operation was one of the most traumatic events of my life, and I don't know if I can go through it again. I want to cry with the frustration and misery of it all. But that would be silly.

All these pretty villages, with their clear signposts to the next one, and more or less a straight line south-eastwards, so there are no navigational difficulties. But the villages are all too small and shuttered to have bakeries and coffee outlets on a Monday morning. I keep getting excited by small crowds, but they're not at coffee shops. They're at the *Mairies*, apparently casting their votes in local elections, and being sociable about it. They must be doing something different, though – the elections were yesterday.

There's a family of four, the parents walking unhurriedly, pleased at having performed their civic duty, the two small children each holding a parental hand and not giving anything away. They're behaving as though it's Sunday; but I'm *sure* it's Monday. I pull up beside them, with a cheerful greeting, to ask where I might get coffee today. I know there isn't a bar in this village, because I've already been right round it. Am I just practising my French, or am I half hoping their appearance of general goodwill towards the world might translate into an invitation to a clearly weary cyclist?

A Gallic shrug from him. A half-hearted suggestion from her that five kilometres in the wrong direction there just might be… It was worth a try.

So I've gone thirty miles, on these lovely sunny roads, when at last a big cathedral appears on the top of a hill in the distance. That's good. Where there's a cathedral there must be coffee – it's a rule. Never mind that I've already got nearly seventy miles to go today, and it's a hill, and it must be off route. I'm not on any deadline, except I've got nowhere to stay tonight, and today – surely – must be a good day for the *would you like to offer me a bed* notice.

As it gets nearer, the hill gets bigger. And the road wants to skirt round the bottom, and just wave to the cathedral *en passant*. But then a half-hidden sign pointing to a "medieval city" up the hill decides it. I shouldn't miss a cathedral *and* a medieval city – which will mean a choice of coffee shops, surely.

It's a daunting climb up a 25% slope, which turns into a flight of nearly impassable steps. But these come out on a nice gentle switchback road – the road which I should have found from the bottom, if two gardeners in the *Rue des Jardinières* hadn't misdirected me earlier.

And what a medieval city it is! Laon has enough cobbled streets to shake a bicycle to death, and yes, they make coffee here. In the end, too much of it.

I sat in the shade, admiring the magnificent cathedral in its little square, and sensibly opted for *petit* when offered the choice of *petit* or *grand*. The bike is propped up by the cathedral, and locked in case I decide to wander. The streets I can see look highly wanderable. To my left the narrow main thoroughfare is seductively curved, to make you want to explore round the bend. A large flock of coloured lanterns fills the space, strung between the buildings, dappling the street and promising an intimate evening.

I'm looking into the cathedral square, a small space bounded by the necessary palaces and chapter houses required to support a medieval cathedral. This was once an important place, a strategically steep hill overlooking the wide plain of Picardy. Julius Caesar fortified it, and the Romans successfully repelled invasions by Franks, Burgundians, Vandals, Alans, and Huns. It has been fought over in every century since, until the Allies expelled the Germans in 1918. It's amazing the cathedral and its square still stand.

In the end I didn't wander far. All that violent history exhausted me, and Libre was impatient to be played. She likes cathedrals. So I sat on a step in the shade, centre stage, and Libre filled the little square with Bach, and Fauré, and Saint-Saëns.

Soon I'd sold two CDs and been given a second cup of coffee, this time *grand*, not *petit*. That might be a bit much for safe driving, I thought. Then back down the wrist-wrenching cobbled streets, and the sweeping switchback, to rejoin the route to Reims.

French pronunciation can be tricky. I thought it would sound something like *Rem*, as in Rembrandt. But then no-one knows where I mean. No, it's more like *Hhhrrrrrrans*, like the beginning of Ransome, but with an unseemly excess of hawking first. If you're a foreigner it requires practice, and an abandonment of your natural English reserve. So I'm practising it, aloud, as I cycle the quiet road across the Picardy plain, hawking and spitting onto the grass beside the road.

Then disaster. A bolt attaching the front rack to the frame sheared off. The bike can't be ridden. It needs drilling out, a new thread cutting in the hole, and a larger bolt in the enlarged hole. That needs a workshop, and it's lunchtime in the middle of nowhere. At least it isn't Sunday. Surprisingly, I'm fairly calm. I could be shouting, and kicking things, and wondering aloud why the universe hates me. Instead, I'm just quietly assessing the (mostly non-existent) options and wondering if this wouldn't perhaps be a good time for lunch anyway.

But after hardly ten minutes of assessing those non-existent options, Rafael pulls up in his blue van, to see if I need help. He grasps the issue immediately. "I live one kilometre this way. Put the bike in the van. We'll mend it."

The van is thankfully empty. Libre sticks, undignified, out of the open back door, and off we go. It was fiddly, but in half an hour it was fixed, even down to cutting an old bolt to the right length to fit. Thanks to the angel Rafael.

Back on the road to Reims, pronounced *Hhhrrrrans*, where I've nowhere to stay. More of the same kind of roads, until, now in the rather blazing sunshine, we re-join the unflexing, unflinching, Roman road for the last several miles.

Actually it's more than several. Again, you can see a monstrous cathedral from a long way off, but it doesn't seem to get any nearer. I'm very hot. I'm very tired.

But here we are, outside a cathedral of really excessive proportions. Libre likes cathedrals, as you know, so we set up, with the hopeful notice in plain sight, and play, trying to look as though the wrist isn't hellishly painful, and we could easily wipe the dust off our feet and carry on to the next town if you don't want us.

So what sort of people are passing through the square, in front of the huge cathedral? Where is the offer of a bed going to come from?

Nowhere. There are plenty of tourists, looking tired and bored by this time of day, wandering without much purpose. They have no rooms to offer, of course. There are quite a few – mostly men – smart, briefcased, who look as though they probably work for a public employer, in a hurry to get home. There are the old and lonely, who sit, and take a non-committal interest, but only at a distance. Clearly this isn't going to work as I'd imagined.

I stopped playing halfway through a Bach *Allemande*, rather rudely. I don't *want* it to work, I realised. I don't want any of these strangers to welcome me into their homes. I don't want to play for them this evening. I want a quiet, still evening to myself. So I stopped trying to engage, to entice. I packed up quickly, to go in search of a hotel. I haven't had, I realised, a quiet evening since I left home.

I didn't even pause to go into Reims's great and famous cathedral. That's two cathedrals I've played outside today, without going into either. That won't do my pilgrim's *bona fides* any good, if anyone asks.

CHAPTER 27

The wrong Chaumont

WEDNESDAY 15 JUNE

Today promises to be the first proper hot day. The forecast is for a balmy 27C, which some people might think I'm barmy to cycle in. But I like it. It's going to be thirty-eight degrees by the weekend. So I need to push on South, where with any luck it will be forty-two, or something like that.

Champagne. There's a lot of it about. Mostly it's still in the fields, soaking up the sun, acquiring its flavour, growing. But there's an air of expectation. And a lot of people encouraging it, mostly with various kinds of trimming, it seems.

Somehow you can tell it's champagne, even without the proud signs announcing which *grand cru* it is, and exactly how big the field is, and who owns it. It all just looks expensive.

It's intoxicating, too. And confusing. Here, for instance, is a road that's clearly going downhill, so why is it such hard work? The head wind has died down a bit, so it should be fast and satisfyingly effortless. I find the page on the GPS thingy that shows gradients, and it says we're actually going uphill at 2.9%. I have to believe the GPS, rather than my own eyes. I remember this kind of optical illusion in other parts of the world, where they charge tourists to watch a car rolling uphill, defying gravity. This is definitely a more striking example than any of those.

I'm wondering how it happens. Not how a car rolls uphill, silly,

191

but how we lose our normally rigorous sense of the horizontal. I suppose this landscape is one that really does deserve to be called rolling. It's all an intricate pattern of curves – hills, fields, roads, and these odd passages between the fields that are too small to be roads, but too smart to be tracks. And superimposed on all that curving, the uncompromisingly straight wired rows of champagne vines. Something about it addles the brain, so you don't know properly which way is up. I love it. It reminds me of that freefall feeling you get in dreams.

The aptly-named Bouzy will be the place to go, surely. I'm not wrong. On the road leading to Bouzy even the lampposts are drunk. In Bouzy itself, every other house is advertising champagne in one way or another, and the church spire seems to lean in homage. The church is locked, so perhaps it's having a day off. Everything looks a bit hungover, actually.

Then the grandly named V52, a newly-tarmacked cycle path along the Marne Canal. What's in a name? There must be some deep-seated psychological resonance in the designation V52 – you can buy a V52 motorboat, a V52 aeroplane (don't try and buy a B52 by mistake), a V52 wind-turbine, or a V52 electric guitar. The water is an unfeasible, enticing, and possibly dangerous, aquamarine. But there are fish in it, and lots of weed, so it's probably clean enough.

This is heavenly. I wonder if this is how the Dutch experience cycling. No hills, no need to change gear; only sweating when you want to. It's completely flat, straight, smooth, traffic-free, with the calm water on one side, and a gently evolving landscape of trees, with the occasional glimpse of river, on the other. The River Marne is the complete opposite of this smooth canal and the V52. I've never seen a wigglier waterway. You couldn't navigate much of a boat there. But if you engineer a straight canal along the same valley you don't have to build bridges and tunnels for it, and you get a ready supply of water to keep it topped up. Clever.

I want to go fast, just because it's so easy and satisfying. I want to go slow, so it doesn't end, and send me back to earth.

The V52 is nicely way-marked, though you couldn't really go wrong. Periodically there are little notices encouraging you to leave the canal, and go and explore and spend money in a village a mile or two to one side or the other. Then the canal goes through, instead of skirting around, a town; perhaps even a city.

What you first see, unsurprisingly, is a magnificent spire, close to the water. This is Notre-Dame-en-Vaux, an old parish church. There's also a cathedral, St. Etienne's, but you can't see it from here. The city was renamed in 1998. It used to be Chalôns-sur-Marne. But who's heard of the Marne? Call it Chalôns-en-Champagne instead – that will surely double our tourist numbers. What's in a name? Wasn't that about the same time Homer Simpson changed his name to Max Power (the name he got off a hairdryer) and saw his status rocket as a result?

The first rule of swimming in a canal is to know where you're going to get out. I could definitely get in. But the neat, shuttered bank looks too high to climb out by. A few miles – I'm not really counting – further along, past a heron that doesn't move when I cycle within ten feet of it, and the bank is lower. So I swim, in a nearly weedless section of the unfeasibly aquamarine water, down and back to an old bridge that only carries a footpath going nowhere.

It's warm and wonderful, and I could stay here all day if I didn't have miles to go before I sleep.

The original plan for today was to make for Vitry-le-Francois, fifty miles in total. But I've no accommodation there, and it would leave me with seventy miles tomorrow, ending with a couple of serious hills, followed by a concert. So it would be better to go further today, if possible. I was keeping an open mind about it, but fifty miles of this smooth flatness would hardly count as a day's work.

So instead it's a late lunch in Vitry. I can't eat much, even though it's late, because of the Crystal Hotel's rather overwhelming breakfast in Reims. If this were a proper holiday I'd then be sleeping in the sun. But I'd better press on and see how much I can shorten tomorrow's itinerary.

After Vitry, away from the Marne and the smooth V52, we're entering a country of beautiful half-timbered houses. Some of them, usually a *melange* of dwelling and farm building, are in need of attention. Some have been beautifully restored. Some have been unbeautifully restored – and some look like inexpensive last-century imitations – usually with white plastic windows. Oh dear.

Another thirty miles, at Brienne-le-Chateau, and I need to think about resting. I couldn't go much further, and it looks as though hotels are going to be thin on the ground for a bit, so I'll just collapse here.

By chance it's a good stopping place. The town is deeply interesting, and would repay a much longer visit. It's named for the Chateau, an enormous and magnificent building, completed – with spectacularly bad timing – in 1788, four years after Napoleon Bonaparte had graduated from the Military Academy in the town, and the year before a notable Revolution imperilled all chateaux and their ruling inhabitants.

They did things differently in those days, and the Military Academy was run by Benedictine monks (yes, really). They were apparently a mildly sadistic bunch, who required the students to be completely cut off from their families for the five years of their residence, and who took no notice of Napoleon's further isolation and bullying, on account of his poverty and his Corsican accent.

Napoleon nevertheless conceived a strong attachment to Brienne. The town makes much of the fact that he stopped there again, briefly, in 1805, on his way to be crowned King of Italy, and that he later occupied the Chateau itself, directing the Battle of Brienne from there in 1814. He bequeathed a significant sum of money to the town, enabling the construction of a rather handsome *Hotel de Ville*, which is now graced with a statue of the man himself as a fifteen-year-old boy, complete with the trademark hand-stuck-in-waistcoat, and with long hair and a very insolent stance.

I don't have Napoleon's choice of accommodation, however, and it's this hotel or nothing much else. It's cheap. But you wouldn't call it cheerful. The *patron* wants his guests – there are only about five of us – to appreciate that he is greatly overworked, and that anything would be too much trouble. He berated me for sitting down at a table unnecessarily laid for three, when I could have sat at a table laid for two. I moved, but I must have been tired – I asked him if he was always rude to his guests.

Or maybe it was the pain I was in. The carpal tunnel wrist is worse again after today's eighty miles. If I played the cello now, I'd be holding the bow like a knife, or a saw – which wouldn't inspire confidence in an audience. But Libre hasn't been out of her case all day, so I'm bound to be feeling a bit miserable and lonely.

Talking of pains, in the wrist and other places, have you seen the *Pains Artisanales* they make in France these days? *Delicieux. Mon Dieu.*

More of that in the morning.

I eschewed the grim-looking breakfast and had a pie and pastry from the *boulangerie* instead. I ate them both in the little garden opposite, by the bronze of Marshal Valée; another of Brienne's claims to pugilistic fame.

Sylvain-Charles Valée was born in Brienne-le-Chateau, gained a military command in the Revolution, and somehow managed to advance his military career when it looked as though the Revolution had failed, and did so again when it returned. He's a proper hero of France.

I've got a *pain artisanal*, a beautiful heavy black bread, much longer-lasting than a feeble *baguette*, and very suitable for a military campaign, in my bag for later.

Setting off South, into the rapidly warming sun, the thought of that bread was greatly encouraging. The forecast is for a balmy thirty-three degrees, but early in the morning there's just a blue sky of beckoning promise.

These D roads are often wide and empty, usually straight, and nearly always smooth. They're a pleasure to ride. Hay bailing is in full stride, and the smell of a field being bailed is intoxicating.

The warm sun brings out all the smells of the French countryside – mostly lovely, and occasionally disgusting. Have you noticed that at the right stage of decomposition a pile of manure has the same sweet pungency as the rind of the best soft French cheese? Yes, truly.

It's getting hillier, and more up than down. At Eguilly-sous-Bois there's a locked church that looks as though it would have been worth a peek. There's a little old chateau, with flute-playing cherubs on the arched gateway guarding a bridge over something that might be a moat, which absolutely demands a peek. It looks just the place Miss Havisham would have lived in. But there are probably guard dogs, so I'll not go too far in.

Towards the end of the morning I find myself suddenly in the small town of Essoyes, by a bridge that seems familiar. Then the dawning revelation – this is where Renoir lived and loved and painted, and it's magical.

Is the light really different here, or are we just seeing it through the eyes of the great painter? Everything is alive and shimmering with Impressionistic intensity. I've always loved Renoir. Libre just has to play in sight of that famous bridge.

Then across the river, and up into the bright and empty woods of the national park. Miles and miles of almost nothing but trees, with some welcome shade on a couple of long climbs. This morning's *boulangerie* bread, and some cheese, sitting on the grass in a butterfly-filled clearing. And maybe I closed my eyes for a moment or two.

Now it's really hot, and I'm not pedalling fast, but it isn't so far to Chaumont. Somehow the place isn't as big as I was expecting. It's a small village, so I ask a local for the address I've got for tonight's concert.

Non, Monsieur, there is no Rue de Temple in Chaumont.

It dawns on me. I'm in the wrong Chaumont.

This is Chaumont-*le-Bois*, and I should be in Chaumont *without* the Bois. Hopefully it's just down the road.

But it isn't. Ever-helpful Google Maps says it's forty miles away, but that I could get there in a little over three hours, if I really tried.

Not in thirty-three degrees, I couldn't. And the concert is scheduled to start in three hours exactly.

Berating myself for such unbelievable stupidity, I knock on a couple of doors looking for cold water while I work out what to do.

It's quickly clear the concert has to be cancelled. They won't think well of me, but there's nothing else I can do.

While Clement – who didn't open the door when I knocked, but who came out later to see what the fuss was about – is giving me repeated and very loud instructions on how to reach the right Chaumont, and I'm trying to make calls to limit the damage, an implausible solution is offered. Elie will come and collect me in his van. The show must go on. *Wait by the church*, he says, *and I'll come for you in an hour*.

He couldn't possibly get here in an hour, but at least we will have tried, I'm thinking.

Clement gives me an ice cream, in exchange for a surprisingly calm rendering of *The Swan*, to the accompaniment of the neighbour's jackhammer. He shows me the hairs on his arm standing on end as a result, or so he claims, and then leaves me in peace.

How could I be so stupid?

Elie arrives in a little over an hour and a half, and dismantles the innards of his van in order to get the bike inside. We'll only be half an hour or so late for the performance, and he drives like a Frenchman from an earlier era, trying to make up the time.

They're all waiting in the sunshine. The local press wants a mock-up of me arriving by bike (to save my embarrassment, I suppose), and I go straight on to perform, unwashed, and in my cycling clothes. The pain and weakness in my bowing arm is much worse than yesterday, and I can scarcely hold the bow. It could hardly, I feel, be any worse.

The concert is in the United Protestant Church of France, and most of the audience are members. One of them knew all three of the French pieces I played (the other two were Fauré, and Debussy's *Syrinx*). Afterwards they set up a table on the grass, and half of them stayed for the most restorative dinner of my life. It would have been perfect if I weren't still unwashed and in my cycling clothes.

The United Protestants of Chaumont (NOT le Bois) are wonderful, wonderful people. *Merci a tous*.

CHAPTER 28

Some film music, incidentally

I begin my delayed and sweaty performance in Chaumont's United Protestant Church of France with *James Bond*. It's always a good opener. After all, it opened every James Bond film, except *Casino Royale*, in that signature "gun-barrel sequence". Everyone recognises it, from its fanfare opening, through its slow crawling semitones, ascending and then descending, to its famous *dum-di-di-dum-dum* rhythm – a killer argument in all the libel actions Monty Norman has fought and won against claims that the arranger John Barry actually wrote it.

But it's not what people are expecting, from a solo cello and a small and inoffensive-looking cyclist. In other circumstances – a rugby club dinner, say – it would be recognised before the end of the first fanfare bar. I was asked, by the way, to play at a rugby club dinner – a fit-looking player in Cambridge heard *James Bond* on the street and tried to book me. When I'm playing it at a sit-down concert, some people get it in the semitones, and some not until the *dum-di-di-dum-dum*. Because it's not what they're expecting. I can see them thinking that, and then wondering what they should have been expecting, before they settle down for the ride and pass round the popcorn.

It's a good opener for me, too. I can look them in the eye, make them think I'm the barrel of that gun. I can sweep the room, in an exaggerated Bond appraisal of the scene. I can go on repeating those three elements, in any order, without getting lost, because that's the nature of this music. From its first appearance in *Dr. No*, in 1962, it's been through innumerable iterations. It's been arranged and re-arranged and covered so many times you would think it would be like George Washington's axe – three new handles and two new heads since George Washington himself cut down that cherry tree. But still George Washington's axe.

Yes, still Monty Norman's original tune. In a proper arrangement for solo cello by the great cello arranger Ilse de Ziah. It's lost none of its zap in all those years. Don't disparage film music. It may be incidental, but don't think it's *just* incidental.

If it's any good, like Monty Norman's theme for *Dr. No*, it soon migrates away from the screen and stands on its own. Like incidental music in the classical repertoire. The most famous is probably Mendelssohn's *A Midsummer Night's Dream*. But Handel, Purcell, Beethoven, too – they all wrote it. And youth orchestras all over the world now play John Williams' *Harry Potter* music. And what about Bernard Herrmann? Maybe not a well-known name, but you can't imagine Alfred Hitchcock's *Psycho*, or *The Man Who Knew Too Much*, without Herrmann's music.

So *James Bond* is a good opener. In Chaumont I couldn't of course pair it with the poem you heard all those miles ago in Buntingford – *My Lonely Heart* doesn't translate well. But I've got a bit more film music lined up for later. It's by Ennio Morricone, one of the most prolific and successful of them all, and a composer who seemed to be able to make himself at home anywhere. I don't know how he had the time, or the energy, or the creativity to do it, but in one year – 1968 – he wrote the scores for twenty films. He was closely associated with Sergio Leone, and with Quentin Tarantino, as well as writing for Roman Polanski and Franco Zeffirelli, along with a host of others.

There were lots of not entirely memorable spaghetti Westerns, but a great number of very well-known titles too: *A Fistful of Dollars, The Untouchables, The Good, the Bad and the Ugly, Once Upon a Time in the West, Cinema Paradiso...* And of course, in

HIGHWAY CELLO

1986, *The Mission*.

It's always a risk to identify something as the "most famous" of someone's works, but I'm sticking my neck out, and calling *Gabriel's Oboe*, the main theme of *The Mission*, Morricone's most famous work. It has a life way beyond the film. To the extent that many more people have heard of the music than the film. And there are probably lots of people who play the oboe just because of this music.

The film, beautiful though it is in its cinematography, and stellar though its cast was, wasn't hugely successful when it appeared in 1986. And it's sunk a long way since. Set in the 1750s, it dealt with colonial atrocities in a way that highlighted some of the horrors of that era, but didn't wear the further passage of time well. The Guarani Indians, as they were called, were people who had things done to them. The actors, and agents, in the film were the likes of Jeremy Irons and Robert de Niro. The Guarani weren't even given proper names.

The protagonist, Gabriel, was a Jesuit priest, whose mission was to make Christians of the Guarani. Even that concept is now so problematic it would take a Boris Pasternak, rather than a Roland Joffré, to tell the story. Ostensibly the Jesuits were trying to rescue the Guarani, and others, from the enslavement practised by less religious Spanish and Portuguese. In practice, their policy of *reducción* was itself an enslavement, and the Jesuits have been implicated in appalling abuses of their own.

So it's not a surprise the Guarani were suspicious of Gabriel when he arrived. Early in the film you watch him climbing the Iguazu falls – the largest waterfall system in the world, with a maximum flow five times the maximum flow of Niagara – in order to play his oboe to attract the Guarani. It would of course have been more impressive if he'd carried a cello, rather than a tiddly oboe, halfway round the world, and up the Iguazu falls. Then Morricone would have written *Gabriel's Cello*, which would have been a much better idea.

201

You might think I'm brave to play it. After the trouble I got into borrowing a flute piece, here I am moving straight on to something that is clearly, properly and unarguably, for the oboe – though only, as I've just implied, because Jeremy Irons couldn't play the cello, or wasn't man enough to carry it up Iguazu.

I went to Iguazu once, by the way. Twice, actually. On consecutive days –first from the Argentinian side, and then from the Brazilian. And if I'd known what I know now I would have brought my cello with me. But I'd been playing at a cello-fest in Buenos Aires on a borrowed instrument, and you can't take a borrowed cello up Iguazu. All those rainbows are there because it's like being in a very rainy rainforest without all the trees. Everything is permanently saturated, and the borrowed cello wouldn't have survived in good shape. Libre, on the other hand, robustly carbon fibre, like a boat, would have revelled in it. It's a pity I didn't know her then.

Anyway, I'm playing *Gabriel's Oboe*, in another of Ilse de Ziah's beautiful solo cello arrangements. Everyone recognises the tune, though it's one of those tunes that's sometimes not as easy to place as it is to recognise. It isn't fair to let people suffer the *I know that tune what is it* feeling in the hope they can work it out before the end, when someone's going to ask them whether they enjoyed the original film, and they'll be found out. So I tell them. And then afterwards, of course, I have to poke a bit of harmless fun at the oboe – which made Jeremy Irons look effete, which a cello would never have done.

Gabriel's Oboe

Gabriel, my angel,
read the job description –
on a cloud (they're all
numbered) with a harp.
Yes, a bloody harp.

No, there is no summer
holiday, read the
contract. Does the meaning
of "eternity"
elude your subtle mind?

Harp. H.A.R.P.
Why? Read the contract
please: Happy. Alpha.
Romeo. Paradise.
Not that devil's OBOE.
This is heaven. There are rules.
No. Don't even ask, of course
you can't play God's own CELLO.

You remember I called my journey through England the *First Movement*, and now in France we're playing the *Second Movement*. One of the main differences, of course, is that in France there's no poetry. This changes things. There isn't the counter-play and counter-balance. There's no time to re-group. The music has to do all the work. Sometimes that makes it seem like harder work, and I miss a little bit of poetical respite. At other times I think I'm putting more into the music, so it speaks for itself.

After all, I'm thinking, what does a poem like *Gabriel's Oboe* add to the music? Maybe it doesn't add anything. It's a subversion, a self-deprecating ironic diversion, a deflation, a distraction. A waste of space, perhaps. Who's to say?

Not all my poetry is quite so silly as this. Some of it is decidedly serious, even depressing. When I play *Carrickfergus*, and follow it with *I live in fear*, I have to be very careful. We need at the very least a friendly hand to hold after that. Maybe I'll play *Carrickfergus* later – we'll see how we go.

Well. If you think film music isn't quite dignified enough, or just a bit ephemeral, you're not going to be very impressed with this. Maybe you should skip to the next chapter, where with any luck I'll get to Langres, Dijon, maybe even Chalon. Though I need to check first which Chalon I'm heading for – sur-Marne, or sur-Saone?

What about the music to accompany a TV series? I'm not talking those jingles that run every day for forty years, like neighbours becoming good friends, even though they're irritating as a mosquito on a summer night. Yes, there is some ephemeral music here. But increasingly – it seems to me – there's real music. The whole industry knows it now. You can't sell a TV series without a good soundtrack. You can't sell a video game without it. If you think they're not listening, you're wrong. Or at least underestimating.

Benedict Cumberbatch and Martin Freeman made a great pair in the BBC series *Sherlock*. Mark Gatiss is a fabulous writer, which definitely helped. And Sir Arthur Conan Doyle shouldn't be forgotten in the roll of honour. But imagine it without the music. It ran to four seasons, albeit disappointingly short ones, and the music I'm going to play is from Series Three. It's the *Waltz for John and Mary*, from an episode called *The Sign of Three* – the music Sherlock Holmes plays on his violin for the wedding of his friend Dr. Watson.

If you know your Conan Doyle, you'll know that Sir Arthur's original was called *The Sign of Four*. Maybe the BBC didn't have the budget, and reduced it to three, or maybe there was a different point being made. A waltz is archetypal three-beat music. And there are three people involved in this.

Sherlock Homes didn't have friends, until John Watson came along. Dr Watson is his only friend. And then along comes Mary Morstan, to change John Watson's life. In the BBC series Holmes plays his own compositions on the violin, and Watson remarks that he isn't very good at cheerful music. So partly this is his attempt to write cheerful music. And partly it succeeds. A waltz is fundamentally an unthreatening thing – even in the hands of a Johann Strauss.

But like the three-beat music, there's a triangle here; a love triangle of sorts. You can see the fight within Holmes. He desperately wants to wish his friend unalloyed permanent happiness, and to do so from an unalloyed and pure generosity. And partly he succeeds. But underlying it you can hear the forlorn inner loneliness of the friendless man who found a friend and knows he's now losing him.

That's why, in my view, it's such good music. Music should never, I feel, communicate anything uncomplicatedly. It's beautiful, it's gentle, and it's happy; but it leaves us with an uncomfortable melancholy. It always leads me into a contemplation of my own loneliness – something this journey is rather underlining, with its daily meeting of new people, and its daily renunciation and moving on.

So when I have an English audience, I pair this beautiful Waltz with my most uncomplicatedly happy poem – wishing that sometimes, just sometimes, even if only for a day, we could be happily ever after.

Happily Ever After

He was the slam of my door,
the short of my fuse,
the sting at my tail,
and the flash to my point.

He was the spectre at my feast,
the cuckoo to my nest,
the snake in my grass –
the arse at my elbow.

He was the mote in my eye,
the plastic in my ocean,
the storm in my tea-cup,
the dark night in my soul.

205

But you – you are the Dark Knight of my shining,
the swell of my ocean,
the ginger in my tea,
and the tonic of my gin.

You are the leaves on my tree,
the apple in my eye;
you are the snow, and the beau, of my ball,
the feather to my nest.

you are the dew to my grass,
and the salve to my sore,
the moat to my castle,
and the beam to my face.

You are the lead to my pencil,
the ink to my well,
the truss to my roof,
and the thrust to my play,
the flash to my quick,
the tingle to my skin,
the short of my breath,
and the slam of my dunk.

You are my fairytale ending,
the happily of my ever after.

CHAPTER 29

No mustard in Dijon

FRIDAY 17 JUNE

After the concert at the United Protestant Church of France in Chaumont, and the splendid, convivial and highly restorative dinner in the garden – so much more than a picnic in the park – all organised by the friendly and redoubtable Evelyne, she handed me over to the care of Martine. I couldn't follow the conversation, but she seemed to be giving Martine lots of instruction for my proper care. Clearly someone who could go to the wrong Chaumont was not going to be generally expert at looking after himself.

Martine spoke little English, and my long-forgotten school French was exhausted. We walked the short way to her immaculate fifth floor flat in a companionable, smiley, silence. A cup of tea, a proper wash, and a comfortable, quiet, bed – three of the best things in any language.

Today is a real holiday. I'm cycling slowly, sometimes along the river, and sometimes along the canal that shadows it nearly all the way from Chaumont to Langres, counting the herons, and looking for places to swim. It's warm, and blue – by which I mean the sky as well as the canal. It's only thirty miles to Langres and I feel I've got all the time in the world. Elie, who rescued me yesterday, has made the arrangements in Langres – accommodation with a retired Scottish-French couple, and a concert in some unspecified venue.

So there's not a lot to worry about.

I divert from the canal every few miles to pedal around a quiet village, admire a church, and a *Mairie*, and anything else that is admirable. Luzy-sur-Marne, population 273; Foulain, population 687. Foulain has a very new shop, with coffee and Post Office, white walls and handmade rustic fittings. Perfect place to stop, where everyone coming in says *bonjour* to everyone already there.

Vesaignes-sur-Marne, population 101; Rolampont, population 1413; Humes-Jorquenay, population 579, up a small steep hill, the *Rue des Lilas*, to a little church with a view of Langres on another hill in the distance. And in between, a couple of leisurely swims, bread and cheese in the shade and maybe – I forget – a moment's shut-eye. You would think the summer must go on for ever here, but there are serious stacks of firewood that tell a different story.

The flatness comes to an abrupt and brutal end. Langres is set on a hill, 400ft above the canal – which is rather pedantically named the *Canal between Champagne and Bourgogne* – the main road, the railway and the Marne itself. It's a short road up, so it's very steep. It requires two stops. If the bike were lighter I could get off and push, but you can't push this great beast up a hill like this.

Langres is utterly beautiful. A long straight main street is lined with interesting and useful shops. One has several glossy magazines celebrating Queen Elizabeth's Jubilee, next to one featuring Liverpool United Football Club on its cover. How ignorant can you be? I thought it was just a bit of low news in the summer – *Liverpool in Colour*. It was no such thing. It was *Liverpool in Anger* – *colore*, not *couleur*. Well, I didn't know the French police had pepper-sprayed Liverpool fans at the Stade de France three weeks ago, and everyone – except the police – was saying it was the police's fault, not Liverpool's. If you knew about these things you would apparently know it was a special occasion. The other team was Spanish, and they'd insisted on the Stade de France being specially re-turfed with twenty-four refrigerated truckloads of Spanish turf for the occasion. And the press had been reporting from the day before that Liverpool fans would stage a pitch invasion, which I understand is frowned upon.

Well, I've been to Liverpool, so I'm not taking sides.

I've parked the bike, bought a brace – a splint – for this troublesome wrist, in one of the several pharmacies, shuddered at the fierce austerity of the former Jesuit College, eaten an ice cream and a few fresh apricots, and now I'm sitting in the shade watching the world go by at a leisurely pace whilst admiring the statue of Diderot. I need to sit for quite a while, because Diderot and the Jesuits are big subjects.

Diderot deserves more attention than he perhaps gets outside of France, and maybe Russia. When it comes to Enlightenment, he's one of the best. He was educated, and beaten, at the Jesuit College in Langres, the town of his birth. It was perhaps the Jesuits, trying to make him into one of their own, who made him instead a lawyer, and then an artist, a Bohemian, a philanderer, a writer and an atheist.

Diderot founded the *Encyclopédie* in 1751, at the age of thirty-eight. In these days of information on tap it's easy to underestimate how important the *Encyclopédie* was. It framed a new approach to the ordering and dissemination of knowledge. Diderot assembled a formidable cast of writers and researchers, and himself contributed more than seven thousand articles. Most of his team melted away in the face of ecclesiastical and official displeasure, and Diderot himself was imprisoned for the subversive and godless work. (He would like us to be reminded that his *Encyclopédie* predates the *Encyclopaedia Britannica* by seventeen years.)

Wonderfully – he wouldn't like it if we said *miraculously* – he was rescued by Catherine the Great, who summoned him to St. Petersburg, kept him there for five months, and made him discuss philosophy and rationalism with her nearly every day. Noting the lack of funds, and sympathy, from the French authorities, she bought his library – which, she said, was to remain in France until his death, when it could be brought to Russia – and appointed him, on a big salary, as its librarian. And just so that her intentions could not be misunderstood, she advanced the first fifty years of that salary.

I noted, incidentally, that the trouble-making Jesuits were expelled from France in 1762, five years before they were booted out of South America.

Then suddenly it's time to go and find my hosts, Elizabeth and Dominique, in an altogether splendid house with long views over the Marne valley. They designed and built the house themselves, in a tucked-away corner, thirty years ago, and it's the very definition of perfection.

"You could see a lot more water when we built it," Elizabeth tells me. "But you can't stop the trees growing on your neighbours' land, and soon we won't be able to see the river at all. We're too old to move, though."

Half an hour later, Elie is here with his van, to take us all to the concert. I've no idea where it is, or what to expect, but I'm just going with the flow and hoping the wrist will hold out. Elie used to be a monk – possibly a Jesuit, though I'm not going to ask, just in case – but he gave it up in order to fall in love and marry. At least I think that's the story. He's not *persona non grata* in the Catholic Church, though, because here we are in some sort of Diocesan building, setting up in a fine, high-ceilinged room with a bright acoustic, where the audience is already helping itself to chairs and setting them up around three sides of it.

I don't know where to position myself in the face of a three-sided audience, but we work something out, and I set to. Elizabeth is willing to translate my introductions and general trivia, in her beautiful Scottish accent which, she says, she's given up telling people isn't English.

In the morning I take the long way down the hill from Langres, to rejoin the canal further South. But they haven't got as far as this with the cycle-surfacing of the canal path, and it's rough and stony, slow and unsuitable. So I wave goodbye to the water, and revert to some proper roads. It's a good thing it's flat. The weather is getting seriously warm – thirty-six degrees today – and I think the accumulating tiredness is more than I'm giving it credit for. I'm not such a young fellow, after all.

I haven't gone more than thirty miles on the road, through a litany of beautiful but not over-active villages – Cohons (isn't that a rude word?), Heuilley-Cotton (presumably the kind of rag you use on a bicycle), Villegusien, Danmarien, Cusey, Sacquenay, and the best of them all, Chazeuil, where my front wheel falls off – when I begin to miss the canal.

The falling-off of the front wheel was a surprise, and an inconvenience. I was lifting the bike onto the pavement, and the wheel just stayed behind. It wasn't serious – I wasn't riding down the middle of a busy road at the time – and it's an easy matter to put a wheel back into its forks and tighten the quick-release mechanism. But I shouldn't have allowed it to get loose without noticing. And it isn't so easy when you've got such a fully-loaded bike. I was thankful for the shuttering of hot French houses, though – no-one to giggle out of a window.

The reason I was missing the canal wasn't the hills. They were gentle, and just as much down as up. It was the absence of water. It's getting hot again, and a little dip would be just the thing.

As though the landscape is reading my mind, suddenly there's water. A beautiful lake, the Perte de la Venelle, right beside the D28. It must be a weekend spot – there are trees in organised rows, a couple of picnic tables, and a lone camping fisherman on the far side.

The willow-clad island in the middle is perfect for swimming around, far enough from the fisherman not to disturb. Perhaps I'll even lie in the sun for a while (it turns out to be a very short while – it's very hot) and then swim again…

I'm getting out of the warm green water the second time when a low-slung but once-expensive French car comes dustily down the track from the road, a bit too fast, and stops beside the bike propped up on the picnic table. The man getting out of it, leaving the door open in an unmistakably aggressive gesture, wants to speak to me. Swimming, he says, is Not Allowed. Why not, I wonder, in a place clearly designated for leisure? Security, he says. "If the police come, they will give you a ticket. Only they might not because you're a foreigner. Read the Notice."

I did read the notice, on my way back to the road. It said *Private Property please take your litter home*.

The mystery is two-fold – why he wanted to prevent the swimming, and how he knew I was there. I couldn't be seen from the road, and his visit was clearly purposeful rather than *ad hoc*.

The miles go quickly by when you're trying to solve a mystery. By lunchtime I've reached St. Julien. There's a very shady bench, with a view of the church – unusually not old in any way – and a war memorial, and a little parade of children going home from school.

There's also a restaurant, with a very new-looking marquee over its equally new-looking asphalt. This outside space is packed, with a happy mix of – I'm guessing – local retirees and hi-vis workers (presumably from the business-like plant parked up on the green).

It looks a perfect place for a *pop-up* performance, but the *patron* says she doesn't have a licence, and it wouldn't be allowed. This is France, and there are rules.

Yes, rules, like the no-swimming rule. Like the rules of the road, which are scrupulously observed here now. Not like I remember Paris, when I came to see the Renoirs at the Tuilleries as a student. Cars actually stop when instructed by road markings to do so, even if it's clear there's no other vehicle within a mile. And they don't try to push past bicycles when there isn't quite enough room. They're polite, and sober, with very few exceptions, mostly open-topped. Even that most lawless of cars, the 2CV, though few and far between now, is no longer lawless. I'm generalising from a low base here – I've only actually seen one, which looked as though its current driver had had it from new, and was driving with the discretion appropriate to both its age and his.

Dijon is a city in crisis. And it's not just Dijon – the whole of France is in the grip of it. The French way of life – this is hardly an exaggeration – is under threat. Without Dijon mustard, *la moutarde de Dijon*, you can't make a proper *vinaigrette*, or *mayonnaise*, or a *steak tartare*. And they've run out. The shelves are empty. It's no good telling them the English make a very good mustard. That would be on a par with claiming the English make perfectly good lovers.

Dijon, as a result, is in disgrace. Quietly, without telling anyone, they'd stopped growing the important brown and black mustard plants, and bought it all in from the Canadian prairies. Which is fine, until a drought in Alberta and Saskatchewan halves the crop, and the French, mortifyingly, find they're not at the front of the queue. This is what Isabelle is telling me, to explain the hunted look in Dijon's once-pretty streets, its residents scuttling like rats out of the limelight. I told her I thought Dijon looked very fine in the summer sun, but she sidled off, shaking her head, and muttering about *les Anglais*, and what did they know about *la moutarde?*

I parked up outside the Beaux Arts museum and played on a bench in the shade. Libre was hardly warmed up though, before – I couldn't believe it – a Punjabi Bhangra band came out to do a wedding. Libre will compete with some things, but not with a phalanx of *dhols*. So I moved on. After I'd said *bonjour* to the cyclists I'd met near Essoyes the other day, now strolling around with ice cream as though it were nearly the weekend, I stopped by the cathedral to listen to Bademba playing the kora.

He wasn't getting much attention, which was a pity because he played beautifully. He was, he said, a professor of music, and he liked to play on the street, where few of his audience had seen a kora before. Well – a Senegalese kora, and a Punjabi Bhangra band, both on the streets of Dijon, a little city that had once been the seat of the Dukes of Burgundy, and was now in disgrace for its mustard failure, on a Friday afternoon.

Bademba was about to pack up, he said, so maybe I'll play here, in the shadow of the cathedral, rather than further down, among the sunny crowds. I like the idea of making music in the wake of Indian Bhangra and African kora. So I play for an hour, occasionally distracted by the absorbing re-arrangement of the window display in the fashion shop opposite, until it was time to go and seek out my *Warmshowers* hosts a couple of miles out of town. I've been wearing the Langres brace most of the day today, and it seems to have done some good.

I made sure to leave enough time to pay my proper respects to St. Benignus, local martyr and patron saint of Dijon, for whom the cathedral is named. I wouldn't like it on my conscience if I'd played outside *three* cathedrals without venturing in.

CHAPTER 30

A thousand miles from home

SATURDAY 18 JUNE

Warmshowers does not discourage eccentricity. I suppose if your constituency is round-the-world cyclists, you're not really going to fill your books if you only accept rigorously conventional applicants. So when you knock on a front door, or push your bike through a back gate, looking for your *Warmshowers* host, you need to keep an open mind as to who, exactly, you might meet.

I'm sitting at a kitchen table in Claire and Youri's house. But I haven't met either of them. The kitchen, in another self-built but definitely unfinished house, looks like the office of a revolutionary organisation that has just received a tip-off of an imminent raid and been vacated in a great hurry. There are old revolutionary posters, revolutionary books, revolutionary chaos, and the remnants of revolutionary food.

Youri and Claire were on their way back from Lausanne, they told me, where they'd been attending a conference – which they said was academic, but which I'm guessing was probably revolutionary – and I should just make myself at home. They seemed surprised that I should wonder aloud how I might do that, when they weren't there to let me in. "Just go through the front door," Claire said. "It's open."

The bathroom, an idiosyncratic work of improvised revolutionary art, doesn't have an instruction manual, and I can't work out how to

215

flush the loo. But I do find hot water, so I wash some clothes, make a cup of tea, and sit down at the table to await my hosts.

Claire and Youri, when they arrive a couple of hours later than promised, and a trumpet-playing daughter, are as open and welcoming as their lovely house.

The conversation, I confess, is more academic than revolutionary, but I reckon it could have gone either way. And when I eventually bed down in the basement, Youri is quite vague about how many people might be in the house later. A couple of names are mentioned, and at least one of these other beds would almost certainly be occupied by a young African refugee in the morning. The openness of their never-locked house is an order of magnitude beyond anything I've known before.

There are pros and cons to a headwind at thirty-seven Celsius. You need quite a bit of wind to achieve any kind of cooling effect, and to combat the waves of pizza-oven heat rolling up off the road. But it increases the effort required, and therefore the loss of water. I find it hard to take in enough liquid to replace what's lost. So I've learnt to keep an eye out for little supermarkets – which are always very discreetly hidden – to buy a litre of juice, and down it in one.

I'm not using the GPS thingy, because it's in a sulk again. If it really wanted to provoke, to prove its indispensability, it would have looked at the route and worked out it was going to be fairly superfluous today anyway. I'm in wine country again, which means a fairly well-defined valley, nothing much that's high enough to obscure a view, and lots and lots and lots of little un-trafficked roads between the vineyards. Would you call them roads, or are they just tracks? If you make the right judgement you're rewarded with smooth emptiness. If your choice is wrong, the way quickly deteriorates into dusty stony impassibility.

But the country is so open you can see well ahead, and usually make the right call. And if your judgement is wrong, well, it's never more than a hundred yards to another junction and a different choice. And we're between two main roads – one in the valley below and one higher up, so it's easy to keep to the right general direction.

This area claims to have more wine tourists than Champagne has, and there are plenty of signs for various routes *Grand Cru,* and names you recognise from the wine shelves of your favourite local supermarket.

I stopped at Nuits St. Georges for coffee. I sat in the shade of a big umbrella, between two well-padded e-bikers and a three-generation French family, the two older generations of which were arguing loudly while the youngest swung their feet under the table in silent embarrassment.

I waved off the e-bikers, and then leapfrogged them several times as we employed the same navigational strategy through the vineyards, making variously better and worse decisions at each junction.

The last time I saw them, they were deciding to view the collections of old aeroplanes at the Chateau de Savigny-les-Beaune. I was deciding not to. It's a very pretty chateau, built around three sides of a courtyard, with four lovely round towers in a beautiful pale stone, with the vineyards right up to the back wall. The windows are small, though, which suggests a turbulent history, and the rooms are now full – I heard the e-bikers saying – of motorcycles, tractors, and important old Fiat prototypes.

The town of Beaune, a bit further on, is a gem. There's an enormous market on a Saturday, and the whole world is here, in holiday mood. A good place to play some Bach, and a few dances. And a good place to buy cheese, and apricots, and black bread – and a thousand other presumably edible exotic and expensive things that look mouldy on the outside so must be divine on the inside.

I was intending to bike another hour after Beaune before lunch, but when I saw water I was of course distracted. The road is on a dyke between two broad lakes. The bigger one looks rather windswept, but the other, with more trees, and some wiggly walkways around it, just looks warm and inviting. Black bread and liquid cheese on the grass in the shade after a very warm swim.

It really is extremely hot now. After lunch the bike seems to have developed a Rice Krispies noise – there's a crackle from somewhere low down as I cycle on the hot black road. I stop a couple of times to try to locate the source of the noise, and see whether it portends trouble ahead if it isn't fixed. Then I work it out. Tiny bubbles of boiling asphalt are popping under the tyres.

It's not far to Chalon-sur-Saone. There are muscles in these legs now, after three weeks; so fifty miles of moderately flat land – even into a hot headwind – doesn't seem like so much. The *Mairie* has allocated me a place to play, in Chalon-sur-Saone, but when I ride through it I don't really like the look of it. Like so many city places it's too big, and too noisy, for a lone cello. I played enough in lovely Beaune anyway, so why bother?

So instead I opt for ice cream and tea. Why do you look surprised? It's the perfect combination for a hot day. The *salon de thé* was wonderfully pretentious, with prices to match, but the teapots were big, and they seemed to understand that tea needs properly boiling water. They give me a tray, with a triad of egg-timers, which they explain registered three, five and seven minutes respectively. *For this tea, monsieur, we recommend three minutes precisely*, they say gravely. I nod, with the same respectful gravity, to indicate I would not transgress in the matter of timing the tea.

I was intending to go a bit further, since I've no accommodation in Chalon. Whether it was the tea, or the ice cream, or the heat, I don't know, but after sitting for half an hour I find myself completely disinclined to cycle on. I look for a hotel. I cycle gently down to the wide Saone river, and think maybe Chalon isn't such a bad place. In fact it's quite attractive.

The Villa Boucicaut is tucked away and hard to find. I follow the map and end up in a dodgy-looking back street. This can't be right. This is a very short-stay hotel, where you don't bring your own companion. The Villa Boucicaut was somewhere else entirely. I find it on the third attempt. It has a little garden, which might be nice later. And it's officially *Acceuil Velo*, which means cyclists get their washing done for them.

Laure in reception, seeing the cello, suggests a concert later, in the lobby-cum-salon, for the guests. She presumes I've come to Chalon to scope it out for next month's street performance festival. I can't tell if she's offended, or just surprised, that I don't know about Chalon's street performance festival. The town is home to the *National Centre for Street Arts and Public Space*, she tells me, and for five days in July Chalon becomes a seething cauldron of open-air art and entertainment – like Edinburgh, but all outside, and much better, if not yet quite so big.

"Come back for it," she suggests, looking at me – I thought, perhaps – more directly than a casual friendliness required.

She was giving me, she said, the biggest room, and charging me for the smallest. Ten minutes later there is a conference notice board in the lobby advertising the concert, and an hour and a half after that Libre is doing her best in front of a very appreciative, though select, audience. Laure herself is there, in between a couple of brief exits to answer the phone, for which she apologised volubly afterwards, transfixing me with those sparkly eyes.

Afterwards, wondering if it was regret I was feeling that I hadn't asked her to come with me, I walk out alone to find a quiet restaurant to mark the moment of being a thousand miles from home. My energetic waiter, Bek, said he was an Uzbek from Samarkhand. We talk about his beautiful, romantic, city, and I leave him a large and not completely sober tip.

When I get back to the Villa Boucicaut, the reception is dark and Laure has gone. I thought about playing Sinatra's *Strangers in the Night*, imagining in some silly way it might bring her back. But it's late, and it would just have disturbed the other guests, and spoiled the day.

CHAPTER 31

A heavenly grotto

MONDAY 20 JUNE

Twenty-three days and a thousand miles from home. I said yesterday that fifty miles was now easy, with these leg muscles that I soon won't be able to get my trousers on over.

That was a premature claim.

I had fried eggs for breakfast in the Villa Boucicaut in Chalon-sur-Saone. I had friendly greetings, requests for cello-on-a-bike photos, and for CDs, from last night's audience. But there was no reason to delay. Laure was busily absorbed. It was time to go, across the wide Saone, and further South, into the wind.

According to the weather app the wind was 40mph and rising. The temperature, 36C and rising. I'm riding into the wind, into the sun. My mother used to say I was a delicate flower and today, in the face of this onslaught, I'm wilting.

Libre, sticking out behind me, acts like a sail. It's not her fault, but it's not safe going uphill at 6mph, and it's simply dangerous going downhill at 20mph. The roads are getting hillier. I'm not beset by rules, as French drivers now seem to be, but as a guide I aim to go one-third of the day's distance before a proper cake stop, and two-thirds before a proper lunch stop. But on some days that's just impossible, and I've already had one unscheduled pause for recovery before coffee in Cuisery.

I'm coasting downhill towards the river, hot and cross, and deaf because of the roaring wind, past the Rue d'Arquebus, and the Place d'Armes, thinking what a military place this must be, when I spot the Rue des Livres. On the map it's called Grande Rue, but on the street itself it's Rue des Livres. And when everything else is shut and sleeping, on a Sunday morning, this street is a throng of commercial activity. Every shop, apart from the *bistrot*, is a second-hand bookshop, and many of them are spilling out onto the hot windy street.

The patron of the *Librairie Charabias* – which I think translates as the *Gobbledygook Bookshop* – who looks like a character from Middle Earth, all beard and oddly dressed, is sitting at the table next to me, keeping an eye on his shop and entertaining his friends. He's very good at judging the people wandering into the shop. If they're not going to buy anything he stays where he is. If they're going to make a purchase, he excuses himself and goes to attend them. How does he know? Or does his simple presence turn browsers into purchasers?

I should get going. The wind is strengthening further. The four friends lean into each other over the table and confer. *Monsieur*, the *patron* of the *librairie* says, as I'm turning the bike, *we thought you might play for us*.

So, Fauré, Bach, and then, by special request, *God Save the Queen*. He stood up as I began to play that, and I thought he was standing up for the Queen. But he wasn't; he'd seen some customers and he was going to make a sale.

I press on, hot and tired. There aren't many roads here, so there's no choice of route. There's no shelter from the wind. It's straight; it would be fast in a car. I find myself longing for the trucks that whoosh past at speed, providing an instant's respite from the wind.

By the time I reach Mantenay-Montlin I think I'm suffering delusions and hallucinations. I have to battle a strong urge to turn round and go the other way, just so that I can feel the wind behind me. I'm so exhausted I think I would have cried if I hadn't been too exhausted to do so. I stop at the summit of a long, low, pointless and dispiriting climb to wonder at Mantenay-Montlin's silver chicken.

It stands in the middle of a raised flower bed, beside the road, its tail feathers erect and displayed in the direction of Mantenay-Montlin's unremarkable church. It's a truly magnificent rooster, a *coq magnifique*, big enough to be a Trojan horse. Who needs a *coq* that big, I wondered? The rooster is a symbol of France, of course, along with – on the Ministry of *Affaires Étrangères'* list – the Marseillaise, Bastille Day, the *tricouleur*, and Marianne. It became particularly important in the First War, when it was a cartoonist's gift – the Gallic rooster standing up to the Prussian eagle. The Ministry explains modestly that it stands for a "France sprung from peasant origins, proud, opinionated, courageous and prolific".

My experience of roosters, having had one at home to look after half a dozen hens, is that they make a lot of unnecessary noise, attack people without provocation, and have an unreconstructed sense of entitlement.

The road carries on – there's a limit to how long a break you can justify for a fat silver chicken – straight, and hot, and windy. There's no shelter; there's nowhere to stop. The road now seems to be on a ridge, with the country falling away on both sides. In the distance, down below, I can see water between the trees. I'm past caring that a diversion will mean a climb back up to the road. I need to be in that water, out of this wind.

I go in, in all my clothes. I don't so much swim as drift. There's a stern notice that forbids swimming anyway, as well as *all kinds of boating, for safety reasons*. I didn't feel too unsafe, though perhaps I should have done. This isn't just an arbitrary rule, I discover afterwards; the lake at Montrevel-en-Bresse is a place where they exercise and train sea-planes. In my lake-wet clothes I eat cheese, and the garlic-fried potatoes I bought earlier at a village fête.

My body temperature reduced to normal, and feeling almost restored, I go back up the hill in my freshly re-soaked clothes, aiming for the supermarket I'd noted on the way down. Obviously it's shut; it's Sunday afternoon.

But McDonalds, nearby, is open. They can't sell me a litre of juice, but in their air-conditioned departure lounge they can do a pretty tall coffee. Until that moment I hadn't really believed that only America has more McDonalds per head of population than France. Why would you eat hamburgers in the land of *coq-au-vin*? But this coffee is as good as it gets, anywhere.

I stagger into Bourg-en-Bresse, late, and find a hotel. I can hardly get up the steps to the front door. I lie down on the bed, to gather enough strength to go out to eat. But the strength never comes. I'm too tired to eat anyway. Surely tomorrow will be a better day.

A bad day, a day to forget, is generally followed by a good day, a day to remember. So I'm getting up optimistically, a bit light-headed from hunger, but looking to remedy that without delay. Today the French hills start. Not yet quite Alps, of course, but precursors, preparation, warnings.

The wind has blown itself out overnight, and the stillness is wonderful.

Today's route looks good, too. The map shows proper twists and turns, meanders, wiggles, changes of heart. A complete contrast to yesterday's relentless straightness, straight into the wind. Progress always seems slower on a straight road – you can see too far ahead, and the landscape changes too gradually. On the kind of roads the map promises for today, every bend and corner is a revelation. The view is quite different when a feature moves from your right to your left, when a hill appears suddenly in front of you, instead of advancing towards you for half an hour. That lack of warning is like a kind of spontaneity, even caprice. Hills are easier when they don't loom.

So I'm impatient with breakfast, watching through the window the cyclists already on the road. These aren't lycra-leisure cyclists, though, they're going to work. There seem to be a lot of cyclists in Bourg-en-Bresse. I'm looking forward to overtaking them.

The legs are heavy this morning, and it's hard to get going. But I loosen up on the main road out of Bourg, then plunge off into a glorious French countryside. Suddenly I'm light-headed with a completely different light-headedness from yesterday's hunger and exhaustion. There's just a shadow memory of that, a kind of open-mouthed sense of wonder that I got through it, a kind of release-from-prison feeling. I want to shout, just because I'm alive.

Given a choice between a 40mph headwind and a long slog uphill, I'm going to choose the hill. Every time. The real hills, up to Hauteville – there's a clue in the name – aren't until after the Ain river crossing, but I'm excited about them, rather than intimidated. Hills are all in the head anyway, remember?

I'm hurtling downhill, overtaking a bevy of touring cyclists, towards the little bridge over the Ain river at Poncin, fifteen miles into the day. Before the crossing the road goes under a fabulous soaring viaduct carrying the A40. The main span of the pre-stressed concrete is more than 150 meters. How is it possible to make concrete in such lengths, and so graceful?

A quick five miles, and suddenly the road is overcome with a fit of the wiggles. I look at the map. It's a hieroglyphic across the landscape, snaking upwards. In total, the GPS thingy counsels, I'm going to climb just over four thousand feet today. *Bring it on*, I want to shout at all the road signs telling me I have to have snow tyres between November and April. Where's this bravura coming from? Presumably it's a pendulum overreaction to yesterday's misery. Don't knock it.

The French know how to make hill roads. They would rather climb at a steady 6%, even if it means a convoluted route around all the points of the compass, than a head-on assault at a 20% slope. Not like the English, who are far too Cartesian when it comes to hills, and maintain – sometimes against all common sense – that the shortest distance between two points is always a straight line.

A lot of the day's four thousand feet is on well-wooded and shady routes. In truth I'm plodding, rather than racing, up. But I have got forty-four kilos of cello-on-a-bike, and I need strength for a two-set concert later, so shut up, OK?

And if you plod, without stopping, you get there in the end. Sometimes even before you expect to. Sometimes even before the racers, who might get distracted. Aesop wrote a story about it. *Col de la Berche, 864m*, says the sign. It's a tiddler, of course; that's not even three thousand feet. But it's quite a long way up from the Ain river at Poncin, in the temperatures, and with the forty-four kilos, that you already know about. Hauteville itself isn't spectacularly beautiful, but there's a fine view from the sunny bench in front of the church. Though of course you don't see so much of the view when you're lying down with your eyes shut.

I'm going to stay with Serge tonight. I've never met him, but in these out of the way places you can sometimes find a friend of a friend, if you look hard enough, or if you've got very widely connected friends. He has sent me a message to say an audience has been summoned for this evening, so if the mountains are too much, and I need rescuing, I must definitely call him. He'll come with the van, and no-one need know. Maybe word has got around.

But no, no rescue is needed, thank you. I've just got to get over the *Col de la Lebé, 914m*, which I calculate to be 2999ft. I left the bike at that height, and jumped another foot, so I could say I'd reached three thousand.

I arrived at Serge's house on the dot of the estimated time, having been diverted a mile or two by some surfacing work that's turned the road into a lake of impassable tar.

Serge's house – the address says it's a "grotto" – is hard to find, but a neighbour in her garden directs me. It's a place of artistry and endeavour, of ancient-beamed ceilings and thick stone walls, with a newly-constructed hemp cob summerhouse in the garden and a three-hundred-year-old communal bread oven on the road outside.

There's a little concrete pool, which Serge excavated and lined himself, with water bubbling up at a cooling twenty-six degrees, where the wasps come to drink. Apple pies are cooking, and there's proper tea to drink. I'm drying off after a dip, late in the afternoon, when the sun gives just the warmth you want and not any more, looking up at the nearest hill, which Serge says is legendary in local cycling circles because you can go up it three times in one day by different routes.

I didn't tell him I once went up Hartside six times in a day.

Serge's garden is beautiful – though his raspberries are small for lack of water – and, five minutes before the concert, he's shaking me gently awake. Chairs are set out under a gazebo in the garden, and there's a table set with drinks and the apple pies. More chairs have had to be brought, then more again, as more and more people arrive. In the end there are seven times the number he'd expected.

I couldn't have warmed up – by which I mean played a few scales – beforehand anyway. The bowing wrist is too painful. I'm going to have to play with the splint on it, which is not ideal. I've learned that the carefully-programmed sets I performed in England should give way to the inspiration of the moment, and the look of the audience. The Second Movement is, I shouldn't forget, a set of variations on the First.

All in a Garden Green, a bouncy Tudor tune, seems like a good starting point, with the kids running about the garden in a different world from the rest of us clustered around the gazebo.

The apple pies are eaten and the wine drunk in the interval. The sun goes slowly behind the hill and, even when a sudden gust blows the music stand over, the music goes on uninterrupted. I do play *Strangers in the Night*, even though I promised myself I wouldn't, and I finish with the *Ashokan Farewell*, explaining that I would be sorry to leave Valserhone.

There are lots of positive things about a journey. There's progress, there's discovery, there's adventure. And so on. But every moving on is also a leaving behind. Human beings are adapted to stability, staying put. We gave up the itinerant imperative when we stopped being hunter-gathers and took up agriculture, however many thousands of years ago that was. Moving on is moving into the unknown, with all its risks and dangers.

The rolling stone gathers no moss, etc., etc. But it does tend to bump into things. And the more things you bump into, the higher the chances that sooner or later one of them will hit back.

So the further I go, and the hotter it gets, and the bigger the hills, the wearier I find myself. And I don't think the weariness is just physical. It's mental and emotional. I'm a long way from home, and every day is another Farewell.

Mind you, it could be worse. It could be a lot worse. Jay Ungar wrote *Ashokan Farewell* at the end of one of his musical summer camps of that name. The name reminds us there used to be a village called Ashokan, just down the hill. It's not there anymore, not even in a theoretical, or a dead, way. It was flooded out of existence in 1913 to create the Ashokan Reservoir, to supply water to those thirsty folks in New York City. Ashokan, along with ten other villages, wasn't just emptied of its residents. It was demolished. Even its dead were dug up and carted away.

Afterwards, Serge makes a little speech of thanks to the Highway Cellist, and to the audience which, he points out, ranges in age from four weeks to a little over eighty, and no-one seems in any hurry to vacate the Elysian space.

Eventually they drift away, some of the smaller ones sleep-walking or carried, and we can clear up, and eat Serge's pasta and salad, outside in the dark.

His friend Solen, who lives just the other side of the hill, has stayed for dinner, and we talk about working in Geneva, and giving it up to live in this beautiful place, and running a small-scale musical and artistic association, and inviting people to come and be ayurvedically healed in the grotto – which is a kind of agricultural crypt under the house – and Serge plays his guitar and sings in the dark. We eat some of the insufficiently watered raspberries, finish the wine, and gently drift into the night.

CHAPTER 32

La Fête de la Musique

TUESDAY 21 JUNE

Serge sends me off early with a very good breakfast. There's a long way to go, and a couple of big hills early on.

The first one starts ten miles away, and I think I should try to get to the top before the nine o'clock heat.

It's one of those hills where you use a variety of strategies. Like how many pedal turns to achieve a hundred feet of elevation. At first it's two hundred, which is reasonably comfortable. Then it's a hundred and sixty, which isn't. This is the Col de la Chambotte. I'm not quite sure what counts as a *col*, and what's just a hill. But there's a cyclists' website which gives you gruellingly precise statistics on every *col* you might ever want to climb in France on a bicycle. I'm glad I didn't know about it until afterwards. If I'd studied the form I would have known it just gets steeper and steeper.

The view of the lake below widens out. The Lac du Bourget is periodically the biggest in France, though today its water is very far below any high-water mark. There's a great gash of bare beach most of the way round. The overhanging cliffs get more spectacular, more threatening. There are signs warning of rock falls, and there's a big digger tidying up after one of them. Maybe you'd hear a rock fall coming and have time to throw yourself against the cliff. You'd probably survive.

I'm nearly at the top. It's not much more than a Hartside really

– I don't know what I was making a fuss about. A pale blue car that's clearly seen a number of French summers is trying to drive beside me, gesticulating Frenchly. This is risky for both of us – the road is narrow, with a few sudden and narrower tunnels, and the occasional hairpin bend, and a few freewheeling vehicles coming the other way. Somehow I know it will pull in when there's more space and wait for me. I don't mind a good excuse to stop.

Fillou is very excited to see me. "Come for breakfast at the top of the hill! We're musicians, too, and we also travel by bicycle," he shouts. "But I've never seen anything like this! Respect!"

How could I refuse such an invitation, even so soon after breakfast? So I pedal sternly to the top of the *col*, which is a little further than I would have liked it to be when I'm showing off to Fillou how quickly I ascend these little hills.

Fillou has waited. He sets off, along a rocky dirt track, and I'm expected to follow. By the time he has to abandon the overworked car and strike out across a field, I'm beginning to have second thoughts. I think Fillou senses my hesitation. He takes hold of the bike, to push it himself, and cheer us on.

Soon it's like entering a Robin Hood enchantment. There are caravans among the trees – though I can't imagine how they got there – clearings with fire circles and old arm chairs, and what looks like a few bodies in sleeping bags.

Fillou is summoning the merry men, and a couple of women, and by the time we reach his yurt at the end of the encampment, it's generally come to life.

It's a beautiful yurt, big, well-organised, with a proper wooden floor, a serious stove, and enough insulation to survive a winter in the hills.

Everyone seems to be helping themselves to breakfast in a sleepy way, and there's general consternation – search parties are dispatched – that the English visitor should have proper coffee, and not their usual decaffeinated apology.

So while they're doing that, I go back to the parked-up bike and fetch Libre. We play an Irish lament, and the *Song of the Birds*, by which time nearly a dozen young musicians have materialised, with their instruments – including a souzaphone – and I can drink the proudly-found caffeinated coffee to the accompaniment of a half-dressed New Orleans sound. There's something anarchic and wild, almost prelapsarian, about it all. The music is free, and although it wouldn't be polite to ask if the love is free too, these people really could be a bunch of medieval outlaws, hidden away – just making occasional musical raids into the towns and villages, and then retreating to their hideouts.

They call themselves *Les Oiseaux de Trottoir* – *The Sidewalk Birds* – because that's where they mostly play. Sometimes there are twenty of them, which would quite block the *trottoir*, I imagine.

But I must on. There's another hill to climb, and it's more than sixty miles to Albertville, via a lake which will have to be swum in, and where, due to a mistake, I've two concerts to play.

So reluctantly I'm taking my leave of *Les Oiseaux*. Fillou walks me back to the *col* road, and waves me off down the hill, which is only slightly less terrifyingly steep going down this side as it was coming up the other. But I'm laughing out loud, into the wind, at the absurdity of such an encounter, in the foothills of the serious mountains.

I was expecting the population to be thinning out, fifteen hundred feet above sea level, but it isn't. There are lots of densely-inhabited villages and small towns on this scenic route. The most scenic is Annecy, at the foot of Lake Annecy.

Lake Annecy isn't quite as big as Lake Bourget, so it has to claim a different distinction. At 1446ft above sea level it claims to be the cleanest lake in France. You can certainly believe that when you see it; it's beautiful, with serious mountains on the other side, from which hang-gliders are descending in droves.

There's also a magnificent cycle path along the lake, fast and flat. Well, flat anyway. It would be fast if there weren't quite so many cycles on it. All the way from Valserhone to Annecy, thirty miles,

I saw two other bikes. Now, in a couple of miles, I've counted two hundred. Why am I counting bikes? I don't know. I'll stop.

I'm looking for a place to swim. There are little beaches, and grassy places full of families in swimming attire. But by the time I decide it's time to stop at one of them, the cycle path has diverted from the shore, and there's no way back. Not until I reach the southern tip of the lake, and the clearly very busy restaurant *Chez ma Cousine*, is lake access restored. So I've leant my bike up against a notice by the car park that forbids parking to non-users of the restaurant, and out of the corner of my eye I can see a red-faced, apron-clad, gentleman waddling across the car park in my direction.

I can't park there, he says, unless I'm coming for lunch. By which he clearly meant he didn't want anyone as scruffy-looking as me in his restaurant. He is taken aback when I just laugh. It wasn't an intentionally rude response – it just seemed an absurd thing to worry about a bicycle on the grass beside his car park. Then I remember some of the things I worry about, so I apologise and move it. He retreats, pleased at the effect of his authority.

I swim, among the ducks and coots, in sight of the restaurant and the little boats, in the clear warm water. Afterwards I lie in the sun, on a pontoon that is probably at least as private as the restaurant parking, and count the hang gliders. None of them, it seems, is very expert. A trained hang-glidist stays airborne sometimes for days. Some of these look more like parachutists, trying to get to ground as quickly as possible without being shot. So I reckon it isn't a hang-gliding club, populated by people who know what they're doing. It must be a commercial enterprise, sending novices over the cliff for a big fee and making its money by a swift throughput of customers.

Ten minutes later, when I go off route to follow the signs to a small supermarket, I see the field where they're collecting the gliders and ferrying them back up the hill. It's a slick operation, with everything done in an efficient hurry. They must have a queue of customers at the top, and I calculate their daily turnover in the thousands.

The lakeside cycle track continues, mostly unremarkably, to Albertville. Like a lot of afternoon cycling it's just a bit further than anticipated. Still, I'm too early to meet Clotilde. We are to rendezvous in the Place Commandant Bulle, from where she will take me to their house.

Today, 21 June, is *La Fête de la Musique* in France, a day of general musical mayhem. And in Albertville I am commissioned to be part of it. I'm to play an hour's performance somewhere in the medieval enclave of Conflans, up the hill, followed by a sober performance in a church in the lower part of town.

I'm hoping that a couple of crêpes and cups of tea will fortify me. But I'd rather be lying down. It's been a long hot ride. There's a lot of activity in town, as a variety of uniformed and un-uniformed officials try to keep the traffic at bay long enough to close the roads for the *Fête*. I've parked the bike against a road-closing barrier close to the *crêperie*, and the police aren't at all sure about it. I've watched a lot of consultation, and gesticulating, and radioing, and general looking-around for inspiration, until it feels like the right time to forestall any dramatic or irreversible intervention.

We don't want it blocking our emergency vehicles, they explain. So I negotiate another five minutes and promise to move it. In that five minutes the restaurant next to the *crêperie* manages to erect an awning right across the road that might need emergency vehicle access, and has begun to fill it with tables and chairs. The police ignore it.

Clotilde comes to find me in the Place Commandant Bulle, as arranged. The house is just here, she says, pointing to what looks like the town hall behind me. It's a small palace really, with a *tricouleur* flying from the royal balcony. It goes with the job, she explains, Christophe being the Sub-Prefect – a semi-political role that's impossible to explain in any English terms.

I don't want to boast, but it really is a big house. I've never been on a royal balcony before, under a national flag, overlooking the square, and the populace. I'm practising my royal wave. The stairs, polished stone with a wrought iron banister, are two meters wide. There are thirty of them between the ground floor and the first-floor balcony. You really don't want to forget what you went upstairs for.

There's time for a swift turnaround, before the drive up to the medieval enclave at the top of the hill. I'm to play in the square, which is beginning to come to life. A twenty-piece jazz band in red shirts is to follow, but we can't stay to listen because we're expected at St. Jean Baptiste. The *Fête de la Musique* is being celebrated on the street, with five highly amplified stages, and huge crowds. Even at St. Jean there's a respectable number, to listen to a guitar, the church organ, and a travelling cello.

Suddenly I'm overcome with the exhaustion of two days' hot and hilly riding – I've climbed eight thousand feet altogether over the last two days. And there's the accumulated exhaustion of two weeks' steady progress through France.

Don't misunderstand me – I'm not eight thousand feet higher up than I was two days ago. Cyclists only record the uphill, and not the downhill in between. So I'm not that much higher above sea level, and there are some seriously big climbs to come.

So when Christophe suggests it might be time for a rest day, and there is no reason I shouldn't stay with them another night, I don't have to think about it for very long.

I've also looked at the onward route more carefully, and I'm wondering where the earlier miscalculation was. I thought there was a climb of four thousand feet just ahead. But now it turns out it's six thousand. And the GPS thingy kindly shows the gradients, which aren't friendly.

I definitely couldn't do that without a rest first. Even the Tour de France has a couple of rest days, I've been reminded more than once. There's no certainty I could do it even after a rest day.

The wonderful Neil and Marie have already studied the map,

decided it's impossible, at least for a man of my age and general puniness, and driven halfway across France to rescue me. We've packed a tent, they said, and a bike rack, some tools and a medical kit; you'll need all of that.

And now they're camped up on the outskirts of Albertville, on a nice campsite by the river. So I can't just ride off into the sunrise and leave them in Albertville, can I? Besides, it's Marie's birthday, so the least I can do is take them out for lunch, wouldn't you say?

We potter. We wander around the medieval city. We lunch long and hard. We hobble down the hill for coffee and cake. We go to our separate quiet places to sieste.

And tomorrow they will drive up the hill – starting a few hours after me – and bring me water, and wait for me at the top with lunch, and a full medical crew. And if I don't arrive they will drive down again and pick me up from wherever I've fallen.

Wonderful friends.

That's all to come, tomorrow. Tonight there's just time for a few Bartók duets with Clotilde, who tried to pretend she didn't really play the cello, and to hear her sing some beautiful old French songs, beautifully.

CHAPTER 33

Something we can dance to

How long can you meaningfully debate the chicken-and-egg question? Not very long, in my view, if you're talking about actual eggs and actual chickens. But there are lots of chicken-and-egg questions. And some of them can be debated at great length. Which came first – music or speech? It used to be obvious. Nobody thought you could sing if you couldn't first speak. But what does a baby do before it can speak? And all those chimpanzee hoots. Not to mention their rhythmic movements to human beats. And what's a nightingale doing? Is that like the noise a falling tree makes, maybe not actually music unless there's a human ear to hear it?

Here's another: which came first – music or dance? Perhaps that's two different questions. I've read allegedly scholarly articles that say music emerged thirty-five thousand years ago, and people started dancing four thousand years ago. That's an awfully long introduction. I've read other claims that put the origin of both art forms somewhere round about six million years in the past. There's a more modern question here too. Was this tune written for this dance, or was the dance invented to go with the tune?

Maybe you're not into chicken-and-egg (why does nobody ever say egg-and-chicken?) questions. Maybe it's enough to say dance and music go together like hands and gloves (which clearly isn't a chicken-and-egg question) or bats and balls, socks and shoes, curry and rice, night and day, boys and girls, sour grapes and tummy aches.

My excuse is that when you're pedalling uphill, hour after hour, it helps to distract yourself with profound or pointless questions. And I was thinking about the music-and-dance thing because it followed naturally, or maybe meanderingly, from what I was thinking the other day about the two types of Irish music – the Irish airs, and the Irish dance.

You know I like to play Irish airs. They form quite a proportion of my modest repertoire. And they sound, in my opinion, at least as good on a cello as they do on a fiddle, or a flute, or a *clairseach*, or a *timpan*, or a *feadan*, or a *guthbuinne*, or a *sturgan,* or any other instrument you care to suggest.

When it comes to Irish dance music though – sorry, Libre, sorry – nothing, but nothing, beats a fiddle. Nothing even comes close. When you go to an Irish pub, and you're opening the door, still undecided whether tonight it's going to be stout or whiskey, and the heavenly smell of both assails you, and you hear the music of half a dozen fiddles playing a jig at a hundred miles an hour, almost perfectly in tune, you couldn't entertain a different opinion, could you now?

The cello is such a good instrument, according to the experts, because it approximates so closely, both in tone and range, to the human voice. Well, I'm not that kind of an expert, though I know you wouldn't think this a very strong advertisement if you heard *me* sing, but there's probably something in it. So the cello is unbeatable for slow airs, and other things you might sing, assuming that (unlike me) you can sing. But you wouldn't often want to sing a hornpipe, or a jig, or a reel, would you?

I make no apology for playing *Gabriel's Oboe*, *Syrinx*, *Carrickfergus*, and a host of other things that weren't written for the cello. But when it comes to the Irish dances, maybe I feel I'm trespassing a bit. A fiddle can play with such clarity at speed. It can sound like liquid lightning. You can't *not* dance to it sometimes. But the cello, an octave and a half lower, can't keep up. The human ear doesn't process the sounds quite quick enough in those lower registers. And the lower strings have to vibrate so much further to produce their notes, they trip over themselves, and end up in a bit of a muddle, a muddy puddle of sound.

Of course, you can't discount the greater or lesser skill of the player. However you cut it, though, a fiddle cuts it better.

But music and dance go together, and sometimes I want to play music people can dance to. It takes a pro, or at least someone with a very high self-consciousness threshold, to dance impromptu to *The Swan* in a public place. But anyone can jig along to a jig. The easiest dances have quick steps, not slow ones, and you want sometimes to reel in the punters.

So I have a few dances to play. They're not all Irish. One of my favourites is as English as they come, an old Tudor tune which some people say Henry VIII might have written. In between his acquiring and dispatching of wives, Henry VIII was indeed known to be fond of music, but my personal view is he probably subcontracted the actual composition, even if he did claim the royalties.

On my journey through England I found myself in lots of places Henry was known to have visited, or ordered the pillaging of, so I played it a good deal. And when Serge woke me up in Valserhone to play by the gazebo his audience were already spilling out of, I started with it – partly to wake myself up, and partly in acknowledgement of all the children running wild around us.

All in a Garden Green is jolly; it's catchy, light-hearted and courtly. It's also what's called technically a *kissing dance*. You might dance it more circumspectly in the modern world, but I imagine Henry VIII liked its *try before you buy* possibilities – though I don't make too much of that, you'll be pleased to know, especially when I've got a young and mixed audience.

Later in the programme I cross the water to Ireland and play *College Groves*. This is a demanding reel, which needs fully warmed-up fingers to play. But I have to be calm – warmed up, but not over-excited. It needs to be played with acceleration, and acceleration has to be gauged. It's not like a bicycle. There are no brakes. It's downhill all the way, and every bar has to be faster than the bar before, without hurtling over the edge or crashing out of the race. It takes some concentration to go downhill at this speed, and hear the audience whooping at the end.

Having played England and Ireland, it would be politic, I think, or at least good manners, to play Scotland too. So here's *Mairi's Wedding*. It's an old wedding march, so I like to play this one, too, with a bit of acceleration – to indicate Mairi's impatience to get to the church. Not too much, though; we have to maintain decorum here. This time we can apply the brakes. The final verse is slow. Is that to show the solemnity of the kirk, or the foot-dragging of a possible change of heart? No time to think about that now. It's straight into *The Old Grey Cat*, at the noisy wedding reception afterwards, all foot stomping, bottoms up, abandon.

And if there's an English-speaking audience, a sonnet, looking back on it all afterwards:

Mairi's Wedding

Old, grey, cat-clawed, small,
and swaddled by the fire,
half-hearing, half-sighted,
she should, you'd think, be sour
with bitter loss, disintegration,
the itch of bile-like pus
in poorly dressed leg wounds –
alone, afraid, slipping.

Not so. She lives another life,
raptured, dancing to a lighter sky,
fleet and fleeting as her lashes' flutter
on a wedding day of cake and lust

and flowers – not lost, no, flown,
and screeching wildly to a roaring wind.

And remembering the roaring wind, it must be time to get back on the bicycle.

Onwards and upwards.

CHAPTER 34

Haute cuisine

THURSDAY 23 JUNE

I didn't sleep very well, that second, unexpected and wonderfully welcome night in Albertville. I was worried about the day's climbing, which I calculate to be six thousand feet.

I need a strategy. I know, of course, that no battle plan survives the first contact with the enemy. But I ought to have a plan anyway. Not of course that the mountain should be seen as an enemy. It's part of the journey, and the story, and therefore a friend. That's an important start. Hold that thought.

As you know, I live at the bottom of Hartside, the big climb on the C2C cycle route in England, and Hartside has been my training for the Alps. I live six hundred feet above sea level. Just turn right up the hill, and keep going for four miles, to the summit of Hartside at nineteen hundred feet.

So let's think in terms of Hartsides and approach the mountain accordingly. Six thousand feet is a little over four and a half Hartsides, all in one go. Stage One – one Hartside. Stage Two – another Hartside. Stage Three – ditto. By then I'll be tired. So two more stages, but only a thousand feet each.

Twenty-five miles of steady uphill riding. Do I think I can do it? Well, theoretically, yes, definitely. I've climbed more than this in training, though admittedly without Libre and six bags of stuff. And of course it doesn't matter if I fail. Neil and Marie are convinced failure is inevitable, and they've made their plans accordingly. The mountain rescue arrangements are primed and ready.

Even so, there's something about the prospect of failure that's disturbing. It's not exactly debilitating, but it kept me awake.

This is the Cormet de Roselend I'm aiming for. It's a Category 1 climb in the Tour de France, which is to say it's supposed to be difficult but not impossible for elite race riders. Fourteen Tours have featured it, and people who know about these things recall fond memories of the 1996 Tour, when an important French rider "cracked" (technical term) and bowed out of the race while ascending it, and another rider disappeared over the edge going too fast on the descent.

I'm thinking a bit about the Tour de France, by the way, as I'm trying to prepare myself mentally for the day, and I'm doing what the lawyers call *distinguishing*. First of all, you might like to know I'm exactly two and a quarter times as old as the average TDF winner. Consider also that my bike-and-luggage set-up weighs six and a half times as much as an average TDF bike. My average speed to date is a little bit less than half the average speed of the TDF, and my daily mileage a little bit more than half. When I look at it like that it doesn't seem to me too disgraceful or wimpish a performance, and I feel slightly fortified. Fun fact: these comparisons are examples of what Dr Sheldon Cooper, on my second favourite TV programme, *The Big Bang Theory*, would call *fun facts*.

Clotilde and Christophe wave me off early, after promises to reciprocate the visit. I do hope they come. The first Hartside is the easy one. Cross the fast-flowing Arly river out of town, and then begin the gentle climb up its tributary, the Doron, past white water rafting advertisements, to Beaufort, where the magnificent local cheese comes from, and where a *boulangerie* hails and detains me.

Not for long, though. It's important to keep going. This is where the real climbing begins. But like all the best French hills, it's mostly steady. Don't think of it like an English hill. There is no top to see. Just set the GPS to show the gradient, and keep to the plan.

There are a few other cyclists out today. Mostly we're going at roughly the same speed, and stopping at different points, so there's a friendly game of leapfrog, and lots of mutual encouragement. There are two quite mature ladies on e-bikes. I hope their batteries don't run out before they get to the top.

I don't remember the second Hartside. I must just have put my head down, gritted my teeth, and spoken sternly to myself. The third Hartside, through the trees, with occasional glimpses of real mountains, feels steeper again. But the load seems lighter after the halfway point. The fear of failure recedes. We've left the noisy river behind, and there's a real sense of progress at each tight hairpin on the road.

Suddenly the view opens out completely. The road runs beside the truly magnificent Lac de Roselend. There are German motorbikers (why don't I remember them passing me?) admiring the view and each other's bikes, and motorists sitting at the restaurant tables that seem to be built vertiginously over the cliff beside the lake. Everyone stops here, and the Germans ask for a tune. One of them later sends me a photo. I think this might be the only occasion I played without taking my helmet off – though I don't remember not taking it off.

As I'm packing up, some serious cyclists come by. Why, by the way, has no serious cyclist overtaken me yet today? Where are they, on one of the most important *cols* of the *col*-collectors' wish-list? How much does all this weigh, they want to know; and where am I coming from, and going to? I've got a second wind, so in jest I tell them we must be close enough to race to the top.

They laugh, and let me get a hundred yards ahead. But only two of them catch me, before I stop after a fourth Hartside. Well, OK, maybe they aren't *that* serious. But I think some of them are slightly miffed they hadn't overhauled me before the first bend. Don't write me off yet.

We're all reminded of our place in the cycling hierarchy when six young men in team colours come tearing down past us at 50mph, closely followed by their team car. It takes a lot of skill to go that fast down a mountain.

Now then. Neil and Marie have made a plan. They catch up with me twenty minutes before the top, when I'm stopped by a little bridge, admiring the view, and the flowers, and past caring who's in front of me and who's still behind. Marie has been, she says, in quite a panic. She thought I must have fallen off the road, or something. She'd told Neil several times to turn the car round and go back to find me. Neil (who looks like a cross between a seventeenth-century Spanish aristocrat, and a nineteenth-century English one), unflappably declined to do so until, he said, they'd checked whether by some miracle I hadn't already reached the Cormet de Roselend. Which, he pointed out to Marie with an *I told you so* look, I nearly had.

I first met Neil about thirty years ago, in a Hindi class. He was recovering from a financial trauma, and following an Indian guru whose teachings he was combining with his very considerable martial arts training, to re-calibrate himself. I was just learning Hindi because it seemed like a good idea at the time.

At the top, in a cold wind which the wall-to-wall sunshine couldn't quite compete with, while I played a complete Bach *Suite*, Neil got out his stove. Marie opened the wine, sat me in one of their deckchairs, and plied me with the Beaufort cheese they'd bought on the way up, in Beaufort. Neil, who is a highly accomplished – and slightly flamboyant – chef, cooked pasta and a complicated sauce, and a couple of other things, and we dined splendidly on this most *haute* of *hautes cuisines*, six thousand five hundred feet above sea level.

As the French say, *pourquoi pas* – why not?

A couple of hours later I'm tearing down the other side. At a fairly sedate pace, actually; I don't feel safe at all. There are symphonies of brown cows, all with big bells round their necks.

243

There are views of snow. There are cliffs of monstrous size. There are hairpin bends fit for a James Bond film. The six team cyclists and their team car whizz past again, which makes me think they must have climbed the Col twice, once in each direction. They're much too busy to wave, of course, but then they haven't just had a splendid lunch with a couple of glasses of wine and a couple of nearly-sobering moka-pot coffees.

Then suddenly it's all over, and I'm in Bourg-Saint-Maurice, with nowhere to stay. It's early, so I set up on a quiet and narrow street, and for only the second – or is it the third? – time put out my notice saying *I need somewhere to stay and would you like a concert in your home tonight?*

There are no takers for either, but the contributions in coin are generous. There's applause from a balcony above, and a cup of tea from the ice-cream shop two doors down. So after an hour, when I think Bourg-Saint-Maurice is probably busked out with cello, I set off in search of a little hotel. It isn't hard to find one, and Marie (it's not an uncommon name in France) gives me a proper cellist's discount, and invites me to play on the restaurant terrace later.

I feel in remarkably good shape after yesterday's six thousand feet of climbing, and two hours of music. I think the day of rest before it must have been very restorative.

So today's plan seems light in comparison. Four thousand feet of climbing up to Val d'Isere, a very British ski resort. Val d'Isere isn't actually at the top of the hill. When you look at the GPS's helpful profile of the route, it shows the climb going on, another nearly four thousand feet, over the Col de l'Iseran. And then down, magnificently, for almost twenty miles.

The Col de l'Iseran is one of the biggest and best, and highest and most wonderful. It's so important, they close the road to motor vehicles from time to time, so cyclists can enjoy it unhindered.

So maybe I shouldn't bother to stop at Val d'Isere? Maybe I should do another three Hartsides, and roll on down into

Lanslebourg Mt. Cenis, the conquering hero? Well, we'll see how it goes, shall we? No decision has to be made, of course, until we reach the very British ski resort.

The road is nothing like as beautiful as yesterday's. I expected even more spectacular mountains, since we're gaining height. But there's little to see of them – the road is overshadowed mostly by cliff.

And even where there are views it isn't safe to look at them. This is a main road – the only road – and it isn't very wide. Sometimes there are little concrete barriers, which make it feel a bit safer. But sometimes there aren't, and a swerve in a lorry's slipstream could turn into something a lot worse than a swerve.

The traffic is fairly unrelenting, and to be honest it's not that much fun. And it gets worse as I approach Val d'Isere. There are several avalanche protectors – great pillared roofs across the road – which amplify the traffic noise, and make it feel faster and closer.

And then the tunnels. The tunnels are truly terrifying.

It's three hours' ride. And Val d'Isere is not an appealing town. Perhaps in the winter, when it has a purpose, it would look fine. But now, with the weather closing in, and the skiers elsewhere, the approach is through a ghost town of abandoned hotels and lifeless apartment blocks.

I'm tired. There's a roll of thunder, and the rain starts in earnest. It's cold. I don't really want to stay the rest of the day here. But the conditions are most unsuitable for going any further. I think the weather has to have the last word. It would be pointless to climb the same height again, through very cold rain, and then face a dangerously wet descent. And not be able to see anything from the top of the most iconic of all Alpine passes.

Well maybe the weather made the decision. Or maybe I realised I couldn't actually do it after all.

In the place where I have lunch, thinking about all this, watching the worsening rain, and telling myself it was the weather that decided, and waiting for the Tourist Office to finish its two-hour lunch break so it can tell me if there is actually a functioning hotel in the town at the end of June, there are four young cyclists, sleeping on the couches. It seems to me a trespass on the café's hospitality, until the mother of one of them explains they're on an endurance ride across France, and they've done a thousand miles in the last four days, with virtually no sleep.

I don't think she meant to rub it in; but I can be a sensitive soul, sometimes. I've noted before that an especially bad day is usually followed by a memorably good one. The opposite seems to be true as well. After yesterday's all-round magnificence, today was a hard slog, on a dangerous road which promised views it never delivered, into worsening weather, with a boringly depressing town at the end of it. Up, then down. Like a rollercoaster.

Focus ahead. Tomorrow will be the high point, the Col de l'Iseran. From where, presumably, it's downhill all the way to Rome.

CHAPTER 35

Italy, the Third Movement

SATURDAY 25 JUNE

Another day, another *col*. The Col Mont Cenis is not such a big one, but none of these *cols* can be treated like a walk in the park. It's 6870ft above sea level, but I'm starting at Lanslebourg-Mont-Cenis, which is already above four thousand feet.

These hills are different from the hilly roads at home. There you have gradients that follow the landscape, and change all the time. Even the steepest hills have little points of rest where the slope eases off and you can catch your breath.

Not here. The road is engineered to a more or less constant 7%. So once you start climbing, it's the same constant effort all the way to the top – in this case 2300ft higher up.

The road zigzags under an imposing ski lift, which is stationary and mocking. Half the time I'm riding into the early sun, which is already hot. Half the time the sun is behind me. The Col Mont Cenis has six famously equal hairpin bends.

The mountains slowly reveal themselves. The forest smells like heaven.

I was planning a little music at the top. Mont Cenis is nearly the border with Italy – not that it's a border any more, of course, but something presumably will change. The *Second Movement* of this work should have a proper ending, before Italy, the *Third Movement*, begins.

But the top is undramatic. The road just flattens out. There's a café, and a model train, and a cold wind, and an ominous fog. Oddly there's a little procession of elephants – not real ones, you understand, just an oriental-looking sculpture. Did Hannibal perhaps come this way? Well, maybe. Historians know a lot about Hannibal's great trek, which they now call the Second Punic War, but not his exact route over the Alps. There are five main contenders, of which Mont Cenis is one.

The café is staffed by an old lady wearing traditional Savoie dress. She isn't quite ready for customers when I arrive, and I have to wait for her to tie it cumbersomely over her more comfortable off-duty attire. She wants to show me pictures of her and her husband in racier days, posing raffishly by a blue racing car.

What is this language she's speaking? It's not exactly French, nor exactly Italian. I'm guessing it, too, is traditional Savoyard – a diminishing language that straddles the borders of France, Italy and Switzerland. The Savoyards must have found it hard to keep up with which country they were actually in, and what language they should therefore understand, and just opted out in a kind of mountainous but non-mutinous way.

This was Italy, until a fairly definite annexation by France in 1860. At the Treaty of Paris in 1947 the French gave some of it back, and the border was established at Mont Cenis itself. Now the café is in France again, the border having slipped a few miles further on down the hill. How confusing.

Something, anyway, is being lost in the translation, I feel. The train, she tells me – the station used to be just nine kilometres down the hill – was built by an Englishman. It ran from London to New Delhi. And Queen Victoria used it. Something like that, anyway.

Libre stayed in her case. The *col* was too flat and indefinite, too foggy, too cold. It was disappointingly meaningless.

When I finally get to Italy, past a few redundant fortifications and customs posts, past the beautiful lake, where the water is some meters below where it looks as though it should be, there's nothing to see. Just a little blue and yellow EU road sign. I whizz past it almost without noticing, because the descent has truly begun by then.

And what a descent. It's totally crazy, and much steeper than the French ascent. There are now thousands of motorbikes racing up the hill, overtaking slower vehicles regardless of a bicycle hurtling towards them.

I'm very glad I put new brake blocks on the bike last night. By the end of the day the GPS thingy says I've come down seven thousand feet today.

I planned to catch up the day I took for rest in Albertville, and go straight to Turin, instead of stopping in Susa. I believe there's a particularly fine cathedral there. And the city has a strong and romantic ring to it – *Torino*.

But then I find I'm intimidated by the idea of a big city. In the end I'm not brave enough to venture there. I skirt round the edge, through many miles of dispiriting industrial and commercial squalor.

To get properly beyond reach of Turin I have to go further than I really have energy for. I collapse just before the small town of Poirino, at an anachronistically large and splendid modern hotel. But its restaurant is closed on Sunday. And the town is half a mile away. I eat the last of my cheese, and just go to bed. Libre hasn't been out of her case today, and she's chastising me in a sulky silence.

It's Monday. This is Italy. I'm sitting in the shade of a prolific climber, on one side of a beautiful square in Asti. Yes, where the Spumanti comes from. It's an open and traffic-free square, with fine classical buildings on three sides, and a medieval tower to my left. At the foot of the tower, which is now called the *Torre di Vino*, but perhaps didn't start off like that, my audience is drinking its coffee, or passing by on the phone.

Asti is a good place to be reminded that, despite all its antiquities, Italy is a young country. When you come from England – as I do, and just did – you think of countries as being rather old things. If asked, you might say 1066, or something like that. But there wasn't really a *country* called Italy – whatever you might think from reading Shakespeare – until 1861. Even perhaps 1871, if you want to include Rome, and the last of the Papal States, and all that Franco-Prussian war stuff.

Asti, in the days of such things, was a Free Republic. Then it slipped up and became part of Naples. Then it was French. Then it was Spanish. Then it was German. Then the German Emperor gave it back to Naples. Naples palmed it off as a wedding present to a Portuguese princess when she married into the Savoy dynasty. It's easy to lose track, but it seems then to have been Spanish again for a while, before Napoleon took an interest. And so it goes.

A lady, who I discover is called Lia, is taking an artistic video, panning across the square and settling on the cello. She runs the wine shop on the ground floor of the *Torre di Vino*. When I've finished playing, she says, she will treat me to something from her shop. It's too early for wine, I have to tell her, more than once; but lemonade will do nicely. She presses on me some rather fine chocolate *Amarettos* too.

Drinking the lemonade outside, the proprietor of the bar next door comes scuttling out to tell me I'm sitting on his chair, not hers, and I must move. Guiseppe and Janus, conspicuously handsome young men, who obviously enjoyed the music more than the bar's owner, invite me to share their table instead, which displeases the territorial proprietor. His glowering deepens when we begin to laugh out loud. Clearly he thinks we're laughing at him. But we're not. We're talking about how archetypically Italian Giuseppe looks, with his long dark wavy hair, and how absolutely un-Italian, and Teutonic, Janus looks. Janus is slightly sensitive to the historical connotations of being a tall blonde German in Italy.

Asti is halfway along the day's fifty-mile route to Alessandria. After Asti most of the ride is on the *Via Roma* – you guessed it, straight and true, and going where all roads lead. I ride the straight line for a few miles at a time, then divert – nearly always up a hill – into a little village, and then go back down to the Roman road. There's no hurry.

The Roman road is smooth and quick. The diversions aren't. To slow the traffic, every village and town is paved with painful cobbles, the route further complicated by superfluous speed bumps and other impedimenta. But always the houses, the churches, and all the other signatures of their histories, make the diversions worthwhile.

Alessandria is approached over a fine modern bridge. I'm planning to lay out my stall and hope for an offer of accommodation. But then I get cold feet – metaphorically, that is; it's actually drenchingly hot. I felt the temperature rising steadily as I came down from Mont Cenis, and it's just got hotter every hour since then.

So I scout out a hotel instead, feeling a bit of a coward. This is our first full day in Italy, the beginning of *Highway Cello's Third Movement*, and it should be properly marked. And I'm failing.

Then, suddenly, en route, I find myself in what looks like the perfect place to set up and play. A little open space, with a small monument, some bars, plenty of concrete seats, and a flow of people. So, back to plan A.

After a while, though – I earned the grand total of fifty cents in about forty-five minutes – I begin to think I should prefer the hotel. The crowd is an odd mix of remotely supervised children and elderly gentlemen who might have known better days. There's no-one here likely to offer me accommodation, I suspect. And no-one I would want to stay with, I suspect, if they did.

When I get there, I find the Ostello isn't, despite the advertisement, a hotel. It's just what its name suggests, a hostel. But it's converted from a fifteenth-century monastery, and very beautiful. Marco, who's in charge, explains it's one of the very few old buildings in Alessandria to survive Napoleon's attentions, and it only did so because he found it useful as a secure arms depot.

Since then it has seen service as a prison, a hospital, a school, an orphanage, a nunnery, and I forget what else. Now the government doesn't know what to do with it, and a jumble of good causes shares the space with the hostel itself. Marco invites me to play in the garden, under the trees in the cloister, where the acoustic is just perfect, and the cicadas pause briefly – but only briefly – to listen.

Marco is a real historian. Every question I ask, as I'm drawn into Alessandria's turbulent past, is a springboard for the unleashing of more fascinating stories. Marco is an enthusiast, but he wants to be assured, before he unlocks a heavy door for me, that I will appreciate the treasure he's prepared to show me.

It's a fresco, partly restored, from 1520, at the edges of which you can see traces of an even older one. The fresco shows a boy called Timoteus, entering the monastery as a novice, and donating his very extensive lands (which go from here right up into the hills) to the order. You can see why they thought it worth painting over the older fresco to commemorate such a moment. The sternly-bearded bishop is holding Timoteus in a fiercely protective paternal grip, and trying not to look too graspingly at all the newly-acquired land behind him.

Marco should have gone home after his day's work some time ago, and I'm beginning to feel I'm detaining him. So I make some excuse, and the room with the fresco is locked behind us. I thought I'd have a couple of Lia's *Amarettos* before going out to find a real Italian pizza. But the day's cobbles have reduced the remaining biscuits to a packet of crumbs, and I don't have a spoon.

CHAPTER 36

Last Tango in Genoa

TUESDAY 28 JUNE

The *Ostello Santa Maria di Castello* has no single rooms. I share a large dormitory with Daniel, who has come from Argentina to trace his great-grandfather's roots. Like many Argentines, he spoke nearly as much Italian as Spanish, and almost no English.

Until I visited Argentina – for that cello-fest, with the borrowed cello – I'd mistakenly thought it a country almost entirely rooted in an old Spanish identity. Then I discovered nearly two-thirds of its population claim roots in Italy rather than Spain. Great numbers of Italians emigrated in the decades following the European turmoil of the 1860s and 1870s. Lots more followed those older generations after the Second World War. Argentina is as much Italian as it is Spanish.

Daniel's phone wakes me up five times in the night, and there's no breakfast in the *Ostello*. So I'm not feeling sociable when I set off. I was up early, and I thought about playing Osvaldo Requena's *Porteño*, his *Tango for Double Bass,* in the dorm room before I set off. But Daniel is sleeping like a baby. And I don't want to play tango in anger. So I just creep out quietly.

It's complicated, but there was in fact more than one reason I was thinking about Requena's *Tango*. Yes, I confess, I was thinking about waking Daniel. When you sleep in a dorm you can't really expect a peaceful lie-in, especially if you've parked the only fan in the sweltering room right by your bed, and your phone goes off five times in the night.

Even before Marco said I could stay in his *Ostello*, but only in a shared room, and thus I met an Argentine of Italian ancestry in Italy, I was thinking about the relationship between the two countries – and their music. There's an old view that tango, such a quintessentially Argentine music, originated from a mixing of African and European immigrant underclasses. Those communities in Buenos Aires had significantly more men than women, and tango developed so that men could dance with each other. In tango you could sublimate the choreographed sexuality into a complicated ritual of aggression. Honestly.

There's a *flamenco tango* in Spain, but it doesn't seem to be related closely to Argentine tango. So is there anything tango-*esque* in Italy, I wonder?

I was thinking therefore that if I played *Porteño* a bit, I might encounter some clues. It's the only tango in my street repertoire, and I didn't played it much in France because it isn't an easy piece, so I felt the need of a bit of practice.

I love it that Requena's *Porteño* was written for a solo double bass. It sounds absolutely virtuosic on that noble instrument – a rather lyrical departure from what the bass usually gets to play in a band. There's one bit of it I play way up on the C string, where you would never normally play the cello, but where it sounds just like a double bass. You know that reedy sound of protest a big bass makes as soon as it gets above its basic comfort zone? That's the sound I want. In homage to the double bass.

Breakfast sorted, a mile down the road from the ancient hostel, in one of those magnificent emporiums that's both pizzeria and bakery, where you can get a breakfast, or a lunch, or a dinner, and take it home or eat it on the spot, standing up or sitting down, and then get coffee too. So I'm fully restored in mood by the time I set south, for Genoa. It's going to be fairly flat, except for the Apennine hills just before the city and the sea.

I'm still thinking about tango. I'm trying to work out what it is that makes tango music so recognisable. I feel I should be circumspect here, as I was with the Irish music, because I'm not a native speaker of the language. I'm not qualified in any way. So what do you hear when you hear a tango? Well, there's usually a flowing, chromatic, melody. And underneath it – sometimes as though it was in a different universe – there's a rhythm.

The basic rhythm is the *milonga*. Four beats, with the first lengthened by taking half away from the second – a dotted rhythm. So if you think in half beats, ie eight quavers in place of the four crochet beats, it's 3+1+2+2. That's one way to do it. Then, if you're feeling slinky, sexy, devilish, about it – and here's the stroke of genius – you elide that one-plus-two in the middle, to make a three. Your unmistakeable rhythm is then 3+3+2. Make that strong, accent it, and make the flowing chromatic melody obey it. And there you have a tango.

Well how then – obvious question – can you have a *solo* tango? One instrument can't do both the flowing tune and the accented rhythm, can it? Can't it? What about Osvaldo Requena's *Tango para Contrabajo*, his *Porteño?* I'll play it later. Promise.

It's cloudy, but very warm. It's definitely going to rain. Last night the *Ostello* was so hot I had to soak a T-shirt and wear it wet, just to keep from overheating. I'm hoping the rain will have the same effect.

I'm waiting for it. It keeps threatening, or promising, but not delivering. The road isn't as flat as I thought it would be, and it's hot. So a litre of milk in Gavi is welcome refreshment. And then, at last, the rain. It's a spectacular thunderstorm, and I'm able to start climbing the hills wearing my own cooler. These are nice wooded hills, with meandering and varied roads. So the climb isn't as unrelenting as the carefully engineered Alpine roads.

Even so, an excuse to stop shouldn't be ignored. The climb is just beginning, and judging by the landscape ahead, it's going to take some effort. There's a little hump-backed bridge, over an

255

enthusiastic stream, just off the road. Across the bridge, a multi-coloured village clambers up the steep hill. It's very picturesque. You couldn't get a car across this bridge, so I'm not blocking anyone's way when I pose the bike on it for a photo.

There's a notice that says it's Paganini's bridge. I'm assuming that means Niccolò Paganini, Italy's world-famous early nineteenth-century virtuoso violinist, whose twenty-four *Caprices* are still the test of violin virtuosity today. Paganini was born just up the road in Genoa, contracted syphilis in Paris, which he treated with an alarming mixture of mercury and opium, sold his soul to the Devil (allegedly) so he could play the violin like the Devil himself, and was therefore refused a Catholic burial when he died in 1840. He was a proper rock star.

I suppose I should have played some music on Paganini's bridge. A vertiginous tango, straddling the hump of the little bridge, with the exuberantly Latin-coloured village of Voltaggio behind, would be just the thing. But I didn't want to look silly if it was a different Paganini. The notices don't say. Though they do say it's also called the Roman Bridge, and it's probably thirteenth-century. That's quite confusing.

It's a steamy climb, until the clouds drift off halfway to the top. I stop again, by a laden cherry tree. Unfortunately the tree is growing out of the cliff-sided ravine that channels the *Torrente Lemme*, spanned lower down by Paganini, and it would be suicidal to try and reach the ripe fruit. I think of Paganini and the Devil's temptations. I resist them.

With a bit of effort I can get to the top from here without cherries. The wooded view from the summit is pure Italian – at least it would be, with a bit more sunshine. I'm trying not to speculate about the mismatched couple getting dressed beside their car. Put on a fresh shirt for the descent, and let the wet one flap itself dry strapped to the cello case.

Here the Northern Apennines have southern slopes much steeper than the way I came up, and the descent is swift and brutal.

Suddenly I'm in the built-up valley, looking down on, and then cycling though, what look like dormitories for a big city.

Genoa, or *Genova* in proper Italian, is indeed a fine city, with a large and magnificent port. The steep old town seems to brood over the port, encircling it and protecting it proudly. Even now not all the big ships are tourist vessels. There's a lot of work going on here.

In its heyday, when Italy was a confusing patchwork of city states, Genoa was fairly constantly in conflict with Venice, the other side of the peninsula, both cities trying to establish a maritime trade supremacy. In *The Merchant of Venice*, Shakespeare has Shylock's daughter eloping from Venice to Genoa, and we hear Shylock lamenting the extravagance of her life in that expensive city. It's easy to imagine. Even now Genoa has more than a handful of palaces.

I might have been going to see a representative sample of those palaces. I'm cycling around the port, shouting at unreconstructed Italian drivers, crossing junctions with incomprehensible markings, wondering if Genoan traffic lights perform any function, when I nearly fall off the bike at the sight of a truly magnificent and fully fitted seventeenth-century galleon. This is no longer a time to think of mere palaces.

The *Neptune* looks as though it's just arrived in the port, every one of its many guns pointing out through open portholes, ready for action.

It's the first properly and completely touristical thing I've done. I can't resist spending six Euros to board and inspect. And it really is fabulous. Except that it's a fake.

It's full-sized, and historically accurate, and it can sail the high seas. But it was made in 1985, for a Roman Polanski film you might never have heard of. The guns are plastic. But it's as close to the real thing as I'll ever get – six Euros well spent. *Pirates* was a box office flop. How much that had to do with its idiotic plot, and how much with Polanski's flight from America a few years earlier after his conviction on a charge of having sex with a minor, may be debatable.

But the film doesn't matter. The Tunisian-built ship was described at its launch as one of the most expensive movie props ever commissioned, and it's now something of a symbol of Genoa. There are kids running around having wild piratical adventures, and I'm quietly lamenting that I'm too old for that sort of thing.

Then into the medieval city, where the bike has to be wheeled because the streets are too narrow and full of tourists from the cruise ships below, to look for somewhere to play. The *Via San Lorenzo*, by the cathedral, just down the way from a bored-looking posse of police, looks good.

As soon as I set up, wondering if the police might take any notice, the gentlemen's outfitter across the road puts on its own music, very loud. There's no possibility of competing with it, but I'm wondering if there's an aspect of Italian culture here that's just foreign to me – I don't think I'd ever buy an expensive suit to an accompaniment of full volume heavy metal. Then I realise there are plenty of other things in Italy that don't make sense to me. Like traffic lights, for instance. How do you know when, *per* Antonio Martino, they're *instructions*, and when they're *suggestions*, and when they're just *Christmas decorations*?

That's perhaps a sign to pack up, and go and find Marco and Norma – *Warmshowers* hosts again – who live somewhere up in the hills behind. The place, Marco warned me, is hard to find, and "has many steps."

Google Maps can't find the house. Every route it tries ends up at the foot of a great flight of stairs. Eventually I leave the bike and go on foot. Yes, says Marco, there is an easier way, but it still involves about two hundred steps. You take the luggage; I'll carry the bike.

Later, after a fine dinner, I'm playing Libre for Norma and Marco in their lovely sitting room. What shall I play? Some Bach, to express the perfection of the moment. The *Waltz for John and Mary*, for their quiet companionship on the sofa. *Down by the*

Salley Gardens, for the daughter they put on video phone so she could share the moment. And Osvaldo Requena's *Porteño,* a summary of the day.

Would you like to hear my tango poem, by the way? I should explain it didn't start off as a tango poem. It just ended up that way. It began in one of those little moments you can't afterwards remember if it really happened to you, or if you just read it in *Private Eye's Pseuds Corner.* Small child asking its parent, "Mummy, does Lego have a silent 't', like Merlot?" You couldn't waste that, could you?

Margot

At the table, Margot,
sips her glass of Merlot
(on a Sunday Pernod)
reading Hercule Poirot
(gold and leather foliot
from the Rare Book Depot)
regretting last night's bistrot;
through the open windot
hears the strains of tangot
on her neighbour's cellot
sweeps the children's Legot
feeling like an idiot
(in French) or something faux
which is slightly od
becaux
she isn't —
(French, that is).

Later again, surveying the tightly packed city below, in the near dark, in good company, and with a little sea breeze, I'm thinking maybe sometimes I try a bit too hard to make sense of things.

Tango, Napoleon, phones that ring through the night, galleons and cruise ships, Christmas traffic lights, and heavy metal suits, music, stairs and the hospitality of strangers. Does it make sense? Does it have to?

CHAPTER 37

Play it like Yo-Yo Ma

WEDNESDAY 29 JUNE

I spent a long time that night with Marco, surrounded by his maps on the dining table. I want to get to Pisa, about a hundred and twenty miles away, by the day after tomorrow. But there's no easy way to do it. The Apennines, which form so much of the spine of Italy, curving down from the Alps in a big question mark, block the way. Further South they confine themselves, as mountains should, to the interior. Around the Gulf of Genoa they trespass on the coast itself. Yes, the Ligurian coast is therefore beautiful. But it presents a series of cycling challenges.

Marco is not especially encouraging. It's up and down all the way to Recco, he says. Then there's a big hill where you cut off the Portofino peninsula, and down again to the coast at Rappallo. More hills, and back to sea level *here*, he says, tracing back and forth on the map. And then, after the flat, built-up coast road to Sestri Levante, well, there's your big problem.

I can see it on the map. It's a proper hill, with only one small road. Because of course you can't – and wouldn't anyway – take a bike on the tunnelled motorway. And, Marco warns me, there's nowhere to stay anywhere along those thirty kilometres. You can't get over that hill, and all the way back down to civilisation, in one day.

And if I stop before I get to the big hill, I protest, I won't then be able to get over it and all the way to Pisa the next day. He shrugs. That's what I'm trying to tell you, he says, like a patient teacher whose pupil has just grasped the offside rule.

I've no solution by the time I set off in the morning. After a month of cycling I realise I'm on the verge of exhaustion. Yes, I've got muscles I didn't have before, but there's an accumulation of fatigue. I'm good for a sprint, but not really for a marathon. I'll just have to see how the day goes, and hope a solution presents itself later.

I'm a short way down the hill from Norma and Marco's lovely house in the heights of the Genoan suburbs, when suddenly I hear someone shouting my name. It's such a surprise I nearly fall off the bike. Again; that's twice in two days.

It's Marco and Norma, on a nifty motorbike, on their way to a swim before Norma has to go back to her exam-paper marking.

"Follow me," Marco instructs, and sets off at full speed, weaving through the Genoan traffic as though we're late for a very important meeting. Here comes the sprint. Marco makes absolutely no concession to my absence of motor. The road to the coast, I've already discovered, is more convoluted than I expected, so I do want to keep up with him and not get lost.

There's only one way to deal with Italian traffic. Whatever you intend to do, it has to be done with absolute conviction. You have to proceed with an aura of divine authority. Rules, you have to proclaim, and demonstrate, do not apply to a bicycle conveying a cello.

Well, it works in Genoa, and a couple of miles later I wave to my shining knights as they speed off along the coast for their pre-work swim. It works less well, later, in Rapallo, where an angry Italian car rams me – absolutely deliberately. He doesn't win the shouting that follows, though. A small crowd quickly materialises, and it's clear which side they are on. The angry Italian car screeches away with its tail between its legs.

Apart from that, Rapallo is a lovely place. A monstrous cruise ship is anchored, smoking, out in the bay, and all its cargo are being shepherded, in numbered groups, through the pretty town. I play on a quiet corner, trying to put off the day's difficult decision.

I still don't know how far I'm trying to go, or where I might stay. Marco was right. A steep two-thousand-foot hill at the end of a fifty-mile day, in this heat, with this load, and – I think he was trying politely to imply – at my age, is a big ask. I told him there are always places to stay. No, he says, there aren't.

The coast road is every bit as beautiful as Marco and the brochures describe. Periodically I can see across to Corsica. It's dramatic, in a genteel kind of way. The coastal towns are neat and pretty and, as they disperse up into the hills, they give way to expensive villas tucked among the trees. I expect you could have a nice holiday here.

I don't want to stop in Sestri Levante, except briefly under the shade of an ice-cream umbrella. It isn't far enough. I've made a choice – I'm going to tackle the hill, and sleep under a hedge if necessary. I like comfort at the end of the day, so this is a big decision. Stony ground, biting insects, and who knows what else. But I'm resolved.

Halfway up there's a campsite. I wave to a few people unloading their cars. I haven't got a tent, so I can't stay there. Is that fleeting thought one of disappointment, or of adventurous superiority? Enjoy it while you can, I tell myself. A night under the stars might be romantic in the right company, but alone in the middle of nowhere? Don't expect comfort. Or much sleep.

So I carry on. I can get further. Possibly even to the top.

And I would have done – really – if Franco hadn't beguiled me.

A man with the long silver pony-tailed hair of an old pirate is standing by the open door of a dingy bar, watching the world go by, as though he's seen it all before. He smiles at a cello on a bike, and nods imperceptibly in the direction of the sign that advertises his restaurant and rooms.

Decisions are made in moments. So now here I am, sitting in the bar, which really only looked dingy because I was outside in the full sun, with the bike parked up in the spare dining room, waiting for Franco and his chef to finish their dinner so I can have mine.

Luca, a rugby player on holiday from Milan, has translated a few difficulties. He's staying at his wife's sister's house – that white one, there, where I should drop in for a drink, he says, pointing – and afterwards he's coming back to hear me play the cello. Do I play Irish music? He used to coach an Irish team, and he loves Irish music...

He's as good as his word. A couple of hours later he returns. He brings a present with him – a painting of the cellist in action. After we've had coffee and I forget what else, he makes a special request – *Bach Suite no. 1 in G Major, the way Yo-Yo Ma plays it.*

It might not have been quite how Yo-Yo Ma would have rendered it, but I think it was passable, and the terrace restaurant applauds appreciatively. Everyone here likes the idea of the English cellist on his way to Rome.

It's late before we exhaust the nuances of all the recent rule changes in rugby, and I sleep with the windows wide open to the sea breeze coming up from way, way, below. And to think I might have slept under a tree, and never met Luca, or been surprised by the Davidin restaurant where they gave me stewed rabbit with an explanation I couldn't understand, or played Bach like Yo-Yo Ma, looking across to Corsica fading into the sea at the end of the day.

In the morning it's only half an hour's climb to the top, before it's downhill all the way to the sea again. Here the prettiness of the Ligurian coast is suddenly gone. Twenty miles of flat road with an unbroken line of bars and clubs and restaurants blocking the way to their private beaches. Just occasionally there's a narrow break between all the privacy, and a low status public beach allows us *hoi polloi* to reach the water. So I stop for a quick swim, and an ice cream or two.

Only a quick one, though. This relentless high-octane

beachiness discourages dawdling, and I've ridden fifty miles by lunchtime. Ten more and I need to divert inland to look for gentler ice cream. Frederica, with a degree in linguistics and a fluency in four languages, recommends the chocolate. She wants to know why – *why* – I'm cycling all this way with a cello. She looks to the boss with a raised eyebrow, and they agree. Such madness should not pay for its ice cream.

Twenty more blissfully flat and fast, but blisteringly hot, miles after that and the famous leaning tower hoves into view.

It's been stabilised since I was last here, at great expense, and at the angle agreed to be just safe enough. You wouldn't want to upright it too much, would you? That would risk killing the golden-egg-laying goose.

I ask a man with a machine gun, as I've learned to do, and he sends me to a hidden-away office.

"Such things are not allowed, of course," explains Francesco with the stars on his shoulders. "But I will see if we can make an exception."

After three phone calls he's ready to make the exception and, presenting me with a bottle of very cold water, he directs one of his officers to accompany me, to take, he said, such videos and photos as I require. Whether he was expecting trouble I don't know, but he couldn't stay for the concert himself, he explains, because he had to be somewhere else in a hurry. The last I see of him he's almost running, out of an armed side gate.

The officer thinks we should still keep off the forbidden grass, but I persuade him that if I'm on the grass it will set less of a precedent, which is what they seem to be worried about. He thinks it's a good argument. So Bach on the smooth and fenced-off grass of the Leaning Tower it is. Not as good as last night's, because I've just got off the bike after eighty hot miles, and the bowing wrist is weak and sore, but I do try to make it in the style of Yo-Yo Ma.

That was a moment of triumph. If you don't ask, you don't get, as I tell myself again when the nice little hotel I find is more expensive than I think a travelling troubadour should allow himself. Well, there *is* another room, she says, but it isn't air-conditioned. She says it as though that would be like selling the Black Hole of Calcutta. But now I know the trick of putting on a wet T-shirt, I'm effectively carrying my own air-conditioning kit. That would do nicely, I tell her, if it were just twenty Euros less. Negotiation concluded, she hands over the key with obvious misgiving. I think she's expecting me to expire in the night, and worried how that will look in the next day's papers.

But I've no time for her hesitation. I just want to get freshened up, and out onto the streets of Pisa, to find a proper Pisan pizza. *Do you realise*, I'm saying to Libre, *this is our fifth night in Italy, and we haven't had even a single pizza yet?*

CHAPTER 38

Don't upset the Mafia

SATURDAY 2 JULY

Am I taking this improvisation too far? I've called this journey a work in Three Movements – England, France, and Italy. The First Movement was highly structured. It set out all the themes – cycling, music and story – in proper order. Then France, the Second Movement, allowed variations on the themes. It was still quite structured. Usually I knew where I was going. I had places to stay, places to play, deadlines to meet, with only the occasional blank page.

The Third Movement was intended to be more improvisatory – the same themes, but more experimental, exploratory. Turn up and see. I was more prepared to do what I would not have dared do nearer home – set off for the day not knowing where it might end. Without a place to stay.

I think the realisation the other day, that I could have slept under a hedge if really necessary, was a moment of discovery, a permission to be free of some of the normal worry of travel. I've discovered there are, after all, lots of places to stay in this country. It's fine to improvise.

But am I taking it too far? Have I lost all sense of responsibility?

I'm aiming for Siena. It's seventy miles away, inland, and so the final twenty miles is entirely uphill. In this forty-degree heat that's a bit much. This is the same question I faced when I left Genoa a couple of days ago. Then it seemed a big deal. But today I hardly care. I'll just set off, see how far I get, and call it a day when I've had about enough. In some suitably attractive place, I'm going to draw a line, and just stop. It might be an interrupted cadence, but no-one's perfect – today, anyway. See what I mean?

It's the first day of July, and definitely the hottest of this journey so far. I like heat. But forty degrees, on a bike, uphill, is, I acknowledge, *too hot*.

The Tuscan road is pretty flat, but it's in very bad condition. Is this the effect of unrelenting summers, or the siphoning-off of funds to organised networks that we read about? These roads have the profile of farm tracks. They sink into wide ruts where the wheels pass over them, and rise up at either side. And in the ruts the top surface cracks, and crazes, and disintegrates. Sometimes I can count three or four generations of patching in these ruts, and often it's impossible to cycle in them.

This means a choice. Try to find a narrow, smoother route right at the edge of the road. Or migrate into the middle of the lane. Go to the edge and you risk falling off into a ditch, or riding over glass, or into thorn bushes. Be bold, take the centre, and you risk *contretemps* with the traffic. There's never a good option.

I'm in the valley of the River Arno, until the hill-top village of Santa Maria a Monte beckons me off route. It's an almost perfectly circular, naturally fortified settlement, with long views over the valley in all directions. But it's just too hot.

There's an instant's relief, freewheeling down from Santa Maria back to the plain. The River Arno has taken a different route. Now even the sunflowers are turning their backs on the sun. Another, bigger, climb to San Miniato, equally historic, equally fortified by nature, and birthplace of the father of Galileo Galilei. Vincenzo Galilei, his plaque says, was a master of the lute and, by his enquiries into musical theory, set his son on the quest to understand the music of the spheres.

There's a library, and a bookshop, and a music school, and an earnest cultural association putting up notices for a forthcoming lecture and general extravaganza. And a sliver of shade nearly wide enough for a cyclist and his cello. The cultural association pauses briefly in his postering round to listen. The music school, which turns out to be the same thing as the cultural association, offers lessons in piano, "modern" singing, and hip hop.

San Miniato – which could also market itself as an outdoor museum of weird and wonderful door-knockers – stretches out along the road South and East. Even if I hadn't seen the unexpected sign for the *Via Francigena*, like a long-lost friend, directing me off to the right, I would have stopped here for lunch, between the deli and the *gelateria*. I buy something magnificently Italian, which I shouldn't really eat with my fingers, and a plateful of olives, and sit down on the stone bench.

I refill my empty water bottles with cold water from a roadside fountain, stretch out on the bench, and shut my eyes against the sun which bounces off the buildings opposite. It's a bit public, and an occasional car coming down the pedestrian street passes uncomfortably close. But I feel like a proper vagabonding vagrant, entitled to sleep anywhere.

The temptation to sleep the rest of the day on that warm shaded bench is almost too strong to resist. But I see two cheerfully vigorous and heavily-laden pilgrims setting off up the hill at a seriously brisk walk. The heat seems not to affect them. They only glance at me, but their assumption is plain – here is a pilgrim who can't stay the course, who's fallen by the wayside. They check each other, to be sure that falling by the wayside isn't something that could ever happen to them.

Did I see all that in one glance, when my own eyes weren't even fully open? Or just imagine it? I don't know. But by the time I get to my feet, and they're halfway up the hill, they're certainly holding hands. I half wish I still knew how to pray. I would have offered a prayer for them – Lord, let them stay the course.

I wasn't going to fall by the wayside today, though. At least not yet. This is just a slightly extended lunch break. But I remember many other fallings, by other waysides.

Down by the Salley Gardens. When I feel these feelings strongly, I sometimes play that tune. It's quite a well-known tune and most people who know it know it in relation to the W.B. Yeats poem. You'd think the music was written for his famous words. But it wasn't. The tune is much older. It was called *The Maids of Mourne Shore* until twenty years after Yeats published his poem in 1889, when Herbert Hughes put the two together.

I can't remember all the words. But there are two lines that stands out:

She bid me take love easy, as the leaves grow on the tree,
But I, being young and foolish, with her would not agree.

So before I set off, up the little hill signposted *Via Francigena*, I did the next best thing to saying a prayer. I asked Libre if she wouldn't mind just playing *Down by the Salley Gardens*.

And then I tried to distract myself from the hill – which to be honest was only tiddly – by reciting my own irreverent and disrespectful take on the original poem.

In Sally's garden

Witching, once, in Sally's garden
loosely handed, late at night
we heard a frog
croak: croak, croak.

Sally stopped, loosed our hands
and sighed, "my oh-so-handsome Prince!"
I – charming – smiled;
I turned to take her kiss.

"He was, once," she said. "What days those were –
and nights – the royal house of somewhere –
I forget."
She waved her pretty fingers.

"Easy, take it easy, Love,
I told him, over, often, but…
he wouldn't listen,
foolish, foolish man.

"Thinking he was young, he went
and came the way young lovers come,
and go, until –"
she flashed her eyes, and sighed again,

her wand-like fingers willow waved
and caught the pale moon's light –
she said "some spell
just broke,
and handsome
though he was…
he croaked."

I wave to the handsome young couple, no longer holding sweaty hands, as I overtake them outside the lovely chapel of San Sebastiano, just beyond the pretty Piazza Buonaparte. But I don't stop. I've miles to go. Maybe I should aim for Siena after all.

Twenty miles further, though, at Certaldo, I'm collapsing from heat exhaustion. Siena is out of the question. The road goes through Certaldo, and it doesn't look inspiring. The medieval town is to one side, up another of these steep hills. It's called Certaldo Alto, which is a bit of a clue, and I can see from here there's even a funicular railway. It's that steep.

Certaldo, I think, doesn't meet the criteria for being stoppablein. I wanted somewhere as pretty, and quiet, and interesting, as San Miniato. So I take stock, exhausted, in Certaldo. I look at the map and pinpoint some hotels. There appear only to be two options. The choice is between Monteriggioni, maybe twenty miles away, and San Gimignano, about half as far, but twelve hundred feet up. Oh dear. I lie down for half an hour to think about it.

And now here I am, in San Gimignano. And I'm staying in a palace.

It's not an ostentatious palace. In fact it's so discreet it's almost impossible to find. Google Maps is precise about its location, but when I arrive there's nothing there. I go round the little block several times. There's one firmly shut door in the anonymous street façade, and a young man sitting on the step with nothing to do. He looks as though he's been there all day. He's never heard of the palace.

I'm squinting at the three little polished door plates, wondering which bell I might ring in desperation to see if they've heard of the palace which is supposed to be here. One of the doorbells *is* the palace.

The Palazzo Buonacorssi began life in 1200. Marzia's family bought it in 1900. It's not an expensive hotel, because that would require lots of bathrooms, and other unconscionable alterations to the historical structure. But it's just the best place to stay. A totally anonymous face to the street, and a heavenly sheltered courtyard within. Marzia is very welcoming and solicitous towards an overheated and exhausted cyclist.

And just look at all the places to play in San Gimignano, with its piazzas and towers and churches and walls and cisterns. It's a UNESCO World Heritage Site. All medieval Italian towns used to have towers, and if they hadn't been so much at war with each other they still might have them. From a distance San Gimignano looks like a power station on a hill. Only when you get a bit closer can you see it's not a modern power station – obviously – but fourteen stupendously magnificent towers. No other town in Italy has so many still standing.

So I think I'll make a weekend of it – well, at least stay another night. San Gimignano is a town of great beauty, and even though I'm here by accident, I could definitely do worse than stay. Besides, I've just discovered a very good reason not to go to Siena tomorrow.

Tomorrow, Siena will be transformed into a Dantian hell for the annual *Palio*, the mad horse-racing through town that's only slightly less dangerous than Pamplona's bull-running. Dante, by the way, didn't live in Siena. He lived in San Gimignano.

This is what I imagined Italy would be like – turn up in a beautiful square, play for a while, and earn enough for lunch, maybe even dinner.

It hasn't been like that anywhere, yet. But it would have worked out in San Gimignano, which has the most beautiful old square it's possible to imagine, with a lovely open acoustic. Except for the local Mafia.

I don't know, of course, whether they were Mafia with a capital M, but he was quite gently definite. "We are a local association, and we play here," he said. "You cannot play here."

He said it in such a way it was clear he had no doubt I would understand.

He was setting up his steel drums, and he allowed me to play while he did so. Then, of course, I moved. He couldn't chase me around town and play his steel drums at the same time.

I can see why you would protect such a spot. The tourists in San Gimignano are cultured and generous. But it's not a small place, and there are lots of tourists, so it wasn't too much of a problem. I played lots of Bach – twice by request. I played *Down by the Salley Gardens*, more than once. I earned enough for lunch *and* a good dinner.

Then Libre had a rest, while I strolled around town with an ice cream, or maybe two. Well, you couldn't put the raspberry flavoured with rosemary in the same cone as the almond and

273

saffron, could you?

I might even have slept after lunch, in the incomparably wonderful Palazzo Buonaccorsi, when the temperature reached thirty-eight again. I planned the rest of the route. Three and a half days to Rome, all being well. De-mob happy.

CHAPTER 39

Blocking the street in Siena

SUNDAY 3 JULY

You perhaps think a bit too much of my music is either serious or sad. I can see why you might think that. You've heard me play a lot of Bach, and although we could argue about how serious some of those dances really are... Yes, OK, it's serious music.

And then you've heard all that slow Irish stuff, which isn't generally cheerful and sunny, I agree. And *The Swan*; and *Syrinx*; and *Ashokan Farewell*. The list goes on.

Maybe you're forgetting *James Bond*, because I haven't played that for a while. Or Henry VIII's *All in a Garden Green*. And a few other dances, from Scotland, and Ireland, and Argentina.

I'm not trying to contradict you. I think a bit too much of my music *is* either serious or sad. So I've been trying to redress the balance a bit, with a couple of numbers from the musicals. My absolute favourite is *Thoroughly Modern Millie*, though that didn't in fact begin as a stage musical. It was a film before it went to the stage. Julie Andrews starred, in 1967, hot on the heels of her more famous *Mary Poppins*, and her even famouser *The Sound of Music*. It wasn't a stage musical until 2002.

The thing about it, which makes the theme tune so beautifully playable, is that it's set in 1922. So we can swing it about, and swoop into the notes with a gay glissando, and knock it out as though we're a big band. It's fun to play. But it comes with a health warning, or at least a performance warning. The first verse is in the key of A. Then it slides up a semitone into B flat. You have to keep your wits about you.

Millie thought she was thoroughly modern in 1922, when she moved from her small town to the bright lights of New York. She liked short skirts and short hair, and – perhaps most of all – the way they kissed in the movies. She planned to get a job with a rich boss, and marry him for his money. Indeed, thoroughly modern.

Perhaps the basic problems don't really change. What about an update, a hundred years on?

Her list, or
Good at bedtime stories

Good at bedtime stories,
scratched her mental pen,
loud across the parchment
in her head.

Was that on the list?
She scratched again, a bit
distracted from his even tone,
some long and moral tale.

"In conclusion" (happy word,
she thought) "what you
need to understand," he said,
his tone now earnest, pressing, full –

"is I am not like other men.
I do not patronise, explain, or spell out
words like non-apotheotic (meaning,
by the way, just ordinary).

HIGHWAY CELLO

"Respect is what you need,
and get from men like me,
who understand you're more than capable
of independent thought."

His thought could run and run, she sighed,
and sighed again, and smiled
a sidelong smile – apology if he could see it
through his manly flow.

But the manly flow flowed undiminished
true and straight.
Reluctantly her pen
scratched out his name, his promise,

all his untried bedtime stories,
noting, wistfully, he's handsome,
but I think I'd better take
that parachute.

There's a Conservatory of Music in Siena, along with all the better-known things like *duomos* and *palazzos*. The young men studying my performance with critical generosity were, I discovered when I stopped, its students and alumni.

If I'd known, perhaps I would have been more self-conscious. And then I would have forgotten the notes. You mustn't, I've learned, be too self-conscious playing on the street. You need to be alert to the passing audience, to engage with it, to encourage it.

When a shy person surreptitiously films from the side, not sure if it's allowed, or if it's chargeable, you need to direct the performance towards them, and make sure they know you don't mind.

When a child, who's probably never seen a cello before, wants to detain its parents, you give it every encouragement. If possible, you get it to dance.

And when a slightly frazzled teacher stops his young charges and begins – standing right in front of you – to lecture them, you create a dramatic ending that causes them to interrupt him with spirited applause.

And when an ambulance comes wailing up the narrow pedestrian street, you quickly back against the wall and watch it drive over your artfully placed CDs. (Actually, it was only the very edge of one, and no damage was done; let's not exaggerate.)

Siena, like San Gimignano yesterday, is a happy place to play. I set off early from the *palazzo*. I wanted to get the twenty-three miles, and Siena's big hill, out of the way before the real heat of the day. In fact the GPS thingy's profile of the route was quite intimidating. There wasn't just a hill up to Siena. There was nothing *but* hill, all day. And it was going to be hot again.

But I've had a rest day, and I'm a sucker for punishment. Down the hill from San Gimignano, after a breakfast of coffee and heavenly *panforte* – a cake that looks as though it might be chocolate but turns out to be a chewy mixture of nuts and fruit and candied peel and spices, sold by weight, and probably the densest concentration of calories it's possible to devise.

Then straight up the hill to La Grazie. Down. Up. Down. Up to Monteriggioni, a wonderfully perfect, nearly circular, fortified bastion on a natural hill. The walls are intact. They enclose a tiny collection of houses and gardens, a little church, and a square. There's a car park outside the walls, and a couple of tourist coaches. The walls were built in 1213 to keep the Florentines out, and they're good at keeping the coaches out too. All these visitors don't come so much because Monteriggioni features in Dante's *Divine Comedy*. It's the appearance – albeit with some poetic licence – in *Assassin's Creed* that has put it on the coach itineraries.

And if you want to call your visit *ancient and modern*, stop by the Formula 1 inspired *Pit Stop 17* cocktail bar. Move one of its chairs from the sun to the shade on the other side of the street, and take coffee with the establishment's owner, and listen to him complain about the heat.

Down. Up. Down. Up. Up, to hilly Siena. I thought Siena would be straightforward to navigate – another old city, with everything important on the top of its hill. But the medieval streets seem to traverse several hills, and getting from one to another isn't easy with a bicycle. A good proportion of the town's streets aren't streets at all, but flights of stairs. In the end, after a bit of backtracking and bemusement, I wonder why I'm doing it. I don't need to find the Duomo, or the Piazza del Campo, or the Palazzo Pubblico, to prove I've been to Siena. I'm trying to prove something quite different.

I want to convince myself that yesterday's performances on the streets of San Gimignano were not an outlying fluke. I want to believe I could do it again – to spot the right place to play, and to play in a way that inspires the opening of wallets and purses. So I'm looking for the right *kind* of place, not necessarily a famous place. I choose a narrow street, at the entrance to a square. So there's a lot of foot traffic, and it's moving, but not too quickly.

A narrow street makes for a good acoustic (as the Conservatory students noted). So those coming up the street are alerted to my presence, with plenty of time to get their purses out if they want to. And they generously detain and encourage those coming down from the square.

I shouldn't really be thinking about the money, of course. I should be playing just because this is what I want to do, and this is where I want to do it. But it's hard not to look for validation. When a hundred people go by with their noses in their phones, it's discouraging. And when I get this much notice, and I hear the frequent chink of coins, I admit it makes me feel good.

There's something about Bach, of course, that makes people think it's the right response to these old stones and bricks. It also makes them feel good about themselves in a place like this – look at us, we've come on a culture holiday, and here we are, listening to Bach on a cello. Double culture. Gold stars, and an extra *gelato*, all round.

So I play lots of Bach. And lots of dances, too, so the kids will stop and jig about, and block the narrow street, which works a treat. And *Thoroughly Modern Millie*, and all those other cheerful things you complained earlier you haven't heard yet. And I did well again, monetarily speaking. So I treat myself to a proper Sunday lunch, counting out the bill in heavy coinage.

In the afternoon the roads are hot – very hot. The forecast says thirty-six, but when I reach San Quirico d'Orcia, an ancient fortified town on the top of *another* steep hill, everyone says it has definitely been forty today.

When I say everyone, I mean the staff of the Capitano Hotel, which seems to own most of the old town.

The Capitano Hotel is a long shot. The staff in reception are being very professional, and almost managing to disguise their understandable distaste at the sweaty figure in front of them. I'm not the kind of guest they're accustomed to. Most of their visitors arrive in properly stylish Italian cars, either owned or hired for the duration, with properly expensive hats, and shoes, and luggage. I sense an alertness to the passage of any such guests, who might need to be diverted for a moment.

These rooms, I'm trying to explain, are too expensive, as I hand back the glass they kindly gave me, and ask for a refill. And then another. They're too expensive even for a meaningful negotiation. But there isn't another hotel I've any chance of reaching in my current heat-exhausted state. Is there any other option, I'm asking? I'm trying to give the polite impression that I'm not moving until they find one.

Please wait in the garden, for just a moment, she says, glancing up the stairs towards the measured tread of more salubrious guests. Her colleague gently hustles me out through the garden door. Could I have another glass of water while I wait? When this one comes with ice I think perhaps the strategy is working – I'm trying to make myself so much at home they can't possibly send me away.

And yes, after ten minutes, there is another option. It's in the annexe down the hill. She explains quietly, so that no other guests should overhear, and with the same care and uncertainty as they did in Pisa, that this is not an air-conditioned room. Subtext: don't think of suing us if you expire in the night.

So I exit discreetly, not to be seen by the proper guests, and bow to the reception staff to acknowledge their kindness. I go back down the hill, past the eleventh-century Chiesa di Santa Maria Asunta, which marks the *Via Francigena*, to find the little annexe.

Now I've had a couple of cups of tea, and I'm back in the garden, properly dressed and looking quite respectable, surrounded by huge terracotta pots of rosemary, with shady walks covered in wisteria and vines and olives. The garden vista is backed by those characteristically needle-shaped cypresses, and there's enough breeze to keep the mosquitoes at bay, and to point out it's still well over thirty degrees at nearly eight o'clock, and definitely time therefore to go in search of some dinner.

The staff, quite impressed and only momentarily wrong-footed by my transformation into something resembling a *bona fide* resident, suggest a little light music in the garden. It would have been a nice place to play, among the rosemary and wisteria, and backed by those needle cypresses. But I can't. I'm too tired to bring Libre back up from the annexe.

I make my apologies and walk slowly in the direction of the square, pausing for a moment to look into another walled garden, where drums and microphones are being packed up and put away. I've just missed a school performance, one of the tidying-up teachers explains. Yes, we've had a good time, she says, though they're mostly just beginners, so you never quite know what's going to happen.

I thought I was recovered from the day. But I find I'm not. I need to eat, but when the exhaustion shows itself in a queasy dizziness it seems wise to go slowly home and eat the remains of lunch – bread and cheese and apricots – rather than risk a table in the public square.

CHAPTER 40

Smelling like the Devil

MONDAY 4 JULY

I smell like the Devil. Literally. It's nothing to do with the heat – though more of that later. It's a real and strong smell of sulphur. And it's coming from me.

When I see the signs to the Bagno San Fillipo, 4km up the hill to the right, I imagine a shaded square, with cold water gushing from ornate fountain heads, sustaining a village, and several bars and restaurants where you can get coffee, which I'm desperately needing. The signpost has a picture of a fountain, or something very like one.

The SS2 – that's the name of the road I'm on – begins (or ends) in Rome. The signs are counting down the kilometres, and I've reached 160. One hundred miles to Rome.

At this rate, though, I'll never make it. I've been exhausted before. Life, after all, is an exhausting business. But I've never been exhausted like this.

The road goes through a desert, and I'm parched and fading. Should I go off route – and climb 500ft – to enjoy the relief of San Fillipo's Bagno?

I change my mind twice before I actually begin the climb. And when I get there, I find the whole thing has been mis-sold.

There was no mention, at the bottom of the hill, of the word *termico*, "thermal", which is now everywhere. These are hot

282

springs, not cold mountain waters, and there's a strong smell of sulphur in the air. The last thing anyone would want, cycling in this heat, is a hot bath. Even without the sulphur, that would be a recognisable definition of hell.

But I've come all this way, and there's no shady square, and no coffee. And it's an excuse not to get back on the bike straightaway. I chain the bike to a fence and walk down the path through the wood, to take the waters.

The result is that now I'm enveloped in this strong sulphurous perfume, which is going to accompany me for the rest of the day.

Back on the low road, and the Tuscan countryside is parched and without shade. A small wasp gets inside my shirt. By the time I've stopped and ripped off my helmet, and struggled with the sodden shirt, it stings me twice in that little bit of the back you just can't reach.

The road – the *Via Cassia* – is straight, and in much better condition than most I've ridden in the last few days. But it doesn't pay much attention to the countryside, and it always goes over the hills instead of round. It's hard to decide whether it's a modern imposition on the landscape, or whether it's Roman. Then I realise there's a clue in the name – it's the work of Emperor Cassius.

There's not much traffic, so it goes fast. A smart car whizzes past, does a U-turn ahead, and whizzes past again. I can hear it doing another U-turn behind me, and then it comes more slowly.

"Can I take a picture?" The driver is leaning excitedly across his passenger to ask. I'm not in a state to care whether he wants to take a picture, or whether this is a highway robbery. At least it's an excuse to stop.

Enrico is, he says, a professional photographer. So putting his equipment together is more complicated than just taking a phone out of his pocket. He shows me a picture I nearly took myself – a few round hay bales by the road, highlighting the straw-coloured landscape – except I couldn't be bothered to stop. Then suddenly he's in professional mode, directing the photos he wants. The result, which he sends me later, is quite expressive – a wasp-coloured cyclist, Libre, and half the picture a cruelly blue sky.

The green flashing sign outside the chemist in Acquapendente says it's thirty-nine degrees. The red flashing sign outside the discount supermarket directly across the road says it's forty-one. They're flashing at different rates, and the effect is like two drunken men sparring without ever landing a punch. Why can't they just call it a draw and agree it's round about forty degrees? It's too hot to fight about anything.

When it's this hot, waves of heat, way above body temperature, sweep up off the black road. You notice it most on the ears – they're constantly burning, as though the dry countryside is talking about you, mocking you, hissing quietly about the lack of shade.

The grass beside the road gave up long ago. It's the same straw colour as the emptied fields. This landscape, with its curves and needle cypresses, might be beautiful in the Spring. It's hard to see it that way now.

Still, Bolsena, by the lake of the same name, is somewhere to aim for. I can see the lake from a distance. That much water must, I feel, cool the surrounding air just a little.

Entering the town, with its stupendous old castle on one side, I aim for the lake on the other. I'm looking for a little hotel as close to the water as possible. Let me in that water!

The lake, it turns out, after I've found a hotel right beside it, is a slightly cool bath temperature. The air is a quite warm sauna. Don't you just love the summer?

I wash off most of the sulphur in the lake, so I think I can walk up to the old castle, through the avenue of the grandest and biggest plane trees I've ever seen, without crosses being waved at me. But I'm afraid Libre is staying behind. One of us is just too tired.

I stop at a shop selling beautiful things made from highly figured olive wood. What an intoxicating smell. There's a table top I really, really like. But it has a lot of noughts on the price label, and I laugh out loud when I imagine the table and Libre fighting over the space on the back of the bike. The shopkeeper looks at me oddly, perhaps nervously. These things happen when you can practically smell the destination, two days away.

The proximity of Rome is emphasised at the little roadside table just up the street. I eat *pinsa*, which is known to cause fights. Is it pizza, or is it not pizza? I can't possibly enter that arena, but its slow fermented sourdough mixture, which should include soy and rice flours, and doesn't allow tomatoes in its toppings, makes it quite a different experience. I would have enjoyed it more though if I hadn't been sitting so close to a loud and patriarchal German-Italian who required his whole family – and all the rest of us – to know he was an authority on any subject they could mention. He is loudly offended when I leave without a *buonasera* in his direction.

I sleep well in Bolsena, overlooking the largest volcanic lake in Europe, comforted by knowing the volcano has been inactive since 104BC, and looking forward to my last full day's cycling tomorrow.

Another hilly day. The road up to Montefiascone – which I'm told I can't translate as the *hill of spectacular mistakes* – has a good view of the lake. But whatever the name really means, there is a well-attested historical fiasco to commemorate here. On Good Friday 1670 the magnificent cathedral lost its roof in a fire. The Montefiasconians overcame any suspicions this might have been a divine judgement, and set about replacing it with one of the largest cathedral domes in Italy.

If you want to quibble and point out that St. Paul's in London has a dome almost exactly three times the size, you might like to know that Montefiascone's is a generation older. It took Sir Christopher Wren forty-four years after the Fire of London to get his dome off the ground (his first designs were rejected for being too "Roman"). It took Carlo Fontana and the Montefiasconians just four.

I'm still on the *Via Cassia*, which here, in unpleasant contrast to yesterday's section of it, is in the worst condition of any Italian road I've yet been on. I should have stopped in Viterbo. It's an important place, with enough history to fill a book. But I ride casually through it all, waving to a few stupendously magnificent papal palaces, cathedrals, fountains, castles, museums, churches and piazzas. It's all very splendid, but I just wish some of that money had been spent on this *[word removed]* road instead. It may be suitable for old Roman tractors, but definitely not for bicycles with cellos.

Bracciano is about twenty-seven miles from Rome. If the weather had been different – which I think it sometimes must be, unless all these road signs warning of snow are someone's idea of a joke – I would probably have pedalled on and reached Rome in the early evening. But I know when I'm beaten. Besides, Bracciano appears to have much to recommend it. It looks like a fine place to stop. Like so many of these towns, there's a little medieval heart, with steep, stepped, cobbled streets. There's a castle, too, of course, and a fine collection of churches.

I'm trying to find out why the castle isn't called Castello Bracciano. Instead it has a tongue-twister of a name – Orsini-Odescalchi. I'm also trying to decide if it's a fake, like the Neptune in Genoa's harbour. It's in such good condition it looks as though it can't be more than a hundred years old. Unfortunately they won't let me in to see. It's closing in ten minutes. This is the castle that featured in *Bill & Ted's Excellent Adventure*, which may or may not be why Tom Cruise hired it as the location for one of his weddings. It must be real, then, surely – Tom Cruise wouldn't get married on a film set, would he?

Like Bolsena, Bracciano also has a volcanic lake – not as big as Bolsena's, but handsome enough that it could almost be in Cumbria, and far enough below the medieval town that you can see nearly all of it in one go if you've climbed up as far as the castle.

The castle stands high and protectively over the square, which isn't medieval. I'm sitting on a metal bench facing a fine town hall, with a nice fountain beside me, and children running about. I've played a Bach *Suite*, with all the repeats, for a father and teenage daughter who won't let me stop.

Even at eight o'clock there are people working in the town hall, and from time to time a bunch of them come out on a balcony – I think to listen, but maybe just to take the air.

There are the usual young footballers, too, of course, who are bound to accumulate in such a space. Occasionally their pitch encompasses mine, so it's all slightly hazardous. Nevertheless it was a good way, I decide, to spend a last evening before the end of the journey in Rome, tomorrow.

CHAPTER 41

Improvisation and the meaning of life

Life, goes the old cliché, is not a rehearsal. You don't get to practise the difficult bits ahead of time. You do, however, if you survive them, get to dwell on the mistakes and regret them at some leisure. Unless of course you're Edith Piaf, or one of those few other lucky ones who *ne regrette rien*.

Musically speaking, there are two quite different circumstances of performance without rehearsal. There's sight-reading, where the music is put in front of you and you just have to do your best to play what's written, when you've never seen it before. It's either right, or it's wrong. It's good, or it's bad. If you're doing a music exam, or an audition, there will always be sight-reading. It's a test of technical competence, of how swiftly and accurately you can translate the written music into the sounds the composer intended.

And then there's improvisation. You don't have any music in front of you. The music comes out of your head. What you're trying to do is make something meaningful and beautiful out of a few rules and lots of imagination. If you're improvising in a band, the rules can be quite specific – *this is the pattern we're all following*, or, *the leader decides, and the rest of us fit in*.

When you're on your own the rules can be looser. They can even be almost non-existent.

HIGHWAY CELLO

Life isn't a rehearsal. It's an improvisation. All of us make it up as we go along. Sometimes with more and sometimes with fewer rules; sometimes with more and sometimes with less success. We're definitely not sight-reading, though – there's no script. We're improvising.

I've been thinking about this as the journey has become more improvisatory. Early on there was at least a partial script. There were set lists. So when it came to a performance, I knew what I was going to play, in what order. Further on, I was trying to read an audience, and play what I thought might suit the moment. I never got quite as far as playing something twice because I forgot I'd already played it, but I did once set off to play a piece and found I was playing something else entirely.

Further South, in the general mayhem of heat and dust and exhaustion, the pages in front of me are fading. Or I was blinded by the sun. Whatever it was I felt a permission, and an urge, not always to play the pieces I knew, but to play the music in my head. I'd been trying to select, from my small repertoire, numbers that spoke to the moment. Then I began to want *my* expression of the moment, not something borrowed. Yes, obviously Bach is better music than Wilson, so I didn't ditch the real music altogether. But on the street, in random moments, at first occasionally, and then more often, I made my own.

Sometimes I just want to wander, to watch people passing by, to wonder about the lives they lead, to marvel at their opacity, and their transparency. And to be transparent myself.

I want to be part of the landscape of old stones, and warm trees. I want to be a cloudless sky, and a whimper of complaint about the unrelenting heat.

There isn't time to write poetry, to put all this into words. I'm in the wrong language anyway. There's only the moment. And me and Libre in it. And the old stones and the warm trees. And you, passing by, doing whatever you're doing, distracted, or impervious.

Of course, all the music I've already played for you, the Bach and Debussy and Fauré, the laments and jigs and tango, the musicals, the films, the ballads; all of it speaks to all kinds of things and moments. It's not prescribed, so I can put any feeling into it I want. And you might hear that feeling, or you might hear something else entirely. Once the note leaves the bow, it's yours, not mine.

A small child comes into view. I make my rhythm the same as the child's footsteps. It's amazing how quickly children notice. Sometimes they think the music is coming out of the earth at their command. So they stamp. So the music stamps. Then the music skips. So the child skips. Then the parent wonders what's going on. So the music scurries away and hides, just peeping out from behind an imaginary tree.

It's not just children who hear themselves in the music. A couple arguing, absorbed, alternately angry and defensive. So I make a discordant, staccato, sound. She notices. She's got two people to be angry with now. So I make a little glissando mewing of apology, of reconciliation. She can't help laughing. But he doesn't understand, until she nudges him, pointing in my direction. I give them a musical shrug and look innocently away. He pecks her on the cheek, and I waltz them off the stage.

Sometimes it's more – more than the wandering, the landscape, the people, the conversations.

Sometimes I want to improvise a more basic commentary, on life, the universe, and everything. Yes, in Bracciano, by the fountain, I'm playing to that very attentive father and daughter. And then suddenly I'm not. I'm in quite a different place, playing only for myself, looking back over forty days of a journey from the edge of Empire to its heart, and wondering about tomorrow morning's arrival in Rome.

I've never been a great improviser. I'm a lot less musical than I would like to be. In fact, in many respects, I'm hardly musical at all. Some of my musical friends have been open-mouthed at what I can't do. I have great difficulty pitching a note. I have no idea of a chord sequence in the simplest of songs. I failed Grade IV aural tests. Real musicians hear all kinds of things that just pass me by. Real musicians know where they are, and what's going on. They follow the structure of the music, and it makes sense to them.

Not to me, it doesn't. I just like beautiful sound. I hear it in my head, in my fingers, in the hills. And I want to make those sounds. And throw them out there, to the winds, to the world.

So when it comes to improvisation, I'm hopeless in a band. Worse than hopeless. It would be like asking me to fly a plane.

All I can do is play a tune, a feeling. I try to stay in a proper key, or at least modulate to something recognisably related to where I started. But it doesn't always work. I tell myself it doesn't matter – there's no band behind me to get confused, or cross. This is just the raw feeling of the moment. Is the soundtrack of your life an example of good harmonic order? Well, mine isn't. Sorry.

Don't lose sight of where I'm going with this. Yes, improvising some music is about catching hold of a moment, and expressing it, and releasing it. But more than that, it's also about trying to cope with, to accept, to submit to, the improvisatory nature of all existence.

There is no divine plan, no goal, no happily ever after. Teleological explanations of the universe, or any individual life in it, are simply redundant. They don't work anymore.

There used to be big religious debates about *free will* – what is it, what are its limits? It's a necessary element in the explanation of sin, and a fallen world. But isn't it then also blasphemous; the suggestion that God might have limited God's own agency in favour of these poor created beings?

If you live in a post-theistic world, as I'm trying to do, the free will question is completely different. It's still an enormous question. But it doesn't take its meaning from any God-question.

Instead it asks what is the meaning, and what are the limits, of my ability to decide what I'm going to do next? While I'm writing this I can get up and make a cup of tea. I can look out of the window. I could smash the computer through the window and destroy it all. I believe I'm making a choice not to do any of those things just at this moment. But we know we're conditioned in so many ways. We're suggestible. We're products of our genes and our environments, and we're predictable, at least in a probabilistic sense. Anarchy does not rule.

But still we choose. We improvise. What note to play next is my choice. My *choice*. *My* choice.

I once met a retired American engineer in the beautiful Mexican city of Oaxaca. Why, I asked him, had he retired to Oaxaca? He'd worked, he said, on engineering projects in seventy countries. When he retired he realised he could live in any one of them. Or nearly any one of the more than seventy others he hadn't worked in. He was free, to choose. "So I chose Oaxaca," he said. "Why? Hard to say – it was just a choice."

This is what my – inexpert, sometimes even feeble – musical improvisation is about. It's commentary, and reflection, on bigger questions of improvisation. I chose to make this journey. I could have stayed at home. Every moment is a moment of uncountable choices. To stop, or keep going. To go faster, or slower. To take this road, or that. To wave, or not to wave. To play, or not to play. To say yes, or to say no. To speak, or not speak. To dare, or not to dare.

When I get home I'm going to buy a book. I'm going to study the art of improvisation and see if my musical inabilities are really as big as I think they are, or whether I could learn to improvise properly, or at least better. Then I might begin to understand the meaning of life.

CHAPTER 42

I'm in Rome!

Bracciano is less than thirty miles from Rome. Romans come here for a day out. You can get from the city to Bracciano's beautiful lake and splendid castle in less than an hour on a suburban train. So I'm nearly there. The end really is almost in sight.

I must have been in a hurry. The miles fly by, and after an hour I'm sixteen miles out of Bracciano, on the edge of the metropolis itself. The roads are bad; they're complicated and confusing. The traffic is mostly on its way to work, impatient commuters resentful of a bicycle on holiday. But I don't care. I find a new lease of life, and I rattle along at much the same speed as the cars. Sometimes, when they queue and crawl, I whizz down the outside with the motorbikes, nipping back into the lane just in time to avoid being grazed by a bus coming the other way. It feels like a fairground ride.

I have to ring the reception committee and tell them I'll be early.

Committee? Not exactly. But Jenny and Alfie are going to meet me at the Vatican. The BBC, who made a little feature of my departure, from Hadrian's Wall, six weeks ago, want to make another of my arrival. But they've sub-contracted it. We have to do it ourselves. Do it on a phone, they said; don't make it look too homemade. So I have to get them out of bed. Tell them to be there on time.

Technically, you might say, the Vatican isn't Rome at all. It isn't even actually Italy. But let's not quibble.

It was Terence who gave me the idea. "Are you going to play for the Pope?" he asked, as he snipped the hair that was a good deal greyer than when I'd last seen him, just before Covid. "Well, you should."

That was a few days before I left home, and Rome seemed a long, long, way off. So I haven't given any thought to a symbolic arrival. But why not? Not the Pope himself, perhaps. But I really should try and play in St. Peter's Square, shouldn't I?

I don't think I've ever cycled so fast. Until I had no choice and had to cycle faster. The roads are confusing; there are too many road signs, and I don't know what they all mean. Without warning I find myself in a tunnel, on a road that looks as though it shouldn't allow bicycles. It's dark. It's terrifying. If bikes, as I suspect, aren't allowed, I just won't be seen. Being overtaken is likely to be a terminal experience. So I have to strobe my lights and go at the same speed as the traffic.

Fortunately it's downhill.

Then I'm spewed out, blinking and shaken, into the daylight. I could be anywhere. But wait, the map says I've come in more or less a straight line, and in exactly the right direction. Vatican City is just over there. And I'm early. There's no committee.

If you don't ask, you don't get. So I approach the Carabinieri, four of them, chatting outside their van with a soldier, his finger on the trigger.

"We don't have jurisdiction," they agree. "You have to ask the police." I don't have to look for the police. When I return to the bike, propped against the colonnade where it shouldn't be, there are half a dozen of them, wondering to each other whether they should arrest it. I suddenly remember that moment in London when I might have been shot – no properly alert security force is going to think there's a cello in that cello case. They'll be looking for the detonator.

So I ask. I've come from Hadrian's Wall, yes, on the bike, yes, with the cello. Please could I play for five minutes in the Square – a fitting end to the journey?

"We don't have jurisdiction," one of them says. "That's another country. You have to talk to the Vatican State Police."

So where, I wonder, aloud, might I find the Vatican Police?

"You don't. I call them for you. Show me your documents."

So with my passport open in front of him, he rings his office, and explains the unusual request. "Normally of course, this isn't allowed. But in your case I think they might say yes."

Ten minutes later the *yes* arrives, a phone call, followed not far behind by a large but un-uniformed Vatican official.

The policeman, from the neighbouring country, and now joined by a couple of colleagues, holds onto my passport until I finish playing. He hands it back with a broad smile. "Complimenti," he says. "Welcome to Rome."

So I've played my cello in St Peter's Square, outside the Vatican. My arrival has been officially filmed, in a homemade kind of a way, and should appear on the BBC later, by way of proof.

I've arrived. And in eighteen hundred miles, and forty days, I haven't had a puncture.

I'm going to lie down.

"Is this the first time you play at the Pantheon?" The question is aggressive. The questioner isn't wearing a uniform, but he has a large *Polizia* badge hanging round his neck and resting on a very authoritatively-sized stomach. The badge isn't much below my eye-line when I stand up.

I don't have time for any of the usually persuasive story about having biked from almost Scotland. "It is the last," he says, wobbling his badge with power. "Here it is forbidden."

You can see why it would be. The crowds are big enough for a football match (though well enough behaved for rugby) and have just been dangerously parted by a parade of three horse-drawn carriages. No authority would be in the mood to tolerate a stationary cellist eliciting mild applause.

Even so, I do get a photo, and a video, to prove I *have* played in front of the Pantheon – which has probably seen worse in the 1897 years it's stood there.

Rome is a city of many superlatives and magnificences like this. The *Highway Cello* journey was conceived as being "from the edge of the Roman Empire to its heart." And here that heart seems still to beat.

I've been in Rome now nearly seventy-two hours, and I'm still trying to believe it's over. I've arrived. I'm *in* Rome.

So I've been going around all the iconic places, and many little hidden corners, shamelessly blocking the tourist traffic, and playing Bach, and Debussy, and old English folk tunes that may or may not have been written by Henry VIII, and Irish love songs, and anything else I can think of, trying to get it into my head that I'm *in Rome*.

The heat has dissipated, and the forecast is for a comfortable thirty-three today. It went out with quite a bang. Jenny and Alfie had put on a little party, and I'd played some stuff out on their terrace, overlooking semi-suburban Rome – yes, *Rome* – and I was sleeping on the same terrace because the bedroom was too hot, when I woke up to find I was being blown away.

We'd seen some lightning in the distance, earlier, and suddenly the storm arrived. The wind was fearsome, and fearsomely sudden, and stuff that wasn't tied or weighted down was banging and crashing and flying away. Rome – yes, *I'm in Rome* – can really put on a show.

They have pizzas here, and *gelato*. And fountains. And a river called the Tiber. And history, and Empire. And tourists who seem sometimes to want a break from all that just to listen to a cello playing in the shade.

And I'm sitting in a heap, reflecting that I've ridden forty days, and eighteen hundred miles, and climbed the height of more than three Everests, to get here. And I'm feeling that odd mixture of finality, and mortality, and emptiness, and accomplishment, that goes with the reaching of a goal.

I should, at my age, know that life isn't about goals. It's only process. And the process continues, and today's another day. So what shall we do today, in between the pizza, the *gelato*, and the fountains, and the amazement?

Don't get completely into holiday mode. I have one serious obligation to perform. That letter from the Mayor of Carlisle, addressed to the Mayor of Rome, which I've carried all the way, through three countries and over an Alp or two, is still in my bag. It's in remarkably good shape, seeing what it's been through, and I have an appointment this morning to present it to the Mayor's Diplomatic Ambassador.

I thought that would be the work of five minutes. *Ah, Mr. Wilson, welcome to Rome. So you made it. It's very kind of the Mayor of Carlisle to write. He could just have sent an email, you know. Have a nice day.*

Despite what I told you in San Quirico – that I looked almost respectable when I was washed and brushed up – I don't have anything smart enough to wear to meet an Ambassador. So I thought I'd better wear my cycling clothes, and go on the bike, with Libre, and make it look as though I'd just arrived – that I would have changed into top hat and tails if I'd had time.

The clothes are unfortunate. But just as well Libre came too. I find I'm expected to give a private concert for the Mayor's Diplomatic Ambassador. On the roof of the Musei Capitolini, in the sunshine, with the ancient city spread out below us.

Actually it isn't that private. It requires a staff of six to organise, escort, take notes, photograph the event, and generally see fair play. As I say to the Ambassador, it makes me feel very welcome in Rome. I'm right to feel that, he says; I am indeed very welcome in Rome.

In the last few days, when I'm supposed to have been resting, recovering, I've biked a lot of miles over Rome's back-breaking cobbles. They look nice, from a distance, those cobbles. But they're not nice for riding on. Libre doesn't like them at all.

Proper Romans ride electric bikes with enormously fat soft tyres. Much better on the cobbles.

I play in the Piazza Navona in front of a famous fountain and a million tourists. I play a couple of times by the Fontana Tortarughe, the Turtle Fountain, serenading a little wedding party with *The Swan* while they take their pictures beside the fountain's rather immodest bronze youths.

I try to negotiate with the police to play in front of the Colosseum, but there's no room for negotiation. Even the suggestion that I'd just play the Italian national anthem doesn't stop the solemn shaking of heads.

So I play instead in front of the "fake Colosseum", the Teatro Marcello. That probably isn't allowed either, but the police are elsewhere.

I play for the shoppers and tourists and stall holders at the Testaccio Market. I play for the evening strollers, and the young and dangerous footballers, in the local piazza, and then stroll with them, carrying Libre and eating *gelato* as slowly as the heat allows.

And tomorrow, my last day in Rome, I really should get back on the bike, for one last hurrah. As the Ambassador is presenting me with a rather fine print of the Piazza Campidoglio, where we're meeting, they are quite clear. Having started from Hadrian's Wall, I should properly finish at Hadrian's Villa.

It's at Tivoli, just twenty miles outside Rome. Hadrian built it so that he could govern the Empire in comfort, not cooped up in the little villas and palaces of the city itself.

I really ought to go. They're very definite, almost insistent, about it. But I think I won't take Libre. I really can't see my little homemade aluminium cello rack surviving any more of these Roman cobbles.

Nobody could accuse Hadrian of being a spendthrift. He puts Imelda Marcos right in the shade. Unfortunately the heyday of his villa – which is more of a large town than the word *villa* suggests, at least to me – is well past.

There are glimpses of a glory that must have been, but mostly the marble is long gone. There are bricks, in a distinctive style, on the diagonal, the occasional pillar and half cupola, a great number of extremely informative notices in several languages, and lots of ruin and dust.

I stay longer than I might have done, partly from the tourist's requirement to get value for money, but mostly because I don't want to face the road back to Rome.

The way out of the city is busy. There are about ten miles before you see a blade of grass. There are some roadside cycle tracks, but you can't use them because the positioning, and occasional emptying, of recycling bins mean they're covered in a confetti of broken glass.

Once out of the city the road narrows, but the traffic doesn't get less. And there's a lot more glass, and plastic, and generally dumped rubbish, some of it burned. Then you reach the travertine stone yards, which generate more heavy traffic, and more dust. I've seen some very beautiful parts of Italy – from Alpine slopes, to medieval hill cities, Tuscan countryside and the sea, the sea – but this reminds me there's an ugly underbelly to all agglomerations of humanity. Take the bus next time.

CHAPTER 43

What on earth am I doing?

According to the screen we're travelling at 249kph, which I calculate is 155mph, about twelve times as fast as I would normally go on a bike, and in a much straighter line. The seat is very comfortable, and the air very conditioned.

I can give my full attention to the view, without worrying about potholes, suicidal or murderous drivers, unleashed roadside dogs, broken glass, sunstroke, dehydration, or any of the other inconveniences that have attended me for the last few weeks. It's quite soporific.

When it comes to travel, a train has many advantages over a bicycle.

Libre is flat out on the luggage rack above me, almost certainly asleep. The bike has been left in the capable hands of Giulia in Rome, who will dismantle it as much as is necessary to fit it in a box and post it home.

Home. I'm on my way. Three hours on the train to Verona, which I keep calling Verano by mistake, then tomorrow a longer journey to Munich, before an early start should get me home a bit after bedtime on Sunday, the day after tomorrow.

Verona, where at least two gentlemen came from, and where Shakespeare also located *Romeo and Juliet*. Do they know it's fiction? You can pay a touristical fee to admire the balcony from which Juliet wherefored her Romeo. Shakespeare, as far as we know, never went to Verona. But we shouldn't spoil a good story.

Libre isn't coming with me. They wouldn't want her at the opera, she said, and I'm afraid I agree. So I'm going to *La Traviata* alone.

We've arrived in Verona at the height of opera season. In the third largest Roman arena left in Italy, and one of the best preserved, they have a summer of *Carmen, Aida, Nabucco, Turandot* and *La Traviata*. It's a big arena, but there aren't many tickets left for tonight. There are lots of tourists in Verona.

Libre didn't come out earlier, either. We were both hot and tired, she said, and anyway her contract ended in Rome. Go and be a tourist, she said, and I'll stay here.

I wasn't at home very long – less than two days – before I had to be off again, driving way down South for an unexpected performance. John had read about *Highway Cello*, and sent me an email before I set off. "Stop at Malvern, on the way," he said, "and perform in the Theatre of Small Curiosities."

I told him to look at a map. It's not on the way to Rome. But I'll bear it in mind for a future occasion, I said. That future occasion arose quite suddenly, when I had to go to Gloucester, for family. John grumbled a bit that it was rather short notice, so he probably wouldn't be able to get an audience, but why not? *Pourquoi pas? Perché no?*

So I play in Malvern. And there is an audience. It's the first test of the success or otherwise of the journey. Do you remember, I ask myself, where it all started? Yes – allowing, of course, that a beginning is a random place, picked generally *post hoc facto*, as a kind of justification. The idea of busking, as a way of training myself to face a real audience without any music in front of me.

Well, to that extent then it was all a failure.

It wasn't completely a waste of time, though. I abandoned that goal. I decided it wasn't the right one. Performance was about connection, and confidence. Communication, and involvement. And that is a multi-faceted thing. The music stand in front of me was just a small part of it. And from that point of view, the concert in Malvern was at least a pass, I thought.

I came to a compromise. Play on the street without music, so you know you can do it. But have the music there, low down in front of you, in a concert. And if you lose your place, distracted by something or nothing, close your eyes and look inward for it, instead of back to the page.

So it is a success to this extent. Remember the stinging critique I gave myself in Edinburgh – so long ago, it seems – that my performance was "unconvincing"? I'm less likely to think that now. It isn't quite the only thing that matters about performance, that it should be convincing. But it's a good summary of the main points. As in life, so on the stage, I'm telling myself. Be convincing, wherever possible. If it doesn't seem possible, then question the foundations.

I haven't kept a strict count, so I don't know which actually scores higher. But there are definitely two questions vying for the top spot. *Why did you do it?* And *what's the next adventure?*

The first question makes sense to me. There is, I have to tell them, no good answer to it. At least, no simple answer. On the face of it a journey like this is not a mainstream, or sensible, response to anything. But I wonder why I'm expected to justify it? I've given you some background, and I've told you a story. On most days, that's all there is to it.

The second question I don't understand at all. There seems to be an assumption that if you do something daft today, then you'll do something double-daft tomorrow. It's an inflationary graph. Like the taking of drugs. *What's the next adventure?*

It's not that there isn't an answer to the question. There may well be. Doesn't every good novel set its protagonist up for a sequel, just in case? But maybe it's a bit like asking a man at his wedding if he would like to give you a heads up on who his *next* wife might be. I suppose you maybe wanted to ask Henry VIII – though you probably didn't, because you wanted to keep your head attached – but you wouldn't normally, would you?

Sometimes I just shrug. Sometimes I fabricate something wild and implausible. I call those responses respectively the defensive gambit and the offensive.

If there's ever a sequel to *Highway Cello* then you'll know. And if there isn't then at least that only leaves two possibilities – either I just faded away, or I died in the attempt.

The third question is rarely asked. I suppose you might see it as subsidiary, or supplemental, to the first. Maybe even as the same question. But it's the one I've tried to answer. Not *why* did I do it, but *what* was it I was doing?

There is overlap, yes. But I don't think it's the same question.

The *what* is about how you describe it, what you call it. Its meaning in its context. The *why* is about its antecedents – how it came about. It wouldn't be true to say I was never asked *what* questions. *Is it a pilgrimage?* That's a *what* question. *Is it for charity?* That's another.

I struggled, as you know, with many things. I struggled with hills, and heat, and exhaustion, and loneliness, and language, and navigation. And in idle moments – if you can call them that – usually going slowly up a hill, I sometimes struggled with the definition question. *What on earth am I doing?*

I thought about this at the beginning, especially in relation to the pilgrimage issue. I decided I was too post-religious (horrid word, sorry) to be allowed to use that language uncomplicatedly. But the *Via Francigena* is a pilgrimage road, and I was following it. So I couldn't totally exclude myself from the tradition. I decided – well, I think I decided – the nearest modern equivalent I could hang my helmet on was *work of art*.

And then I got nervous, because I didn't want to seem to be claiming to *be* something – specifically, an *artist*. The definition of a pilgrimage, despite what the tourism arm of the church says, with its pilgrim passes and special offers and indulgences and straight to heaven without passing Go, is the intention of the heart. Perhaps it's the same with art. It might not be *good* art, but if that's what I'm calling it, if that's my heart's intention, maybe that's enough?

Meaning is so complicated in a post-modern world. In general I think that's a good thing. It allows questions to be asked that were once simply non-questions. Like gender, for instance. That used just to be assigned. Most of us now acknowledge there is at least some element of choice, of how we identify ourselves. But within what limits, if any?

Sometimes you just have to be a Humpty Dumpty about it, to claim *your* meaning for the word you're using. So here's my decision, my final answer, to the question *what on earth am I doing?* Yes, *Highway Cello*, that odd and peculiar mash-up of cello and bicycle and story is, in my self-definition, a *work of art*. There. Colours, and everything else, pinned to the mast.

But hills are seductive and mind-bending things. Three and a bit Everests, remember, between the edge of Empire and its heart. Somewhere along the way, uphill and under the sun, I realised – or decided, I'm not really sure whether it counts as a realisation or a decision – one other small thing. *What on earth am I doing* is the same question, with no difference except word order, as *what am I doing on earth?*

You don't have to agree, of course. Laughter and scorn is just as proper a response as any other. As it is, too, of course, to my *work of art* label.

And Libre, you've never taken me too seriously either, since we set out on this journey. So there's no need to start now. You've been the loveliest of travelling companions, Libre, and you know I'd marry you if I could, but I don't always know what you're *thinking*.

304

Acknowledgements

There are so many people who have helped – sometimes carried, sometimes nudged, sometimes kicked – me to this place: parents, friends, teachers, writers, musicians, store detectives, and all kinds of random influencers. I want to acknowledge them all, though it would be impossible to list them.

In relation to *Highway Cello*, the journey and the writing, let me mention, and thank:

Jenny and Noni, who permitted, encouraged, and washed their hands of it, at nearly all the right moments. Jangus, who recorded music, lent me the GPS thingy, and taught me something about bikes. Alfie, whose birthday party provided the send-off.

Dickon Faux-Nightingale, who designed the *Highway Cello* logo. Steven Allington, and Enrico Coviello, who took photos.

Those who believed, or dared, enough to promote or host a performance: Nick Reed, Danny Knight, Susan Ritchie, Lucie VonCarthy, Fr. Ed Martin, Philip Isaac, Colin Wilson, Christopher and Susan, Richard Field, Hélène Musielak, Evelyne Kempf, Elie Ferrandon, Serge Hediger.

Those who hosted me, old friends and new: Sophie and Daniel, Tim Bramfitt, Fr. Ed Martin, Jordan and James, Colin and Caroline,

Henry and Dawn and Miriam, Susan and Christopher, Richard and David, Rose and Ken, Yves and Caterina, Aline and Gautier, Giles and Marie-Paule, Gaetan and Fleure, Martine, Elizabeth and Dominique, Claire and Youri, Serge Hediger, Clotilde and Christophe, Norma and Marco.

The Angel Rafael, who stopped his van and mended my bike. Fillou, who stopped his car and introduced me to *Les Oiseaux de Trottoir*.

The Mayor of Carlisle, Councillor Mike Mitchelson, who sent me off from Carlisle, and the Mayor's Diplomatic Ambassador in Rome, Mr. Gabrielle Annis, who welcomed me to Rome.

Neil Avery and Marie Ferrandon, who did so much for me in France.

Ilse de Ziah, whose arrangements for cello, especially of Irish music, were so well-received en route. Guy Forrester and Maire Morgan at Linden Studios for recording the *Highway Cello* album.

Everyone who read chapters in development and suggested improvements, or pointed out infelicities – Barbara Nienaber, Larry Culliford, Sophie Johnson, Jo Foley, Lesley Caple, Christine Roberts, Diane Bryson, Bob Morrow, Catherine Makepeace, Gerry O'Brien. Most of all of course my gentle and insightful editor Louise Voss. Jasmine Aurora, who designed the cover. Jack and Christi, who more than once pointed me in the right direction.

Jess and Gwyn, who so wonderfully looked after everything at home while I was away and while they waited for Wren.

About the author

Kenneth Wilson is a poet, a cellist and a dreamer. He is also an ex-vicar, failed property developer and reformed vegetarian who once ran an India travel company. He lives in a treehouse in rural Cumbria, where he plants trees and swims in a cold lake.

Kenneth is the author of *Orange Dust: Journeys after the Buddha* (Blissfool Books, 2011) and a book of poetry, *The Definitions of Kitchen Verbs* (Ravenbridge Books, 2019).

There is a *Highway Cello* album of solo cello music to accompany this book, available from **www.kennethwilsoncello.com**, where you can also see journey photos, the *Highway Cello* blog, and further author information. The album can also be downloaded from **www.kennethwilsoncello.bandcamp.com**.

Kenneth Wilson is available for performances and readings. Please contact him via the website or at kennethwilsoncello@gmail.com. He can also be found on Instagram **@kennethwilsoncello**.